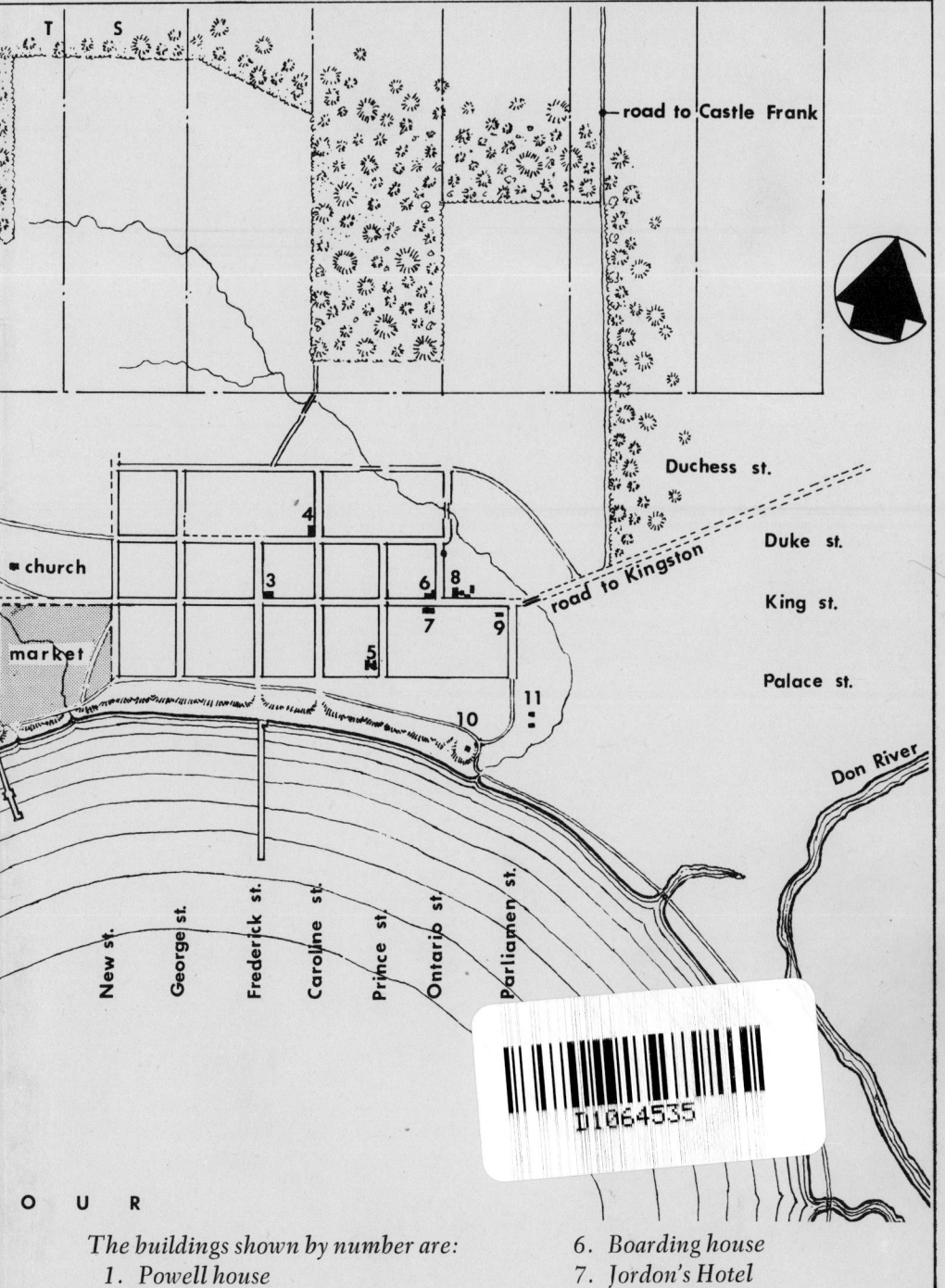

950

T S

road to Castle Frank

4

church

3

Duchess st.

Duke st.

6 8
7   9

King st.

road to Kingston

market

5

Palace st.

11

10

Don River

New st.

George st.

Frederick st.

Caroline st.

Prince st.

Ontario st.

Parliament st.

O   U   R

The buildings shown by number are:
1. *Powell house*
2. *Jesse Ketchum house*
3. *Quetton St. George store and residence*
4. *Jarvis house*
5. *Russell Abbey*

6. *Boarding house*
7. *Jordon's Hotel*
8. *Maryville Lodge*
9. *Berkeley House*
10. *Don blockhouse*
11. *Parliament Buildings*

Toronto
in 1810

ERIC WILFRID HOUNSOM

Toronto in 1810

Illustrated by the author

With a preface by
John C. Parkin

THE RYERSON PRESS   TORONTO / WINNIPEG / VANCOUVER

ISBN 0-7700-0311-7

Printed and bound in Canada by
McCorquodale & Blades Printers Limited

CONTENTS

PREFACE

Toronto in 1810, by architect Eric W. Hounsom, forms an important addition to that small body of current literature dealing with early Toronto and early Ontario; *Toronto, No Mean City* by Eric Arthur, *The Ancestral Roof* by Marion Macrae and Anthony Adamson, and *Rural Ontario* by Verschoyle Benson Blake and Ralph Greenhill. These have mainly to do with buildings of the past. Now we have a book which, happily, encompasses life as a whole.

The author sets the scene against a canvas of life in the colonial era. By focussing the narrative in a single year, he allows us the feeling of stepping through a picture frame right onto the streets of Toronto in 1810. By this means of concentrated attention, he adds authenticity and a more vivid graphic presentation to the tableau of early Toronto life; what the people looked like, how they dressed, what they ate, their attitudes towards government, religion, servants, their surroundings and their entire mode of life in a town which tried to be a transplanted England.

As architect-turned-historian, Eric Hounsom sees our past as a looking-glass whose reflections reveal us as we are today. Canada took 175 years to win the nationhood that the United States achieved by one war. As the author observes, colonial rule and the habit of looking to Britain for example and guidance retarded our coming of age. But he sees this slow growth as beneficial in that it has allowed us to escape the hazards of over-rapid expansion resulting in blighted areas, sprawling industrial complexes and related problems of urbanization.

Through no great brilliance on our part we managed to remain relatively unaffected by the first Industrial Revolution which encompassed first Great Britain and then the United States. In this respect Toronto is indeed unique; when it comes to putting our efforts towards building a great city – "History is on our side."

In my view Eric Hounsom puts architecture in its proper perspective – he deals with architecture in the fullness of life, as incidental to the lives of people. One hopes that future decades will approach architecture in the same humanistic way.

John C. Parkin, P.R.C.A., F.R.A.I.C., F.R.I.B.A.

The purpose of this book is to present a graphic and authentic picture of the first stage in the history of Metropolitan Toronto, which ended with the War of 1812.

In selecting a single year I have attempted to avoid generalizations. The casual reader is often confused when too long a period is covered. Many writers in describing early life in Ontario have been satisfied with such adjectives as "early," or "pioneer," which give the reader no clear and single picture of a generation or a decade – not to mention a single year. Their descriptions fill pioneer life with the ideas and gadgets of three generations, but leave no single impression of one. Toronto was founded in a pioneer era but it was not a pioneer town. Most of the descriptions of pioneer life in Ontario do not apply to Toronto. It did not grow by chance around the location of a gristmill or a sawmill. The site was carefully selected to be the capital of the new province of Upper Canada. Trade was secondary.

This book is not intended to be a history of Toronto from its founding in 1793 to the year 1810, but rather to give a complete picture of life in Toronto in a single year. In attempting to draw this picture of a single year, however, I have made reference to both the past and the future, to place the year 1810 in proper perspective. The reader will also find many comparisons with both Europe and the United States, so that the relative progress of both Toronto and the province may be noted.

Without this balance many readers will compare the town of 1810 with the city of the present – not both the city of the present and the world of 1810. And without it many readers will picture a pioneer people living an uneventful life in a quiet world. This background will also fortify the conviction of many readers that "the good old days" has always been an illusion.

A few of our first citizens were United Empire Loyalists. They had lived and suffered in the new United States. The forests around Toronto would never limit *their* horizon. The lead-merchant, Quetton St. George, had been a French Royalist officer. We may assume that his customers, as well as his friends, were given a vivid, even if a one-sided, picture of

France. And then there was William Berczy, German colonizer, artist, architect-engineer and historian, who considered himself a citizen of the world, who made Ontario and Toronto his home from 1794 to 1799. Garrison officers, who had served in all parts of the Empire, entertained the townspeople with cakes and wine at the mess. All townspeople had travelled across the ocean, or many hundreds of miles from the Atlantic colonies, and a few from Quebec. We may say that the town was isolated geographically but not in spirit. The horizon of the townspeople included both Europe and America. It is probable that they were less local in their thinking and more conscious of the world around them than residents of inland towns of similar size in England.

The reader will find that Torontonians in 1810 were conformists in religion and in politics. Although most of them were intensely loyal to the Crown, they were sometimes irritated by those who represented it. The town was a Tory and Church of England stronghold, surrounded by dissenters and many disloyal settlers. It was an age of wood, cast iron, tin, pewter and brass, with the humble candle and the open fireplace the only source of artificial light. This fireplace was used for cooking and was the sole source of winter heat, if we except the few box stoves.

It was the beginning of our modern age, and in a much smaller world than today. In millions the population was: France 30, Britain 18, the U.S.A. 8, and Canada less than one half million, with about seventy-five thousand of this number in Ontario. This totals less than twenty per cent of the population of these same countries today. Although it was forty-three years before the first railroad in the province, there was a Canadian-built steamboat in regular service on the St. Lawrence. The first Ontario bank was to come in eleven years, house numbering in Toronto in twenty-one years, illuminating gas thirty-one years, water piped to buildings thirty-three years and totally professional fire-fighting sixty-four years.

If we select the greatest single factor influencing the period in North America, we may say it was an age in which the common man had become excited at the prospect of owning land. Indeed, land hunger is given by some historians as the basic cause of the war that was to come two years later, and the reason why most of the land fighting was in Ontario. They presume it was no coincidence that the War of 1812 came when the nearest cheap land that opened for American settlers was west of the Mississippi River. Ontario was nearer.

It is hoped that a broad and authentic picture of the inception of a great city emerges from this narrative and the pen and ink sketches. I am aware of my shortcomings as an illustrator; but no one better qualified has, to my knowledge, attempted to present the town as it appeared in 1810. As an architect endeavouring to be a historian, I have expanded the picture of early Toronto. In drawing these illustrations myself, I have avoided some of the inevitable errors of the retained artist.

The writer is grateful to those who kept diaries, to those who wrote letters, and to their contemporaries who wrote books of travel. I wish to thank those of a later period who tirelessly assembled official documents, and others who have rewritten or edited source history. I am also indebted to those who have collected the artifacts of the daily life of Toronto and the province. The writer has studied and has made his own notes of this material over a period of half a lifetime.

Modern writers of books on Toronto's history owe a great debt to the six volumes of *Landmarks of Toronto* by J. R. Robertson, and to the well-known *Toronto of Old* by the Rev. Henry Scadding. These two works are the major source of the history of Toronto. With access to more source material than these writers possessed, modern research has given us more and more authentic data, and has corrected some of the errors or omissions of these books. The average reader, however, does not have sufficient interest in Toronto's past to read Robertson and Scadding. They are not concise, and are rather heavy going, even for historians. This is also their virtue, however, for in much of the apparently extraneous matter they contain the historian, with painstaking cataloguing, finds much of value.

One other source of information is gratefully acknowledged, the documents, paintings and maps in the Baldwin Room of the Central Library of Toronto, presided over by Miss Edith Firth, who is a recognized authority on Toronto's history. Miss Firth has listened to my reading of portions of this writing, has given advice and has assisted me in searching for documents. The inevitable errors that this book contains, however, are my own.

The writer feels that in many cases the origin of some of the quotations would be helpful to the serious reader, and has included a page of notes at the back of the book.

This book has been written primarily for the modern residents of Toronto, including new Canadians, who are curious about the origin of their city. In the attempt to satisfy the interest of the reader who has no inclination to delve into documentary source history, and desires a fully comprehensive picture of life in Toronto at its inception, the writer has attempted to condense the information found in more than one hundred books. By describing all aspects of life in Toronto in 1810 under thirty-four headings, I have attempted to avoid a wearisome narrative.

It is hoped that both the student and the mature reader, particularly those who desire ready information for both writing and speaking will welcome this classification for quick reference. Repetition of information has been avoided as far as possible. It has been necessary in some cases, however, to present a complete story under its heading, without recourse to others.

E.W.H.

INTRODUCTION

It is not the intention in this brief introduction to trace the history of the site of Toronto from the day of the first French explorers, nor to comment upon the rivalry of British and French fur-traders, or the naval battles on Lake Ontario at that early period. Fort Rouillé, or Fort Toronto, however, must be mentioned, for that trading post on the lakeshore at the foot of the present Dufferin Street, and the circumstance of its erection and its destruction, had a great deal to do with the selection of the site of the present city.

Fort Rouillé was a fortified trading post, rather than a fort, with a staff of only nine men. It was built in 1749, and the French themselves burnt it to the ground ten years later. Rouillé was a lesser fort in a chain stretching from the St. Lawrence to the Gulf of Mexico. It was erected by the French in the same year as the construction of Fort Niagara, situated on the present American side of the Niagara River at its mouth. Rouillé was intended as a trading post to consolidate the fur traffic coming from the north and west by the Credit, Humber and Don and Rouge Rivers, to call them by their present names. A spirited rivalry for the fur trade existed between the French and English, and this was intensified when the French built Fort Niagara. The British then constructed Fort Oswego, at the east end of the lake, on what is now the American side. The French captured this fort, but later in 1759 the British recaptured Oswego, Fort Frontenac and Fort Niagara. They sent a detachment of troops across Lake Ontario to capture Fort Rouillé, but the French, realizing the hopelessness of their position, destroyed it themselves before the British troops arrived. Thus Fort Rouillé, located in the grounds of the present Canadian National Exhibition, had made the location of Toronto a centre of the fur trade long before its selection as a townsite. There is no doubt that a village and town would have eventually arisen in this location, perhaps at the mouth of the Humber River, for many towns in both the old world and the new had their origin with a fort, a mill, or a store. Toronto was also the location of the only sheltered bay between the head of the lake and the Bay of Quinte area, so its eventual selection as a port was assured.

The first military governor of the newly-conquered Quebec was succeeded in 1776 by Sir Guy Carleton (1724-1808). This man, along with the well-known Governor Simcoe, may be regarded as the co-founder of Toronto, as we shall see. It was largely due to Carleton that a conciliatory attitude toward the French Canadians was adopted. He had a great deal to do with the framing of the Quebec Act, passed in 1774, which became a kind of Magna Charta for French Canada. His fair treatment of a conquered people, who were entirely catholic, gave offence to the British colonists to the south who were predominantly protestant. At this time it was the accepted opinion that those of British stock in Canada would always be in the minority. When the War of Independence came in 1776, American armies attacked Quebec, but were repulsed by Carleton. For his services in defending Quebec he was crested K.C.B. He was criticized later for not following the defeated American army and capturing Fort Ticonderoga, and he resigned his post of ten years as governor, and returned to England in 1778.

In 1786 Carleton was created Baron Dorchester, and returned to Quebec City as Governor-in-Chief of British North America, to solve the problems of the Loyalists. In Britain, at this time, there was an increasing dislike of the new United States of America, which believed in government by the people and for the people, and the new turn which the French Revolution was taking strengthened this antipathy in the British ruling class. Dorchester returned to a new world, however. With the expulsion of the Loyalists from the U.S.A., he was forced to modify his outlook upon colonial government, for it was apparent that the most loyal Loyalist expected some measure of participation in it. He also had to change his opinion regarding French Canadians being forever in the majority.

At the beginning Dorchester suggested that the newly-opened Canada West (Ontario), should be divided into districts within the province of Quebec, but this did not satisfy the Loyalists. The British Government, realizing the debt it owned to a people who had lost everything by being loyal to the Crown, decided to divide Quebec into two provinces to be called Upper and Lower Canada; one would be predominantly French and the other British. The bill to bring this about was called the Constitutional Act, because it granted a form of government in which the people had a voice. This act was passed in 1791, and at this date the population of what is now Ontario was twelve thousand, and Quebec one hundred and fifty thousand, and this latter figure included fifteen thousand British.

Long before the act was passed, Dorchester was aware that a new province would be created, and he suggested that the site for the capital be the town of Kingston. He changed his mind, however, when he

1. Typical squared-log house. The census of 1809 lists 11
   one-storey and 27 two-storey squared-log houses. Some of these
   were covered with clapboarding and had plastered interiors.

2. Typical wood construction,
   showing log cabin,
   squared-log building,
   clapboarding on squared log,
   and frame construction.
   When space between upright
   studs was filled with brick
   for insulation, the one-inch
   sheeting under the clapboarding
   was sometimes omitted.

3. *William Jarvis house*

E. W. HOUNSOM

4. Col. James Givins house

E. W. HOUNSOM

5. *Justice Powell house*

6. *Russell Abbey, home of Hon. Peter Russell*

7. *Jordon's York Hotel*

E. W. HOUNSOM

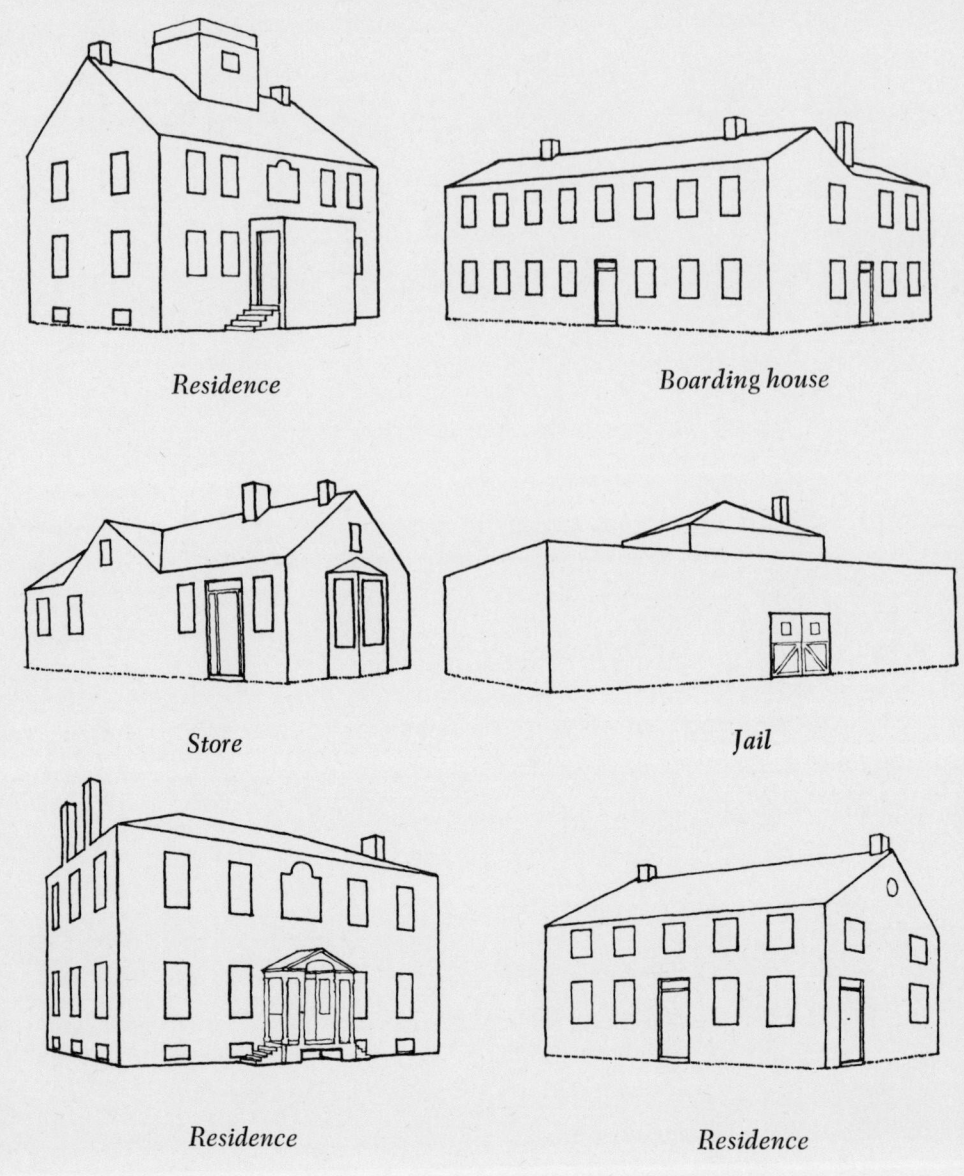

Residence

Boarding house

Store

Jail

Residence

Residence

8. *Diagrammatic perspectives of twelve Toronto buildings, showing diversity of forms. There was no regional architecture in Toronto.*

Governor's residence in Garrison

St. James' Church

Residence and school
(Bow window added after 1810)

Castle Frank

Residence

Residence

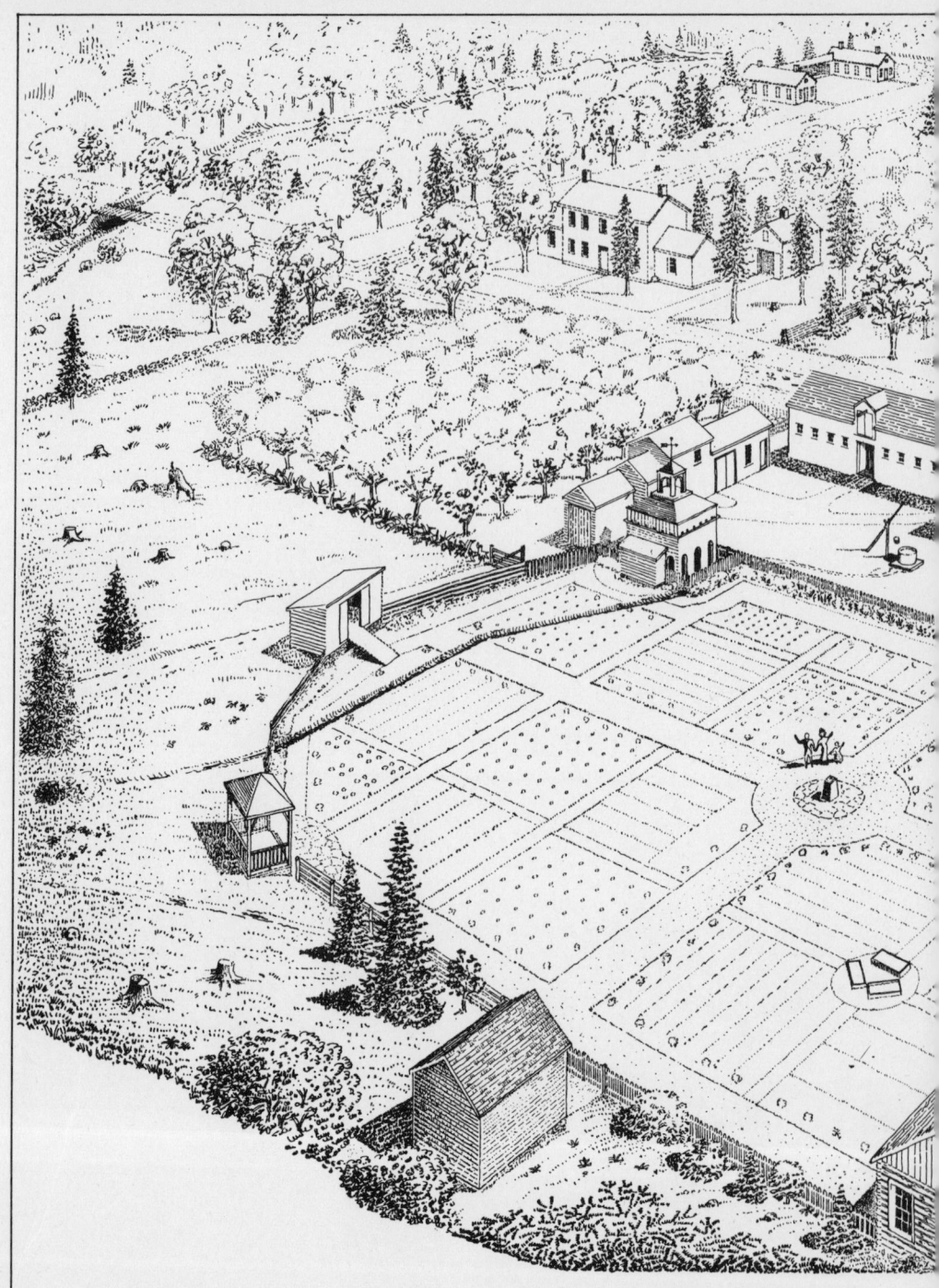

9. *Aerial perspective of Maryville Lodge.*
   The house faced west, and was at the
   northeast corner of King and Ontario
   Streets. The buildings in the service
   court included a building for horses,
   sheep and poultry, two servants rooms,
   coach-house, mill, pigsties and then
   a wagon shed and pigeon-house with
   a privy behind it. The four small
   buildings in the foreground are

root-house, summerhouse, wash-house, and blacksmith shop extending over the street line. At left background is Berkeley House, the Parliament Buildings, and the Don blockhouse on the Bay. The building at right, on the south side of King Street is Jordon's Hotel and the other Mrs. Johnson's boarding house.

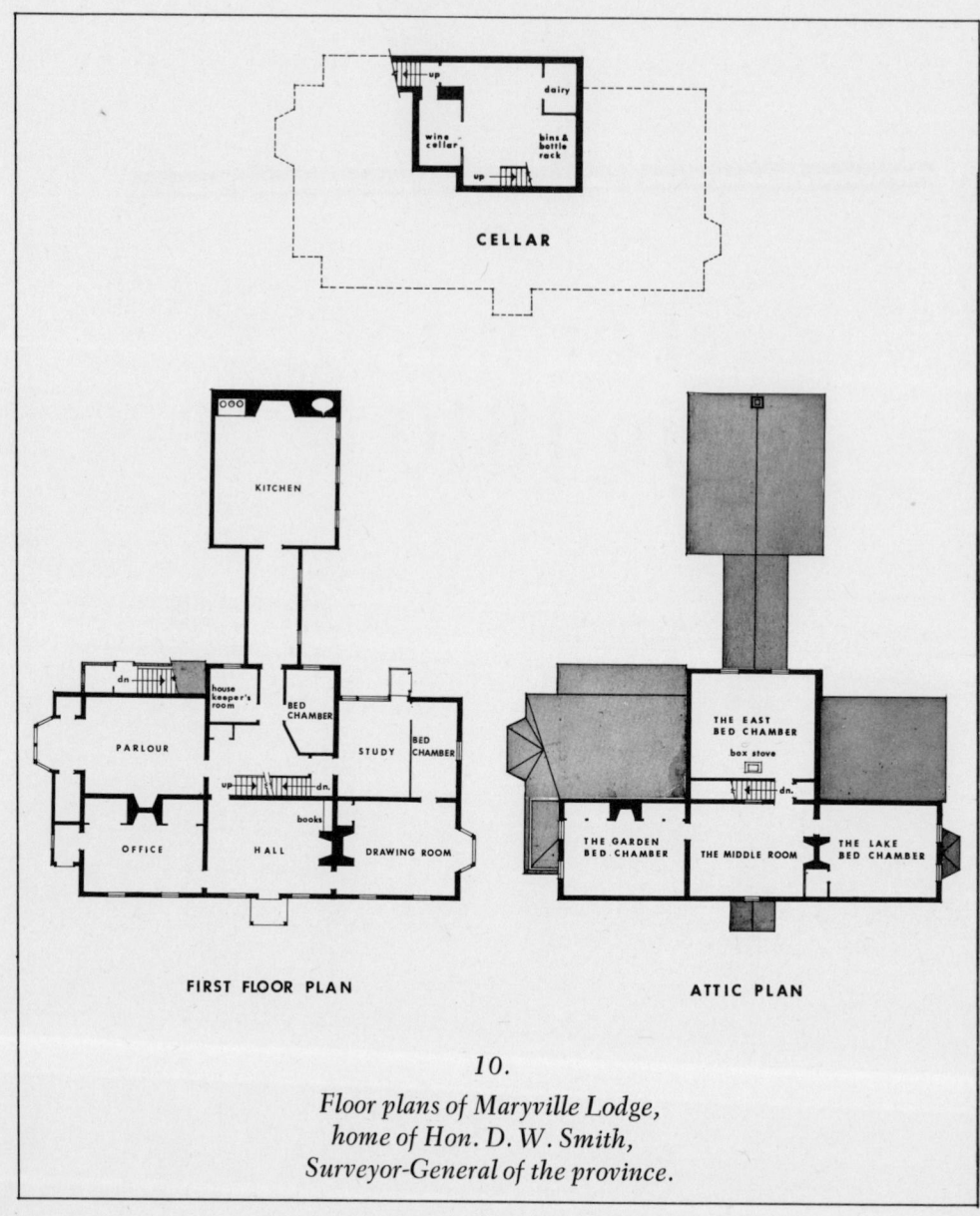

CELLAR

KITCHEN

house keeper's room

BED CHAMBER

STUDY

BED CHAMBER

PARLOUR

OFFICE

HALL

books

DRAWING ROOM

FIRST FLOOR PLAN

THE EAST BED CHAMBER

box stove

THE GARDEN BED CHAMBER

THE MIDDLE ROOM

THE LAKE BED CHAMBER

ATTIC PLAN

10.
Floor plans of Maryville Lodge,
home of Hon. D. W. Smith,
Surveyor-General of the province.

Toronto
in 1810

PART ONE

The Town
in 1810

The Forest

We cannot completely visualize the Toronto of 1810 without considering its background – the hundreds of thousands of square miles of forest land, lakes, swampland and rivers, stretching from the Quebec border to the Detroit River, in which lived the seventy-five thousand people of Ontario. The site of Toronto in 1810 was partially cleared. This forest between the Humber and the Don, on the lakeshore, had never contained the stands of giant timber, such as white and yellow pine, which grew north of the town. A young man from Toronto, visiting in England in June, 1812, had these trees north of Toronto in mind when he wrote to a brother back in Toronto: "How beautiful must the woods begin to be with you. As for these English trees, I hardly think of them as wood. They are so small and stunted . . ." This young man had seen no other trees than those in Ontario.

One writer of this time spoke of the country as one continued forest. He mentioned there were some plains on the borders of Lake Erie and at the head of Lake Ontario, and that a few places were thinly wooded, but in general the land was "heavily loaded" with trees.

Forest fires, caused by lightning and in a few cases by the carelessness of travellers and settlers, had left patches of blackened stumps covering thousands of acres. In these patches, beginning with wild lettuce, a dense mass of bushes soon covered the area until the new forest became thick enough to smother them. These bushes included gooseberries, blackberries, raspberries, and young plum and cherry trees. These cherry trees, of course, are not native to Canada, and may have had their origin in some cultivated orchard in Europe.

Only a few original stands of timber remain in the province today, and relatively few people have seen them. The inhabitants of modern Toronto who have seen these giant trees can understand the emotions of the British settlers and travellers in 1810. The pines were from one foot to six feet in diameter and the largest were five hundred years old and as tall as a seventeen-storey office building. Nothing grew at the base of these enormous trees. The forest shut out all the sunshine and most of the daylight. The interior was a perpetual gloom of vaulted boughs and dead and broken limbs, with no shrubbery on the ground. The earth below was a black vegetable mould, a foot thick, with rank grass here and there sheltering rattlesnakes and lizards.

A solemn roar, like a muffled waterfall, could be heard, day and night. The trunks remained rigid in the greatest wind, but the hidden boughs at the top swayed and threshed about like a storm at sea. A writer of the period gives us a winter picture, and comments upon the deep silence that brooded over the vast solitude, inspiring the mind with a strange awe: "Not a breath of wind stirred the leafless branches, whose shadows – reflected upon the dazzling white covering of snow – lay so perfectly still that it seemed as if nature had suspended her operations, that life and motion had ceased, and that she was sleeping in her winding-sheet, upon the bier of death."

A summer traveller says: "The country has a dreary, cheerless, yet sublime appearance, impressing the mind with an indescribable sensation of awe, loneliness and astonishment, and bringing it back in imagination to the primitive ages of the world."

A third observer stated: "To the mere passing traveller who cares little for the beauties of scenery, there is certainly a monotony in the long and unbroken line of woods, which insensibly inspires a feeling of gloom almost touching on sadness."

These startling impressions were written before railroad trains, motor cars or paved highways when nature, for the settler, was an encompassment – not a tourist attraction.

Awe, sadness, and loneliness : these were the emotions of the settler who secured his location ticket and journeyed with his family to his holding, or walked beside a heavily-laden horse or oxen carrying all of his worldly goods, on a road or trail to his location. Every settler's cabin he passed housed a potential friend and helpmate in the struggle he saw ahead to wrest a sustenance from the soil; every tree became the enemy. When he reached his location his first thought was to unpack his axe.

We may look back with some misgivings at the way this valuable timber was ruthlessly destroyed. Trees of furniture wood were chopped down and burnt where they fell in the race to sow the first grain or corn. The settler had no time to chop squared timber for sale, and he did not possess the equipment to haul it to a distant sawmill. His whole energies were expended in building a cabin, later a squared-log house, and then a log barn. Once he had a roof over his head there was time to salvage the ashes from the burning of trees, and make potash. This potash supplied him with sufficient credit at a store for necessities.

No sentiment was wasted in destroying the forest. These giant trees inspired a primitive fear of nature, and the settler could only become master of his environment by their destruction. He was also spurred on in his task by the fear of forest fire and dread of wolves which hunted in packs and were sometimes bold enough to enter cabins. This anxiety lessened as his clearing became larger. As he lay in his makeshift bed at night, with his family sleeping around him, he brooded over the slow progress in enlarging his clearing, and to him this was a symbol of progress in his primeval world. The destruction of more trees became an obsession.

After the first logging bee, and seed planting between the stumps in the virgin soil which did not require ploughing, the settler girdled the trees of a few more acres. This meant that he chopped a ring around each trunk of sufficient depth to kill them in a short time. The leafless branches then let in the sunlight to completely change the solemn forest to sentinel-like trunks rising from lush undergrowth.

Most of the United Empire Loyalists who came to Ontario had been settlers or farmers in the former British colonies. These Loyalists and later American immigrants felt at home in Ontario's forests, and usually had their land cleared more quickly than those from overseas. The British immigrant saw his sons grow into silent muscular men, bred to the axe, who took their surroundings for granted. It is the fathers of these sons, however, many of whom were town bred, to whom we look with admiration for the part they played in making the first inroads in the forests of southern Ontario.

These forests maintained a water-level much higher than today. They retained rainfall so that it reached the streams and rivers in a steady flow, not in seasonal torrents as today, turning streams and rivers into turbulent floods of topsoil-filled water. By retaining moisture these forests also created large areas of mosquito-breeding swampland, which postponed settlement in some areas for generations.

Every settler saw many years of work ahead to create the same pattern of tidy farmland he had left in the United States or Europe. A mystical feeling that he was building a new world, as well as the satisfaction of personal ownership, was some compensation for his toil.

It was inevitable that settlers at this time would be a different breed of men from those in Toronto. They saw the stores of Toronto filled with luxuries they could not purchase. They were painfully aware that successful tradesmen and government servants of the town were living a life quite different from their own. Many were indebted to Toronto storekeepers. They were dissatisfied with government land-granting, for it was apparent that those who knew the right people were securing the best land and larger acreages. The settler also had neighbours who were not Loyalists, who had come to Ontario for cheap land, and who were still American in their outlook. These neighbours were often Quakers or

Mennonites, who were not disloyal but simply neutral. The chauvinism of some in Toronto irritated them, and they usually voted in provincial elections for any candidate not popular in Toronto. The bond of mutual aid was also setting them apart from the people of Toronto. Their own mode of life, particularly with young settlers, seemed genuine; that of Toronto with its social climbing and class distinction, artificial. Very few of these settlers were Anglican, yet they could not be married by the church of their own persuasion.

So we can say there was a far greater difference, than today, between the life and outlook of those in Toronto in 1810 and those in rural areas, who were changing the forests of Ontario into farmland.

CHAPTER 1

The Harbour

The following description of the harbour and the "Island" will be based upon its condition in 1810. It should be noted that the harbour area changed considerably from the time of Simcoe's first visit in 1793 to that year. In 1803-4, Lord Selkirk noted that the lake had fallen three and one-half feet since work on the town had begun, and he mentioned hearing the Indians say that Lake Ontario rose continuously for seven years and fell for seven. In 1815 many writers described the lake level as "unusually high." This may surprise some readers who assume that man alone has changed the levels of the Great Lakes.

Several miles west of the town was the historic St. John's (Humber), River. The Humber had a two-hundred-year history before 1810, beginning with Etienne Brûlé, in 1610, the first white man to visit it. East of this river was a large pond, with a steep bank on the west side and sloping land on the east. It is now called Grenadier Pond, for tradition has it that in 1813, a party of British soldiers attempted to cross it on the thin ice of early spring, and were drowned. This pond is now in Toronto's largest park and is beautifully landscaped. In 1810, however, it was surrounded with swamp and rushes.

Six miles east of this river was another, which Simcoe had named the

Don, and both of these rivers still find their course into Lake Ontario. Between these two rivers were six creeks, large and small, which have long since been funnelled into sewers, and have had their ravines filled in. These minor streams are still increasing the cost of downtown buildings by being "discovered" during construction. One of these, we have called the sixth creek, flowed through the grounds of the old Normal School (1852-1963), and caused an "extra" in the building of the present Ryerson Institute on the same site. At the formal opening of the Normal School in 1852, the *Toronto Globe* mentioned that the deep creek at the southeast corner of the grounds had not yet been filled; but this was done within the year.

Some of these creek beds and their ravines (for the shore was twelve to twenty feet above the lake in 1810), were filled in so long ago that no record of their exact course remains, and the fill is now equal to virgin land. In other locations, however, springs have rendered the soil too porous for the structural engineer's calculated loads, where modern high rise buildings are constructed.

Starting at the west side of the town, but east of the Humber river as previously mentioned, was Garrison Creek. This stream was eighteen feet wide at its mouth, which was immediately east of the present "Old Fort York." The ravine of this creek, near the lake was 240 feet wide, and the curve of the present Niagara Street followed the contour of this ravine. Many readers will remember this as a tiny stream flowing through Willowdale Park, at Bloor Street, about the time of World War One.

The second on our list was a small creek which entered the Bay at the foot of the present John Street. The third was called Russell's Creek. It was about one and one-half miles long, and entered the Bay west of the present Simcoe Street. The fourth was nearly as long, and flowed in a southeasterly direction to enter the Bay just east of the present Bay Street. Another creek, originating north of King Street, entered the Bay west of the present Jarvis Street. The sixth creek, which flowed through the grounds of the old Normal School, had its source in the vicinity of the present Bloor Street, near Yonge Street. It flowed southeast to below King and Parliament Streets, and then made an abrupt turn west to enter the Bay at the foot of the present Berkeley Street.

The Don River did not enter the Bay directly, but flowed parallel to the east side of the Bay for about two thousand feet, and then made an abrupt turn west to enter. Where it entered the Bay, the Don was about sixty feet wide, and was crossed on a floating bridge constructed in 1806. The public was warned not to draw sand or loaded carts over this bridge, for it was only strong enough for horseback riders and pedestrians. There was also a similar floating bridge located in the inlet between the Don outlet and the town, and in 1812 both floating bridges were removed and a channel was dug connecting the inlet with the river, and an earthwork defence was thrown up on the town side of this new channel. This insignificant cut later became, by natural process, another Don outlet, also about sixty feet wide. The townspeople called it the "Little" or the "Lesser" Don. New bridges over these two Don outlets were not constructed until 1822. Visitors to the peninsula were forced to reach it by boat, or from the mainland, three miles east of the two Don outlets.

The length of the peninsula, at this time, was five and three-quarter miles, from the western tip where the gun platform was located at Gibraltar Point to the present Woodbine Avenue. From Gibraltar Point, across the water to the Garrison on the mainland, was a little less than seven-eighths of a mile. From the mainland to the peninsula, north to south, was one and three-eighths miles. The Bay at this time was much larger than today. As the peninsula appeared to be an island, it was called such from the inception of the town. It actually became one, however, in 1830 when a minor breach occurred which under favourable conditions allowed small vessels to enter the harbour. In 1858 a great storm broke a one-hundred-and-fifty-foot channel, three feet deep, through the hard sand. This was deepened to become the present "Eastern Gap." This channel was used in preference to the wide entrance at the western end of the Bay because of more favourable winds.

To the east of the Don outlet was Ashbridge's Bay, named after an American immigrant whose farm touched the shore. Although this river was a swift tumbling stream in its many branches, with minor waterfalls, the accumulated silt at the mouth slowed it down. The whole of this bay was a shallow marsh of black water with myriads of waterfowl, croaking frogs, and the conical tops of muskrat houses amid the wild rice and rushes. The water flowed lazily around in an ever-changing circuit, depending upon rainfall and the elevation of the lake.

From the inception of the town the "Island" was a place for sport and recreation, and no attempt was made to erect houses or buildings for industry. It was a kind of no-man's-land for fishermen to dry their nets, Indians to recuperate from illness, sportsmen to shoot birds and for horseback riding. Even when the town was incorporated in 1834, the Island was mentioned in the act as belonging to the "Liberties," or suburbs of the community. The city had some jurisdiction over it, but the ownership rested in the Crown.

The lagoons on the Island were shallow, from two to four feet in depth, and they were bordered everywhere with rushes and wild rice which provided food for thousands of fowl, including loons, wild swans and geese, during their migration, in addition to the thousands of birds of all kinds which made it their home. The Island was stocked with goats, which were the offspring of those Governor Simcoe had established at Gibraltar Point. He had seen these animals at Goat Island, adjoining the Falls of Niagara, and this probably gave him the idea.

The trees included willow, pine, and poplar. They were not dense and there was little underbush. Here and there were patches of hard sand, coarse grass and wild strawberry plants. The cool breezes from the lake, over this terrain, made a morning horseback ride exhilarating. There was a favourite run for horses on the Island, and this was on the narrow neck of land between Ashbridge's Bay and York Bay. This run, from the Don to the lakeshore, was nearly three thousand feet, with a width between bay and marsh of about three hundred and fifty feet. Here the trees were spaced far enough apart to permit up to a dozen riders to ride abreast in view of spectators. The grass here was long, which made heavy going for the horses. Its use as a racecourse indicates there was nothing better in the vicinity of the town. Even the streets, which might have provided a better run, were undulating, sloping down to the creek beds, which were spanned with narrow bridges at water level. On the lake side of the Island, a short distance west of this racecourse run, was the "portage" across the Island, where the North-West Fur Company's bateaux were lifted from lake to bay for their journey up the Don River to the long portage on Yonge Street to the Holland River.

The need for a lighthouse to guide ships into Toronto Harbour was felt at the town's inception, and an act was passed by the Provincial Legislature in 1803 for its establishment. It was not constructed, however, until August, 1809, when it became what is probably the first lighthouse on the Great Lakes. The British Government did not pay for such improvements as lighthouses, and the cost and the maintenance was secured by levying a harbour fee upon all boats entering the harbour. The location was the south side of the Island, near the west end. At this time the shoreline was twenty-five feet away, and the limestone used for its building was brought from Queenston on a schooner and unloaded at the site. The height was fifty-four feet from grade to lamp-room floor. The oak and glass lamp cage sat upon the wood platform of larger diameter, enabling the keeper to walk all around the exterior of the cage. Candles were used for illumination; but sometime later the oak cage was replaced with one of cast iron and whale oil was used for a revolving light. On the platform was a flagpole, which was used to warn the harbour master of the approach of vessels to the harbour. A Union Jack was flown if the vessel came from the east of Toronto, and a red ensign fluttered in the breeze if the vessel came from the west.

At the foot of the structure was the lighthouse keeper's cottage. It was a storey-and-a-half building of squared logs faced with clapboarding, and had two small rooms on the first floor, and a winding stair to sleeping attic above. The first lighthouse keeper was murdered, presumably by some drunken soldiers, in 1815. In 1833 the stonework of the lighthouse was raised twelve feet and this heightened structure may still be seen in its original location, although the shoreline has completely changed since 1809.

In 1810 both the Don and the Humber were spanned with bridges constructed the previous year. The Don bridge consisted of ten stone-filled wood cribs across water and ravine, with a plank road platform supported on trusses spanning from crib to crib. This bridge was about twenty feet above the water. From it could be seen an earlier causeway, or floating bridge, partially covered with water. The first means of crossing the Don River had been a scow, which was operated by pulling on a rope stretched across the river. The location of the Don Bridge of 1810 was the road to Kingston. West of this bridge was a smaller one, over what we have called the sixth creek. Before 1810 there was also a bridge across the Don south of the present Bloor Street.

The Humber was spanned with a bridge similar to that over the Don. This river was also crossed by means of a ferry in another location. All of the creeks in the town were spanned on streets with makeshift bridges, close to the water and wide enough for wheeled vehicles. An early map shows Newgate Street (Adelaide), King, York, Duchess and Princess Streets crossing these creek beds.

The number of docks and wharves in Toronto before 1820 appear to be out of proportion to the population of the town, and the amount of trading in a sparsely-settled province. The same could be said of the new town of Newark (Niagara-on-the-Lake) at the mouth of the Niagara River. We must remember, however, that for many years the bulk of transportation, both freight and passenger, was by water. Transportation by land, over the poor roads, was more costly because it was much slower. It is also understandable that Toronto merchants stocked up with goods to carry them through the winter. Any merchant who attempted to import goods by land at any season of the year would have found he could not sell at a competitive price with merchants who secured their stock during the navigation season.

The first wharf in Toronto Harbour was probably a temporary one, constructed at the mouth of Garrison Creek. Within a short time a more permanent wharf was built on the east side of the creek and on the east side of a knoll, and about one hundred feet from the water was situated the first blockhouse, erected in 1797. This wharf was for bateaux, and other small craft, and it was also used by merchants until the construction of the first commercial wharf. A bridge across Garrison Creek was also constructed.

The first commercial wharf was built in 1803 by William Allan, the collector of custom duties. It was originally known as Allan's Wharf, and later as the Merchants' Wharf, and was the earliest landing-place for sloops and schooners. It was located at the foot of Frederick Street, and there was a storehouse beside it at the water's edge.

The second was Cooper's Wharf, at the foot of the present Church Street. There is some doubt about the date of construction which may have been 1808, but more probably 1815. It was large and important looking, and became the favourite landing for schooners to discharge their cargoes. This wharf had a large storehouse upon it, and later a shipyard was built adjacent to it. The first steamboat on Lake Ontario used this wharf in 1816. Cooper's was called Feighan's Wharf in 1834, and Maitland's Wharf in 1845.

Two other wharves built before 1818 are also shown on early Toronto maps. One was the King's, or Navy Wharf, between the present John and Peter Streets; the other, the Commissariat Wharf, at the foot of the present Peter Street.

Water transportation in 1810 was mainly by French-Canadian bateau, which had been long in use before the British conquest. This bateau was rowed, poled, and sailed, using whatever propulsion suitable for the location. Even paddles were sometimes used. Bateaux were usually made at Lachine, Quebec, about nine miles from Montreal. The word "bateau" was originally used to denote all types of craft smaller than barques or schooners, but the word gradually assumed a more exact meaning. In 1810, it was a type of boat, but the size varied considerably. On the Ottawa River a type of bateau was in use up to seventy-five feet in length. On the St. Lawrence, however, they were thirty to forty feet long.

Many readers have ridden in an authentic reproduction of this craft at Upper Canada Village, on the St. Lawrence River, east of Morrisburg, and this was copied from a bateau dredged up from the harbour at Kingston. They were flat-bottomed, five to eight feet wide, and had sides which were nearly vertical. The blunt-nosed bow and stern, which were tapered to permit the craft to be beached, were about one foot higher than the centre of the boat. They were usually steered with an oar of some kind. There were four or more cross seats for passengers or oarsmen, and the craft usually had a stout oak bottom with fir sides.

This craft was gradually evolved for the purpose intended and its main virtue was that it could not be easily capsized. It was well suited for use in the St. Lawrence, where it had to pass rapids. The carrying capacity was about two tons or four families and their luggage. Larger ones carried three tons of freight, or five or six families. As troop-carriers their capacity was twenty-five to thirty men. One traveller mentions leaving Kingston on the 6th of April, 1811, and arriving at Montreal on the 15th. The trip upstream, of course, took much longer. In open water, such as in Lake Ontario, this craft could be rowed at three miles per hour. They usually followed the shoreline, except in clear weather in summer when they went directly to Toronto or the Niagara River. On the St. Lawrence, however, it was a constant struggle against the current, if travelling upstream, and much time was consumed in passing rapids. On this river they were usually manned with a double crew; one crew walking in shallow water, or along the shore, pulling the craft with a rope; the other propelling and steering in rapids, with iron-pointed poles to the river bed. Bateaux usually travelled in "brigades" of twelve boats, each with a crew of five; and there was a "conductor" in charge of each brigade.

At dangerous rapids boat crews took a single boat through, leaving it beached, or at anchor with one crewman, while they went back for the next. At some rapids it was necessary to cut off the tops of trees along the shore as they obstructed the tow rope. Nervous passengers often walked along the shore during these struggles with rapids. Passengers used this craft exclusively on the St. Lawrence, but at Kingston most of them transferred with their luggage to schooners. With calm water, or strong head winds, this schooner trip to Toronto often took a week. When carrying freight only, the bateaux crews usually brought them directly to Toronto without transferring the cargo to a schooner.

These bateaux were propelled in three ways. When used on the St. Lawrence, especially upstream against a strong current, ironshod poles, about nine feet long, were used. An ungainly lug sail often assisted the rowers, and this sail boom was raised five feet above the boat so that the steersman could have an unobstructed view ahead. Passengers were protected from sun and rain with a wooden or canvas awning. As it was an open boat, the freight, usually kegs or barrels, was covered with a tarpaulin.

At night the light-hearted French-Canadian crewmen turned their craft into a creek or an uninhabited island. Fires were lighted, a meal was prepared, and a tent was made of the sail. Songs, laughter and even dancing, if there was a fiddler, were kept up until late into the night.

Sir Thomas Moore wrote his celebrated poem, The Canadian Boat Song, in 1804, after a bateau ride on the St. Lawrence. This craft was used by the Americans to bring their troops across the Niagara River for the attack upon Queenston, and they were also towed by American war vessels for use as landing craft for the attack upon Toronto in 1813. Many American prisoners were sent down the St. Lawrence in bateaux, and they were used extensively for British and Canadian militia troop movements. In 1810, several of this craft could always be seen on Toronto Bay or tied up at the wharves.

The second small craft for passengers and freight on the St. Lawrence and Lake Ontario was the Schenectady boat. The name came from the town on the Mohawk River in the U.S.A. This craft was first brought to Ontario by the Loyalists. They were large open rowboats, and families often built their own for the trip to Canada. They were described as three-handed, if three pairs of oars were used: some were five-handed. This craft had a bluntly-pointed bow and square stern. A sail was usually used and some had a tiny cabin near the stern. These boats were principally used in the Bay of Quinte area in 1810, but could be seen elsewhere. They were used as mail boats between Kingston, Toronto, and Niagara, two of them having been purchased in 1794 for this purpose.

The third small craft was the Durham boat. It was brought to Canadian waters in 1809 from the Mohawk River by Americans. The name came from Robert Durham, its original builder. Although some of this craft were manned by French Canadians, the first crews were usually English-speaking. This was a larger and more sophisticated craft than the bateau, having a length of from eighty to ninety feet, and a beam of ten. It had a slipkeel, and centre board and rudder. The bow was pointed; the stern, sloping but square. It could carry thirty-five tons of freight downstream, and about eight tons, up, when used on the St. Lawrence. It had up to ten times the freight-carrying capacity of the bateau, with a crew of seven.

This craft was also poled and sailed. Each side had a narrow deck at the top of the hull, just wide enough for a crewman to walk along, and these walking decks had cross slats to prevent slipping, for there was only a curb at the side, and no deck rail. The poles used for propulsion were about twenty feet along, and had a pointed steel end. The tops of the poles had large wooden buttons, similar to that on a carpenter's brace, against which the crewman pressed his shoulder. The crew started at both sides of the bow; placing their poles in the river bed, they pushed, as they slowly walked to the stern. They then walked back to the bow to again begin this monotonous poling. Some boats used shorter poles, with cross bars.

A sail was used when possible. The mast had a joint, which operated as a hinge, about four feet above the deck. This permitted the mast to be lowered when passing under a bridge. There was also a portable mast at the stern. Two-thirds of the deck was open, and covered with tarpaulins.

This Durham boat was primarily for freight. It afforded miserable accommodation for any passengers. They huddled around a table in the boxlike skipper's cabin at the stern. The crew slept under the forward deck, as a cookstove was included in this craft, it was not necessary to land to prepare a hot meal. Only a few Durham boats would have visited Toronto harbour by 1810.

It is quite evident that a bateau, with a crew of five, moving two tons of freight at an average speed of less than one mile per hour, from Montreal to Toronto, made the expense of transporting merchandise very high. The Durham boat cost was lower, but still very high by modern standards. The Hudson's Bay Company abandoned canoes in 1823, when they found they could reduce their transportation cost fifty per cent by using boats. The prohibitive cost of transportation was brought into sharp focus during the War of 1812, when ordnance was sent from Britain to Ontario at a freight charge of up to ten times its original cost. Part of this tremendous cost was due to the necessity, in many cases, of transporting by land.

Just as today, there was a continual striving to do the job of transporting merchandise more quickly, and hence more cheaply. Transportation cost at this time may be more readily appreciated with the following: when the Erie Canal opened in 1825, the time of travel from New York City to Buffalo dropped from twenty to six days, and the freight cost dropped to one-twentieth. With this Erie Canal, the isolation of the American West was ended, for they could now buy and sell to the East. The next means of transportation was the railroad, and it was not until our own day that roads began to compete with water and railroads for freight and passengers.

Canada took the lead in shipbuilding on both Lake Ontario and Lake Erie. As early as 1796 a Canadian-built vessel on Lake Ontario was purchased by Americans, and they did not build a commercial vessel on either lake until 1797. These early vessels were either sloops or schooners. They were small, by modern standards, ranging from 15 to 87 tons burthen. The largest was the schooner *Simcoe*, of 87 tons launched at Kingston in 1794, and it was the first vessel built on Lake Ontario exclusively for trade. It plied between Kingston and Niagara, and Toronto was a port of call. The *Simcoe* was designed for the mounting of eight four-pounder, and eight swivel guns, should it be necessary to convert it into a war vessel. It was originally intended for the North-West Company's fur trade. There was also a later vessel, the *Governor Simcoe* of 136 tons, which was launched in 1808.

Another vessel of the period was the *Toronto Yacht*, a schooner built in 1799 on the Humber River. The *Gazette* mentioned that she would soon be ready for her first trip and stated, "She is one of the handsomest vessels of her size that ever swam upon the Ontario; and if we are permitted to judge from her appearance, to to do her justice, we must say, she bids fair to be one of the swiftest sailing vessels . . . Her master builder was Mr. Denison, an American, upon whom she reflects much honour." She was freqently mentioned in the *Gazette*, and the Lieutenant-Governors and General Brock used this vessel – probably because it was so fast. It is recorded to have crossed from Toronto to Niagara in four hours, when some other vessels took up to two and one-half days for the same trip. At this period, sailing time was uncertain. The *Toronto Yacht* was wrecked on the Island in 1812. It was typical of the period that all of the ironwork on this ill-fated schooner was removed and used on new boats. Another well-known vessel in Toronto was the *Speedy*, which sank in a gale in the dead of night with the loss of all passengers and crew.

The schooners announced the time of their departure from the wharves by repeated blasts on a long tin horn. A feature of the times was oversized flags, on both land and sea. Pennants fluttered from the mast-heads of fighting ships. On large ships of war this pennant could be thirty inches wide at the mast, and fifty feet long; on small vessels, fifteen feet or more. A reading of a list of vessels of the period reveals that a surprising number were wrecked, and that drownings frequently occurred, when passengers as well as crewmen were swept overboard. An expert swimmer was an exception, and the percentage who could swim at all was much smaller than today. The vessels of the period were constructed of walnut, red cedar and oak, and gravel was used as ballast. Sometimes green timber was used, instead of the standard well-dried-out wood. In such cases the craft had a short life, even with continual recaulking. With green timber, which had a life of six or seven years, it was too easy to ignore the visible warnings until the strains of a gale were more than the rotting timbers could withstand.

The greatest marine disaster on Lake Ontario, before 1810, was the staggering loss of one hundred and seventy-two lives on the twenty-two-gun warship and transport, *Ontario*, which sailed from Niagara in 1780 and was never heard from again. During the construction of the vessel, one expert claimed that its design was faulty, and that it was too flat-bottomed. It is probable that a gale turned this ship completely upside down before it sank, for only one small article, a bandsman's drum, was ever found on the shore.

With the outbreak of the War of 1812, between Canada and the U.S.A. two years later, both sides immediately commandeered merchant vessels on the lakes to use in the conflict. These included sloops and schooners, and they were used, principally, for moving troops and supplies. Guns were mounted to engage the enemy if necessary. Some schooners were altered to gunboats. As ships of war they supported larger vessels. Work was commenced by both sides upon the construction of new warships of green timber. The largest of these war vessels was the *St. Lawrence*, built in less than a year and launched at Kingston in 1814.

It is ironical that in the first American attack on Toronto, April 27, 1813, two of the cannon used for defence were old French guns without trunions, and the single cannon on the gun platform on the Island had been removed to the mainland because of the shortage of ordnance; yet seventeen months later the 112-gun *St. Lawrence* was launched which never fired a gun except in salute. This warship was launched at Kingston, September 21, 1814, and sailed from that port October 15th as the flagship of Sir James Lucas Yeo, R.N. The size of this vessel was truly astounding if we make the following comparison. During the period from 1790 to 1890, there were 226 vessels on Lake Ontario whose tonnage is known. These 226 had an average tonnage of 336: the smallest was fifteen tons, and the largest, a steam vessel launched in 1884, was 1,900. It is not until we compare these tonnages that we realize what a mighty task it was to build the *St. Lawrence*, whose tonnage was 2,304. When launched she was double the size and gun power of any battleship in the western hemisphere, and this included ships on the Atlantic.

She had three gun decks, mounted 112 guns and had a crew of more than a thousand. Green timber, including oak, elm, maple and pine, were used in her construction. The *St. Lawrence* was a three-masted, square-rigged ship, with mainmasts four feet in diameter at top-deck level. With a deck length of 191 feet, a beam of 52 feet and a draught of 21 feet, she was a very large vessel for the period.

The ship that Nelson wanted for his flagship was the *Foudroyant*, but it was not completed. This warship rated 1971 tons, carried 80 guns and had a crew of 600. The *Victory* carried 74 guns. The well-known American battleship, the *Constitution*, popularly known as *Old Ironsides*, which saw service on the Atlantic in the War of 1812, was a fifteen-hundred-ton frigate of 27 guns, with a crew of 456. Major John Richardson, who saw service in this war and wrote a history of it, said of the *St. Lawrence*, "but war had now been so long carried on in the country as a matter of course, and on so extensive a scale of preparation, that these latter (the *St. Lawrence* and other vessels), were scarcely regarded as anything extraordinary, even on the small and fresh-water sea of Lake Ontario."[1]

While the *St. Lawrence* never engaged the enemy she kept American warships in port, while they feverishly worked at Sackett's Harbour on two warships to meet her on equal terms. The war ended before these American warships were completed. The cost to the British taxpayers was £500,000 sterling, which if translated into the money of today, would be twenty million dollars. While this figure sounds excessive for a wooden vessel, we must remember that it cost ten times the original value to transport the ship's gear and guns from England, for much of this freight handling was by hand. This leviathan, with her escort of smaller vessels, called at the port of Toronto on many occasions.

In 1810 a Canadian-built steamboat had already been in operation on the St. Lawrence for one year. This boat was called the *Accommodation*, and was built at Montreal by John Molson. This first steamboat on Canadian waterways was launched two years after Robert Fulton's steamboat on the Hudson River. These first steamboats operated with paddlewheels, and used wood as fuel. The first steamboat on Lake Ontario was the *Frontenac*, launched at Ernestown, on the Bay of Quinte, in 1816. By 1817 it had visited Toronto. It had a deck length of 170 feet, a beam of 32 feet, and was rated at 700 tons. The *Frontenac* did not come directly to the dock in Toronto, but was brought to a standstill some distance away. Small boats were lowered which brought hawsers to the dock, and these were used to pull the steamer in. Other steamboats quickly followed, so that by 1840 there were fifty on Lake Ontario. It was many years, however, before they entirely superseded bateaux, Durham and Schenectady boats, sloops and schooners. The first propeller-driven steamboats on Lake Ontario came in 1841. The first ferry to the Island from the mainland was a horse boat. Two, and later five, horses activated a treadmill flush with the deck of this sixty-foot scowlike craft, which turned paddlewheels at the sides. This boat operated from 1833 to 1850, and in that year the first steamboat ferry was put into service.

From the beginning of the nineteenth century, many people were aware of the need for canals to provide better travel routes in the province. Rowland Burr, a Pennsylvania engineer who came to Ontario in 1803, published at his own expense his recommendation for a canal to connect Georgian Bay with the Humber River. One report of 1799 mentioned that a future canal may connect the Rouge with the Holland River. The first canal in Ontario (the act for it was passed in 1813), was constructed between Lake Ontario and Burlington Bay. Even the idea of a canal to connect Lake Ontario with Lake Erie is said to have originated with its promoter, The Hon. W. H. Merritt, during his patrolling of the Niagara river as a militia officer during the War of 1812.

Streets, Provincial Roads and Travelling

Our first consideration in discussing the roads of the province and the streets of Toronto is the speed of travel, and the relative speed of travel on roads and streets compared to other means of transportation in 1810. While the modern motor car on a paved highway ranks fastest today, wheeled vehicles rated slowest in 1810.

In 1807, Christopher Schultz made the following comparison of travel time in the U.S.A. It is worth quoting, for it also shows the various kinds of transportation a traveller was forced to use to journey 572 miles. In this example, which is typical, Mr. Schultz was compelled to make six separate arrangements to travel this distance.

	MILES	METHOD	DAYS
New York to Albany	160	Steamboat	1½
Albany to Schenectady	15	Turnpike Road	1½
Schenectady to Utica	104	5-ton keel-boat	5
Utica to Oswego	104	5-ton keel-boat	3
Oswego to Lewiston	172	Lake sailing boats	3
Lewiston to Black Rock	17	Mud road	1½

We can see that this man travelled on roads at little more than an average speed of one mile per hour, but the first steamboat in America carried him against the current of the Hudson River at five to nine miles per hour.

The slowest conveyance of all was oxen, which pulled carts or sleighs at from one to two miles per hour. The fastest travel on roads was by horseback. An army surgeon in Ontario relates that he rode twenty out of the twenty-four hours, and travelled seventy-five miles in one day, but this was unusual.

Roads improved very slowly, for even in 1833 one stagecoach traveller in Ontario calculated that his journey of thirty miles was at a speed of 2-8/11th miles per hour. We can see that the sportsman of 1810, when conditions were favourable, could race his horse-drawn sleigh along the ice of a river or lake at what was to him an exhilarating speed.

The difference between European and North American roads was simply that a thinly-spread population could spend less on both construction and maintenance. Europe had had centuries to improve roads, but American roads were often cut through forests of giant trees, and over thousands of acres of undrained terrain. The freezing and thawing of Ontario soil added still another difficulty to road building which did not exist in most of Europe and large areas of the U.S.A.

Ontario, with its sparse population and little taxation, had very poor roads; but when we consider the ratio of population to the area to be travelled, and the shortage of money to build them, it is remarkable that so many miles of road of any kind existed in 1810. No toll roads (called turnpike roads in England and the eastern U.S.A.) existed in Ontario in 1810, simply because none had reached the state of improvement to warrant toll charges; and there was no private capital with which to construct them. Quebec, however, had one as early as 1805. There was a proposal as early as 1807 to make Yonge Street a toll road, but it did not become one until 1820.

In the reports of Governor Simcoe to his superior, and in other documents, we see a modern progressive attitude toward settling the province as soon as possible. Roads, bridges and canals are discussed, and it was only money that postponed their construction until later. Canals were envisioned as an aid to transportation at this early period. There was never any other attitude toward progress in the early days of the province.

Some writers have classified Ontario roads of 1810 under four headings. First came the bridle roads, which were simply paths through the forest for horsemen, and the winter roads, which were not actually roads in the proper sense, but were routes selected for horsemen with sleighs. With solid ground in the winter, sleighs and sometimes vehicles could take more direct ways across valleys and swampy ground. Next were the corduroy roads, described below, and the common or graded roads, which with fill drainage and surfacing have become the secondary roads of today.

The reader has heard the term corduroy road, and a few of them still existed after nineteen hundred. When the road allowance passed through low lying and swampy ground this type was used, for there was not yet enough wealth to provide earth and gravel fill. This road was constructed by laying logs crosswise on the ground and filling the spaces between with earth or gravel. Log sleepers, parallel to the road, were usually laid under these logs, and a ditch was made on at least one side of the road. Such a roadbed could be relatively smooth and dry when first laid. Unless constantly repaired, however, wagon wheels passing over one side of the road sometimes lifted the log at the other end. This lifted end did not fall back to its original position, but remained a few inches above the other logs. The sand or gravel between the logs was soon washed away in heavy rains, and the resulting spaces between the logs were traps for horses' legs, which were sometimes broken. One writer of the period mentions that the continual jolting, caused by the bobbing up and down of the logs, gave the traveller sore bones and an aching head. In the wet season these logs were sometimes entirely covered with water, and actually floated, so that the driver never knew how far down his wheels would sink.

From the inception of Ontario as a separate province, in 1791, an effort was made to construct a road to connect the upper province with Montreal. Some portions of this road between Montreal and Kingston had been opened as early as 1790, but one traveller stated that no one would think of using it if he could secure conveyance on the St. Lawrence.

The Loyalists who came to Ontario went to the Niagara district, and to Prince Edward County, west of Kingston. The first road from Kingston to the west went through Bath, Adolphustown, to the Carrying Place on the Bay of Quinte, near the present city of Trenton. Most of this original area of United Empire Loyalist settlement is now quiet countryside, for it was later by-passed by the present Kingston Road, Highway Number 2.

The Niagara Loyalists had made a road of sorts from Newark (Niagara-on-the-Lake), to Ancaster, northwest of the present city of Hamilton. Before the end of the century there were two roads. One of these was at the foot of the escarpment, away from the lake. This road had two long stretches of corduroy road, each three miles in length. Mrs. Simcoe called this a "terrible road, full of swamp, fallen trees," etc. Another road was opened from Niagara to Burlington, which followed the shore of the lake. In 1796, Simcoe had construction started on a road at the top of the escarpment. A map of 1815 shows these three roads, and many other farm roads. On this map the long stretches of corduroy road were still on this road below the escarpment.

In 1791, Ontario had settlements at Detroit, along the Niagara River, extending to Ancaster, and along the St. Lawrence and Lake Ontario, as far west as the Bay of Quinte. The Detroit settlement was French, with more than two thousand inhabitants, and was at this time the largest town in the province. When it was surrendered to the U.S.A., in 1796, by the Jay Treaty, however, its population dropped to about five hundred and most of its French-Canadian population moved across the river to live under British rule. The total population of the province in 1791 was about twelve thousand. At is inception, Toronto was virtually isolated between Burlington Bay, to the west, and the Bay of Quinte to the east. In this long stretch of about one hundred and fifty-five miles there was an Indian trail close to the lake, but no road, and there was no road to Lake Simcoe.

As previously mentioned, Governor Simcoe's choice for the location of the capital of the province was the site of the present London, but Toronto, even if it was not to be the permanent capital was a strategic location for army and navy forces, thirty miles by water from the American shore. He also felt that Toronto was the ideal location for a road to Lake Simcoe, which he foresaw as having both commercial and military value, for it would take the fur-traders' route to Lake Huron away from the international border. At any rate, Toronto would be the capital for some years. The area around it must be quickly developed to the extent of supporting it as the capital by bringing farm produce from the north of the town. As Assembly members came to Toronto from as far away as Cornwall to the east and Amherstberg to the west, it was imperative that roads be constructed to all parts of the province.

Simcoe envisioned a road across the province, which he proposed to call Dundas Street, to stretch from the Quebec border to Detroit, and a road from Toronto to Lake Simcoe, which he would name Yonge Street. As something of a scholar, as well as a soldier, he liked the term street, which the Romans had used for their primitive military roads in Britain. Yonge Street was named to honour Sir George Yonge, Secretary of War in 1791, and a personal friend. Dundas Street was named to honour the Right Hon. Henry Dundas, Secretary of State for the colonies in 1794.

Simcoe made a road, of sorts, of the Mississauga trail from Burlington to Toronto. Then in 1793, with one hundred men of the Queen's Rangers he had construction started upon his Dundas Street to London. As early as 1804 tenders were called to improve the lakeshore road, from Toronto to Burlington, and construct bridges. Only a part of this was finished in 1810. At the same time, Dundas Street was also under repair and improvement.

With possible war with the U.S.A. in mind, Governor Simcoe had rest stations constructed in several locations on these new roads. These buildings were fairly large for the times, and were leased to civilians, for a token rental, to keep them in repair, and they were used as general stores and hotels. The primary purpose in constructing them, however, was for use as military storehouses and troop stations in case of war. In 1793, one of these buildings was erected near the mouth of the Credit River and used first as a storehouse and then as a tavern. Another, called the King's Head Tavern, was located at the south end of Burlington Beach, and was built in 1794.

Yonge Street, which had been an Indian trail and a portage road, was cut through as a bush road by thirty men of the Queen's Rangers, from the present Eglinton Avenue to the Holland River, between the fourth of January and the sixteenth of February, 1794. As the distance was thirty miles, it is evident that no real road was constructed in less than six weeks. No gulleys were filled or rivers bridged, and it was many years before it could be safely used.

This unfinished Yonge Street was used to some extent by the North-West Fur Company. Their supplies came from Oswego, in New York State in bateaux which were lifted over the peninsula and travelled up the Don River to York Mills. Here the freight was loaded on wagons for the long road trip up Yonge Street to the Holland River, and finally to Lake Huron. This inland route from Lake Ontario to Lake Huron was forced upon the reluctant fur-traders until the War of 1812 made it a necessity. In 1820, however, the North-West Fur Company merged with the Hudson's Bay Company and the latter company's northern route was adopted, and Yonge Street ceased to be a fur-trader's road. Toronto's future expansion was not to be based upon furs. German settlers from Pennsylvania also used this road. They came to Ontario in Conestoga wagons which they used as boats to cross rivers and streams, to reach their settlement at German Mills, and other locations near Yonge Street.

In 1799 a contract was let to Asa Danforth, an American, for a road from Toronto to the Bay of Quinte, and this was to be completed July 1, 1800. This road was the best. It was thirty-three feet wide, with a road-bed, if such it could be called, sixteen feet six inches wide. Danforth was to receive $90.00 per mile, and forty labourers recommended by him were to receive two hundred acres of Crown Land as well as their wages. Two whole townships were sold to pay for the cost of this road. Although his road was highly praised, Danforth retired in ill humour to the U.S.A. shortly after the road was completed. He sent copies of a printed pamphlet, containing his grievances against the government, to a friend in Ontario for distribution. We are told that the friend did not carry out Danforth's instructions.

His road was called the "York Road" when leaving Kingston, and the "Kingston Road," when leaving Toronto. Some also called it the Danforth or Danforth's Road, while the memory of its builder was still fresh. In most locations, this road was north of the present Kingston Road, Highway Number 2.

All mill machinery was turned by waterwheels at this time, for the Gooderham windmill was not built until 1832. The water-mills were located on rivers, and roads had to be constructed to them. Early maps show "road to Cooper's Mills," constructed in 1801, and situated on the Humber River at the present Dundas Street. This road is shown beginning at the present Richmond Street, west of Garrison Creek. Richmond continued west to the lakeshore to become the road to Burlington.

Another such road led to Timothy Skinner's gristmill on the east bank of the Don, one mile north of Castle Frank, and this mill was built in 1794. This road was located on the edge of the Don Valley, following the route of the present Broadview Avenue. Some claim that the first paper made in Ontario was from this mill in 1826.

In 1810, the main roads of the province could be said to be completed. The main road across the province from Montreal to the present Windsor, and from the head of the lake to Niagara and Queenston, and from Toronto to Lake Simcoe were in use, although major bridges had not been constructed.

Those who have walked, or have driven cars over old logging roads, or over little-used concession "dirt" roads in poor farming districts, will have some idea of the best roads in 1810. Sharp grades or swampy lands were avoided with detours; the gutters were inadequate, or there were none at all; in many stretches the stumps of trees had merely been sawn or chopped at grade level, without removing the roots. In some sections the branches of trees formed a sun-excluding roof. Creeks were crossed with corduroy bridges, which had a life of about six years. Rivers were spanned more often with a raft ferry than a bridge. On Lake Ontario, particularly, the road was an adjunct of water travel, for both bateau and schooner were faster and cheaper for both passengers and freight.

The first stagecoach line from Toronto to Newark, at the mouth of the Niagara River, was inaugurated in 1816, and the journey took four days. In the winter of 1817 the first stage, using sleigh runners, began a regular run between Toronto and Kingston.

The main roads at their inception had been constructed by the Queen's Rangers Regiment, and the government of the province had raised the money, in some cases, by selling whole townships. The streets of Toronto, however, were constructed with statute labour. As there was insufficient wealth in the town to tax, the people themselves had to do this work. Some cash, however, for the cost of this work on the streets was provided from the fines paid by those who neglected to do their statute labour, and public subscription provided money also.

The roadways of the town were simply earth, filled in where stumps had been removed, levelled and graded with shovels, with here and there an attempt to create gutters which experience with torrential rains had suggested. There was no gravel on the streets, at this time, and in the spring, horses, oxen and wagons ploughed through deep ruts and water.

The footpaths were earth, and were worn hard and smooth, in many places with the pedestrian traffic. There was a crude flagstone walk in front of Jordan's Hotel, and tanbark constituted a footpath alongside the tannery property. Some building owners must have placed a few flagstones on the public footpath in front of their property, but there appears to be no record of bringing flagstone from the Humber for "sidewalks." There would be no uniformity, of course, and some footpaths would be neat while others would be neglected. In 1816, however, new regulations to be enforced by the pathmasters provided that footpaths were to be eleven feet in width and "no person shall presume, in front of their premises, to raise the footpath as to occasion a step unless the Magistrates in Session approve . . ."

Hitching posts were placed at the whim of the owner, and ranged from mere log posts set in the ground to neat squared-timber ones, complete with iron rings to fasten reins. Horizontal hitching rails were, no doubt, used at such buildings as hotels.

At the inception of the town, and for many years afterwards, there was no attempt to make the names of streets sound significant or important by borrowing such adjectives as "boulevard," "avenue," etc. Streets were simply named after people, or the name came from some activity upon it. Market Street, later Wellington Street, was the southern boundary of Market Square. Yonge Street and Dundas Street have been mentioned. The town itself was named for Frederick, the popular Duke of York, son of George III. Duke and Frederick became the names of streets. George Street was named for the heir-apparent, George, Prince of Wales and Caroline Street for his wife.

Some of the street names in New and Old Town were later changed. Prince Street became Princess Street, Caroline was changed to Sherbourne Street, New Street became Jarvis, Graves became Simcoe, and Newgate was altered to Adelaide Street. To avoid confusion, both the original and the present names are shown on the map and the text on the front end-paper.

The streets of Toronto may be more easily visualized by referring to this map. The original limits of the town laid out in 1793 by A. Aitken, the surveyor, were Berkeley Street to the east, George Street to the west, and Duke Street to the north. As the town grew, the bed of the creek entering the Bay west of Jarvis Street prevented growth in that direction, so the expansion jumped this creek area to approximately what is now Church Street. What the inhabitants called "New Town" started at the present Victoria Street and extended to Peter Street, in 1810.

In this westward expansion the town blocks created were larger, and some buildings were built back from the street line. Hospital Street (Richmond), became the street which led west to the lakeshore, and the lakeshore road to Burlington. It was seriously proposed in 1800 to close up Lot Street (Queen), because it had no value, being so close to Hospital Street (Richmond). The money from the sale of this street would be used to extend Yonge Street from Queen Street to the Bay. Perhaps it was the owners of the Park Lots (Part 1, Chap. 3) who raised the greatest objection to this recommendation, and it was abandoned.

Neither Queen, Adelaide or Wellington Street crossed the ravine of what we have called the Fifth Creek. Two temporary roads meandered southeast through this area, on the northern bank, to connect with King Street and Jarvis. King was the important street of the town and it led to the Kingston Road. The Fifth Creek was crossed on King Street. This creek valley was eventually filled in so that all east-west streets could be carried through. Such improvement came gradually, for there was a limit to the street work that could be performed by statute labour, fines and subscriptions.

As mentioned, Yonge Street stopped at the present Eglinton Avenue in 1794. In 1796 Berczy's men continued this road south as far as the present Yorkville Avenue, north of Bloor Street. All of this section from Queen to Yorkville was spoken of as the road to Yonge Street. It was narrow, neglected, and full of stumps. The road to Yonge Street stopped at Queen, and the area below was privately-owned land. Farmers from the north turned off Yonge Street at Yorkville, and found a haphazard way across vacant private property on the east bank of the Sixth Creek to the present Parliament and King Street, and then to the market. In 1802 this road to Yonge Street was greatly improved with money raised by private subscription. It stopped at Queen Street, however, and continued south to the east of the present street to avoid private property, such as the tan yard which Jesse Ketchum purchased in 1812. Before 1810 it was projected straight through to Wellington. The owners affected were given parcels of other land in exchange for the right of way through their property.

In 1807 we find that a number of public-spirited citizens held a meeting to raise money to cut down the hill on Yonge Street at Frank's Creek, a minor branch of the Don which crossed Yonge Street in the location of the present Rosedale subway station. The precipitous banks on both sides of this river branch were called the "Blue Hill," referring to the blue clay on the summits. The condition of Yonge Street in this location after autumnal rains and spring thaws was indescribably bad. Other ravines north of the town had to wait their turn for settlement to improve the road with statute labour. Another hill dreaded by farmers was "Gallows Hill," at the present Farnham Avenue, below St. Clair Avenue. The grade of this steep hill had been partially reduced with pick-and-shovel excavation to create a sunken road. Across this cut a large tree had fallen. A gallows, at this time, consisted of two uprights and a cross piece. To many who travelled up this hill under the tree, it suggested a gallows. At the top of the hill was a crude windlass used by the North-West

Company to haul their bateaux on wheels up this hill. The first toll gate on Yonge Street was at the present Bloor Street in 1820. In 1850 the toll gate was moved to the northwest corner of Davenport Road and Yonge.

In 1828 a start was made in putting gravel on the streets, and in 1842 Charles Dickens, on his American tour, mentioned that the streets of Toronto were well paved. The last road surface for streets before the brick, concrete and asphalt surfaces of today was cedar-block paving. This surface was more even and less dusty than the gravel it superseded. It was inaugurated in 1871, when a few streets downtown were paved. Some years later, one writer mentioned grass and weeds six inches high growing between these paving blocks on a residential street. The last cedar-block paving was laid about 1915.

CHAPTER 3

The Town

Speculations made before this present century created many conjectures for the origin and the meaning of the word Toronto. These nineteenth-century historians did not have access to much information available today. Modern analysts now appear to have the correct explanation.

In 1632 the Franciscan missionary, Gabriel Sagard, compiled a dictionary of the Huron language. The word "Toronto" in his lexicon meant, "much or plenty, applied to persons or things." It was not a proper name; in fact the Indians had no proper names of places. Locations were designated by them verbally (for they had no written language) with a brief description or reference to past incidents.

Before 1650 the word Toronto does not appear upon any known maps by the Recollet and Jesuit missions among the Huron Indians of the Georgian Bay area. This Huron country extended from Georgian Bay to Lake Simcoe. The population became thinner toward the south, for the closer to Lake Ontario the greater became the menace of fierce Iroquois of the present New York State. White men in contact with Indians often heard the word Toronto, when their redskin companions pointed to Huronia, the land of the Huron Indians. They began to understand that the word Toronto meant land of plenty.

After Fort Saint Marie was destroyed in 1650, the Hurons were scattered, and the name Toronto began to appear on French maps as the name of Georgian Bay, the name of Lake Simcoe, a trail through the forest, etc. It was never shown on these maps as the name of any Huron village. Later, in the seventeen hundreds, the name Toronto appeared on maps as the name of the present Humber River, the Severn River, Fort Rouillé, etc. It is possible that early French map-makers intended the word as a temporary name until an official selection had been made.

Lord Dorchester, the governor of the Canadas, arranged the Toronto Purchase from the Mississauga Indians in 1787-88. In his agent's discussions with the Mississauga, they used the name Toronto to describe the two hundred and fifty thousand acres of fertile land which changed from Indian to white ownership. Dorchester visited the site in 1788, and saw the silent waters of the bay and the limitless forest behind it. Perhaps after his long terms of office in Canada he was fascinated with words in the Indian language, and to him the unspoiled land of the Purchase was still Indian. At any rate, he intended the name Toronto for the town which would eventually have its inception on the Bay shore.

Five years later a man of different character, fresh from England, saw forest trees crashing down under the axes of the men of the Queen's Rangers, and buildings being erected to create another England in the wilderness of Upper Canada (Ontario). An English name would make the town more English. We may also conjecture that Governor Simcoe's personal dislike of Lord Dorchester provided the motive for seeing in the Duke of York's victory in Holland a good reason for changing the name which his superior had selected.

New York City had been named after the brother of Charles II of England and, of course, there was already a town in England named York. To distinguish it from both of the others he called it "Little York." The prefix was indicative of the little plans which he made for the town. From the beginning most people ignored the "little," and some continued to call the town Toronto. At the date of the naming of the town York, August 27, 1793, twelve houses had been erected.

Later, in 1804, a certain Angus MacDonald unsuccessfully submitted a petition to the Legislature to bring in a bill to restore the name of Toronto. This is indicative of the feeling of a large number of the inhabitants of the town, who finally created sufficient public sentiment to have it restored, when it became an incorporated city.

In 1810 the people of Toronto were living in a town seventeen years old, and the birth of the first white child had taken place sixteen years before. As in all pioneering communities, the men outnumbered the women and the average age of the inhabitants was less than a generation later. The population, if we take the average of the assessment figures for 1809 and 1811, was 630.

This figure does not include the British soldiers of the Garrison and blockhouses, which comprised three companies of the 41st Regiment. The growth to 1810 was slow, for many families moved into the township after a sojourn in the town. Because of the war, the population in 1813 was a few less than in 1810. It began to rise slowly in 1814, so that by 1825 it was 1,677. In 1833 it was nine thousand.

In 1810 the buildings of Toronto included the Houses of Parliament, two blockhouses, buildings of the Garrison, jail, Home District registry office (in a private residence), custom house and post office, one church, six hotels including a boarding house, tanyard, wagon factory, ship-building yard, about six stores including a book store, and a general store in a hotel, an open air market, a potashery, a distillery and a brewery, slaughter house, bakery oven, newspaper office and a printing shop, watchmaker's store and a market garden. The government owned a warehouse for Indian treaty presents and other buildings for military and naval stores. Outside the town were four saw and grist mills on the Don and the Humber Rivers. There were also more than one hundred houses.

Numerous buildings, some at the back of lots, were occupied by furniture and chair-makers, saddlers, carpenters, wheelwrights, coopers, tinsmiths, blacksmiths, bricklayers, and plasterers. Rooms in private houses were used by the government as offices, for which the Crown paid rent. It was not until 1832, when the Houses of Parliament were built on Front Street, that enough office space was available. Usually tailors, milliners, shoemakers, hatters, hairdressers and barbers operated from their own modest dwellings, but in some cases they rented. Sometimes the houses they used had an additional door to the street for privacy, added after construction. All of these trades, crafts and services were necessary to make the town self-sufficient in an age of hand labour and slow transportation.

Most residences had a stable of some kind, usually with haymow above, and some people grew hay on their lots. Haystacks became a fire hazard and were forbidden in 1812. The town lots were one acre in extent and this was large enough to permit the owner's horse to graze. Many householders kept chickens and other fowl. A few had their own cows, and some raised pigs. A few owners had a smokehouse on their property for curing meat, and some had root cellars. Many households had a few squared logs, fence rails or rough-sawn boards on their property drying out for use the following year, for many men made some of their own furniture. Many had flower gardens and most people grew vegetables – if only turnips and potatoes. A few fruit trees on residential lots was usual.

Garbage was a problem for all, for it was not collected. Householders had to cart it away to be dumped or buried, or they burnt it on their own property. There were no tin cans, or cardboard cartons, and bottles were not usually intentionally discarded unless broken. The garbage of the period was fireplace cleaning, housecleaning dust and food refuse. Some, of course, were less conscientious than others in disposing of it before it attracted flies and had a bad odour. It was not until the first cholera epidemic of 1831-32, that a genuine effort was made to clean refuse from private property.

A magistrate's order of 1802 stated that refuse lumber and shavings from carpenter shops must be burnt on Wednesdays and Saturdays at sunset, and that butchers must bury offal or remove it from the town. Readers who have never seen a horse pulling a wagon must be reminded that horses and oxen provided transportation for men and material, and their droppings were not removed by street cleaners until the streets were paved.

As early as 1804 a nursery garden on Duchess Street was advertised for sale, and it contained more than ten thousand apple trees, as well as an assortment of peach, pear, cherry, plum trees, and many varieties of berry bushes.

Cattle, branded on the horns, roamed between the town and the Humber River, and sometimes strayed to Toronto's streets. Board fences, five feet in height, hid back lots from the street, and kept out stray dogs, wild pigs and other marauders. These plank fences were sometimes whitewashed, but more often they were not. Some of the better houses had picket fences at the street line.

Simcoe attempted to push through what would have been Toronto's first property restrictions, with houses of minimum width twelve feet back from street lines to give, as he expressed it, "an architectural uniformity to the town." His recommendations were not carried out. Practically all of the buildings of "Old Town" had their front walls on the street line. In "New Town" a few were built back. There was little planning or order of any kind, except that an effort was made to keep workmen's houses and businesses at the north limit of the town. Generally, the owners of lots built what they wanted. A regulation required that all town lots sold be cleared of underbrush within a short time but trees on lots not built upon were not necessarily cut down.

As the owners of both modest and large frame houses had come from somewhere else, the architecture was not regional but varied. It resulted from the taste of the owner and the skill of the master carpenter. Correspondence of the period reveals that carpenters were very busy tradesmen, receiving what were considered to be exorbitant wages. They often went to new clients as a favour, so it is to be expected that with some buildings lack of time precluded the architectural embellishment which came a decade later. Every residence and every building was unique in form and size, but unlike today there was only one architectural style. This style was interpreted by each master carpenter. Some buildings were exceedingly plain; others had considerable interest and charm. In every example, however, except the two brick buildings, it was the classic tradition of architecture adapted to wood construction. We have since called this the colonial style, although the phrase was not used in 1810.

Records of 1809 reveal there were 14 round log houses, 11 one-storey and 27 two-storey squared-log houses, and 55 one-storey frame houses. This, of course, is an assessment classification. Many of the one-storey frame houses were what today would be described as storey-and-a-half houses, and had rooms and dormer or gable-end windows on a second level. All of the frame buildings and some of the squared-log houses had an exterior of clapboarding, or siding, and these houses were painted. The squared-log houses without clapboarding were seldom painted or whitewashed, and it is a safe guess that none of the round-log houses ever received paint, except on the mortar between the logs. The singleness of style, materials and the uniform scale compensated, to some extent, for the general untidiness on the lots, the absence of paint on some buildings, and the plain board fences.

The above description of Toronto about 1810 will make the reader, familiar with modern residential suburbs, think that the town would be considered very untidy-looking today. Now let us see what the people of the time thought of Toronto. In 1806 a travelling Presbyterian minister called it "a pleasant town." About 1808, John Melish, an American, said it was "a pleasant town containing a good many frame houses, but the land is rather low and unhealthy in its neighbourhood." In 1814 Dr. Dunlap, a British army surgeon, called it "a dirty, straggling village." A young Toronto resident, visiting in England in 1811 wrote to his father: "I am so prejudiced in favour of York (Toronto), that I think it is the neatest and prettiest place I have ever seen."[3] His brother in Toronto, in replying to his letter, however, called his hometown a "miserable hole." But this young lad, no doubt, was envying his brother's tour of England. In 1814 Joseph Bouchette, in his book of travel, noted that "it promises to become a very handsome town."

There were, of course, no public utilities. Even the first public well, which was dug on the market property, did not come until 1822. All houses had a cistern of some kind for washing water. This was a keg or barrel under a roof gutter, or occasionally a brick tank in the cellar. A few had shallow wells on their property, but most secured their drinking water from the Don River or the nearest creek. They went for this water with wood or leather buckets or tin pails; the more prosperous had carters deliver it to their doors. The streets were not lighted, and those visiting at night usually carried lanterns. The footpaths were earth, beaten down by the feet of pedestrians; improved in some locations with gravel or flagstone, or thick planks laid in the pools of water in the spring.

In 1810 the future of Toronto was in doubt. There was considerable caution by private individuals in spending money upon their homes or places of business, for their investment would depreciate if the capital was moved to London or Kingston. As late as 1816 one traveller described the town as wholly useless as a port or a military post. He wrote that it would, "sink into a village, and the seat of government be transferred to Kingston, but for the influence of those whose property in the place would be depreciated by the change."[4] This feeling of apprehension regarding Toronto's future lasted for a considerable time after 1810.

The town, as laid out by Simcoe's surveyor in 1793, consisted of an area north and west of the parliament buildings. It covered ten small blocks or squares, on the north and south sides of King Street, extending from George Street at the west, to Berkeley Street at the east limit. This original area later extended north to Duchess Street, and west to the present Victoria Street. By 1810 the town, on paper at least, extended to Peter Street. A plan by D. W. Smith, the Surveyor General, shows seventy-four lots, large and small, and two large squares between Peter and Graves (Simcoe) Street, from Lot, (Queen) Street to the Bay. This was mostly on paper, however, for a plan of 1814 shows only a dozen buildings in this area. This westward expansion was separated from the original town by the valley of the fifth creek, and was called "New Town." There was much rivalry between the original and the new part of the town, particularly among small boys.

Many surveys had been made of the Toronto area, including the harbour, prior to the arrival of Governor Simcoe, in May, 1793. In 1791, Augustus Jones laid out eleven townships, starting from the River Trent. The most westerly of these was north of Toronto Bay, and was named York, and this township extended from Scarborough to the Humber River. The present Queen Street became a postulated line for land division, and thirty-five township lots, one quarter mile in width from east to west, were shown on this map. Five such quarter-mile lots constituted a "concession," and this concession division of land is still used today.

Simcoe felt that government officials in Niagara deserved compensation for moving to Toronto, and he conceived of a way to reward them. On paper, he created thirty-two one-hundred-acre "park lots" north of the present Queen Street, extending north a distance of one concession to the present Bloor Street. These lots were one-half a township lot, or one-eighth of a mile in width and one and one-quarter miles in depth from south to north. The proportion of width to length was one to ten. They were so narrow because Simcoe wished to obtain the maximum number of park lots close to the town.

Park lots number 1 and 2 were in the location of township lot number 17, and the present Bright Street was the eastern limit. Lots number 31 and 32 were created from township lot number 32, whose boundary was the present Springhurst Avenue in Parkdale. Thus for a distance of four miles, a limit was placed upon the northern expansion of the town. The park lots, along with a town lot were granted free to a select number of people.

At a period when the upper class in England lived upon estates, and Simcoe was in favour of a Canadian aristocracy, such one-hundred-acre park lots would serve the double purpose of rewarding government officials who were forced to sell their homes and move to Toronto, and encourage the creation of an upper class by providing land for "estates." He also made the town lots smaller than originally planned to "prevent the scattering of the Inhabitants in such situations as their fancy or interest might induce them which would ever prevent that compactness in a Town which it seems proper to establish." The area from Peter Street to the Humber River at the west, and from Parliament Street to the Don River was reserved for military and government purposes. The area north of the town presented a solid phalanx of park lots.

When Simcoe's term of office ended, he left Toronto ready to grow like a sleepy provincial village in England. He did not realize, apparently, that because of the rapid expansion of the country as a whole and the low cost of land, no town in America was expanding compactly compared with Europe. He also greatly underestimated the potential growth of Toronto; not realizing that it must grow with the whole province. His park lots were soon swept away.

At the end of his term of office most of the town and park lots had been granted, but few buildings had been erected. Most recipients built their town houses first, in the hope that their fortunes would increase sufficiently to build upon their estate lots. In 1810 only a few had residences upon them, but some were being partially cleared as profitable farms, which supplied Toronto with much of its dairy products and other food. It is probable that much of the firewood sold in the town came from park lots, for some owners wished to have the southern portion of their lots cleared as soon as possible.

In a short time after the War of 1812, however, these lots began to be broken into parcels of land. New streets were projected and thousands of individuals made money from the purchase and sale of this original park lot land. In some cases, members of Toronto's "oldest" families are simply descendants of men who retained large areas of their park lots longer than others. They maintained a large family income by selling portions of their property when it became most valuable.

The retention of this land permitted institutions to acquire large lots for building purposes. One park lot was named Gore Vale, in honour of Governor Gore, and the lower portion of it became the grounds of Trinity College, on Queen Street west, built in 1851.

In 1810 land was not increasing in value, and those who expected it to were disappointed. Perhaps the reason was not as clear then as it is today. Those in Toronto had heard of the rapid increase in land value in the U.S.A. and many expected this to be duplicated in the province. The case of Mrs. White, wife of the Attorney-General, may be illustrative of this seemingly perpetual slump in land value. Mrs. White's husband had been killed in a duel, and she applied for a grant of land in recognition of his former service. Her petition was finally granted, but a year later she applied for cash instead, for she found that her land could neither be rented nor sold. At this time land was being practically given away, with the payment of the surveying fee. Even this fee was remitted if the settler was a United Empire Loyalist. In some locations even an improved farm, with a small house, barn, and fences, did not sell for much more than the surveying fee for one uncleared.

When the Danforth Road was constructed in 1799, the government was forced to sell two entire townships, Dereham and Norwich, in the Long Point settlement, to raise sufficient money for the project. The Mississauga Indians offered to sell sixty-nine thousand acres of their property to the government for a colony of French émigrés, at 1s. 3d. per acre, Halifax currency, equal to $2.50 per acre today. The government declined because the price was considered too high. This slump in land value lasted for some years after 1810, for as long as the population was small the supply exceeded the demand. This land cost was reflected in Toronto. Town lots, of course, had a far greater value per acre than farmland, but even here there was little profit in selling, for the population was increasing very slowly.

As previously mentioned, the six creeks had made miniature valleys, in what is now, downtown Toronto, for the shore of the Bay was twelve to twenty feet above the water. Until 1810, and for generations later, hard slugging with shovel and wheelbarrow went on to level the land by filling in these creek beds. As late as 1842 the valley of Garrison Creek had not been filled in, and buildings stopped at the curving Niagara Street which followed the east side of the valley. In the modern High Park the reader may see the original terrain, and realize the tremendous task to level hills and fill valleys.

Of necessity, at this period, all towns were self contained, in the sense that they were not satellites of larger ones, and Toronto was no exception. Cloth was imported, but men's and women's clothing was made by tailors in town. Some boots and shoes were imported, but the average man depended upon the town shoemaker. No goods were manufactured which required machinery or elaborate equipment, but cabinetmakers made most of the furniture sold in the town, and wheelwrights made vehicles. The blacksmith, who later became dedicated to providing shoes for horses, was an ironmonger in 1810, and made such articles as axe blades and barn hinges. Coopers made kegs and barrels, for such articles were too bulky in proportion to their value to import. Wine, and the best liquor were imported from Europe, but much of the whiskey and beer was made in the town.

Many readers have heard of the so-called Castle Frank (see Illustration No. 8), located below the present Bloor Street, near the west bank of the Don River. While Governor Simcoe was living in his canvas tent, and other temporary locations, he had the Queen's Rangers construct this residence in the forest in 1795. He named it after his infant son, who later, in 1812, died a soldier's death in Spain. Castle Frank was never permanently occupied by Simcoe as a residence; in fact the interior was never finished. It was a kind of retreat, like the modern cottage on a northern lake owned by a city apartment dweller. (His residence at Newark had been a miserable wooden house). The people of Toronto likened Castle Frank to a Greek temple, and so it must have looked from the Don River below it.

It was constructed of squared logs, covered with clapboarding, and was thirty by fifty feet in size. There were four shuttered windows on each side, but only an entrance door under the projecting gable roof forming a porch. This projecting gable roof was supported upon four unbarked pine-tree trunks sixteen feet high, simulating the columns of a Greek temple.

The detailing of this little building was crudely executed. The window shutters and the door consisted of a double thickness of one-inch boards, heavily studded with nails. The exterior was never painted. The single chimney in the centre of the roof took flues from two fireplaces; one facing a living-room, inside the front door, and the other facing a large floor area at the rear used for sleeping and dining. Only this one cross partition was ever constructed.

Peter Russell, upon the invitation from Simcoe writing from England, used Castle Frank as a place to entertain official visitors for a short time after Simcoe returned to England, but by 1808 the building was closed and tenantless. Finally neighbours began to steal lumber from it, and in 1829 some careless fishermen burnt it to the ground. It was a very unimportant little building. Its veneration and fame lie entirely in the fact that it was the only place our first Lieutenant-Governor could call home during his term of office in Canada.

CHAPTER 4

The Garrison

The Toronto of 1810 was expecting an invasion of Canada by the Americans. As today, there was a great disparity in the populations of the United States and Canada, and any realist could be certain that the U.S.A. could conquer Canada, if she so wished. This threat of war had existed since the American Revolution, and when Governor Simcoe became the first Lieutenant-Governor of the Province of Ontario, his first thought was defence. He was convinced, or acted as though he believed, that Canada could be defended, and did his best to bring this about by building roads and military works. He would have gone much farther in military building but for the opposition of Lord Dorchester and the Home Office in London. When Simcoe returned to England in July, 1796, the town had the "Garrison," a mere collection of log huts, and a gun platform on the Peninsula. There was no Fort York in 1810. The garrison on the lakefront developed into the fort of 1816. This restored military work, now called Fort York, is situated in the shadow of the elevated Gardiner Expressway, and is one of the tourist attractions of the present city. The reader is reminded that this fort, restored to its condition in 1816, and three thousand feet from the shore of Lake Ontario, is in its original location. Land fill begun in the railroad era, and further developed since 1913, appears to have moved it far inland.

The reader is referred to the back end-paper, which shows the Garrison in 1810, which consisted of military buildings on level land on both sides of this creek and also in the creek valley. The location was one mile east of the ruins of Fort Toronto, and about two-thirds of a mile west of the most westerly street in Toronto at that time. It was also slightly west of Gibraltar Point, on the peninsula, the location of the gun platform. These two locations, on opposite sides of nearly a mile of water, were intended to permit cross firing upon enemy vessels entering the harbour.

Before the arrival of Simcoe there were no barracks or fortifications of any kind in the Toronto area. Enough of the charred remains of the palisade and the buildings of Fort Toronto, in its three hundred acre clearing, was left to be shown on maps, but the rest of the site of the new town was still a wilderness.

Many of those who have visited the restored "Fort York" may not be aware that a wide stream called Garrison Creek once emptied into the lake on the east side. The shoreline at this time was about eighteen feet above the water, and the creek had made a valley about two hundred and forty feet wide. Simcoe drew a rough sketch, with notes, of his proposal, for a fort or garrison on the west side of the creek, on the site of the existing Fort York, and as early as 1791 wrote to Dorchester that he proposed to construct stone barracks for two hundred and fifty men. His superior did not approve of spending money on military works at Toronto, and Simcoe had to change his plans. In 1793-4 he constructed thirty barracks or huts on this west side of the creek. The outlay for even these modest buildings was questioned, and Simcoe found it necessary to explain in his letters that the cost of labour in Toronto was excessive. These barracks were simply rectangular cabins made of round logs. They had gable roofs and two or three windows, with shutters, on each side. Some contained double-tiered bunks for sleeping, others were used as hospital, canteen, bakehouse, etc. In 1795 a powder magazine was constructed in the location of the east end of the present Fort York. This storage for gunpowder and shot, which certainly should have been of masonry, was built of squared hemlock logs. It replaced the first magazine, a temporary structure whose roof had caved in. Simcoe was aware that this type of log construction had a life of only about seven years.

It is probable that some sort of temporary wharf was built at the mouth of the creek, which proved unsatisfactory because of the changing water level and the prevailing winds.

In 1793 he had his engineers prepare a cost estimate for a combined storehouse and blockhouse on the peninsula, which was to be partially constructed of masonry. This also proved to be too expensive, and a substitute was constructed. About 1796 the first wharf was built on the east side of the creek. Simcoe also planned to erect a blockhouse, and had the framing timbers prepared. Work was stopped, however, probably because of the wording of a letter he received from Dorchester before it was erected. This was the extent of Simcoe's contribution to the military works of Toronto, but it was no fault of his that there was no fort to resist the American attack upon Toronto in 1813.

Russell, the new governor, now attempted to strengthen the Garrison. In 1797 he had his engineers use the framing timbers, which Simcoe had prepared, to construct a blockhouse on the projection of land on the east side of the creek. This defensible barracks was two floors in height, and appears to have been less than thirty-five feet square. It was intended to accommodate seventy men. This situation on the projection of land on the east side of the creek was the most prominent location at the entrance to the harbour. Russell also constructed additional huts, on this side and enclosed this area, on three sides, with a palisade. In writing to his superior, Russell said that he intended to place a navigation light on top of this building. This light is not shown on the sketches of the British Army officer, later mentioned, or on a sketch of 1803. It is possible, however, that this artist omitted it from his drawings for pictorial reasons. If this light was constructed it was probably a large lantern on a crude frame and platform, raised some feet above the blockhouse roof.

This blockhouse, mentioned by eyewitnesses to the American attack in 1813, and situated on the east side of the creek, has been confused with the east blockhouse within the present Fort York. Until recently this Fort York blockhouse was considered to have been constructed by Simcoe in 1793, or even earlier. A Toronto newspaper plan of the "Old Fort", published in 1930 before restoration, stated that this east blockhouse within the present fort was constructed in 1749, and that the date of the west blockhouse was unknown. More authentic accounts gave the date of this east blockhouse within "Fort York" as 1793, and the date of the west blockhouse within the fort as 1813. These latter dates were accepted for a considerable time, and it was thought that when the Americans made their first attack upon Toronto in 1813 the soldiers' barracks and the blockhouse were in this west side of creek area.

Because of this misunderstanding it was assumed that the Garrison Wharf was actually in the creek bed, and some nineteenth-century historians have mentioned that it was widened at the mouth and that canal locks were constructed.

An inventory of military property made in 1880 mentioned the "Canal, locks and wharf at the Garrison." It does not appear that these locks were referred to in any other source account. This is the basis for the assumption that the canal and locks were in the mouth of the creek, and this supposition was also based upon the creek mouth being the nearest sheltered water to the supposed location of the Garrison.

Recent research has established that there was no blockhouse in 1793. The blockhouse erected by President Russell in 1797, and burnt by the Americans in 1813, was actually on the east side of the creek, and both blockhouses within the restored fort were constructed after the first attack in 1813. This creek has been described as eighteen feet wide and also thirty feet in width. On a large scale plan of the new fort, drawn in 1816, it scales only twelve feet. The "mouth of the creek" was apparently taken too literally by nineteenth-century historians, for this wharf was actually at the east side of the knoll upon which Russell's blockhouse was situated, and on the east side of the creek. This location seems reasonable for the prevailing winds are from the west. As soon as the "Eastern Gap" was opened in 1858 this eastern entrance to the harbour was used almost exclusively. In selecting the location for the first wharf, which was mostly used to supply the Garrison, the east side of this tongue of land projecting into the lake was the logical location, for it was protected from prevailing winds, and was located at the base of the blockhouse.

Three watercolour sketches by Lieut. Sempronius Stretton, of the 49th Regiment, made in 1803-4-5, show this blockhouse on the east side of the creek, and the Governor's residence on the west side. His sketch of 1805 shows a palisade on the east side of the creek carried down the steep bank and continuing into the water of the lake. A dock is shown east of this palisade, and a road leads up the bank to the blockhouse and Garrison buildings above. It is reasonable to suppose that the "canal locks" consisted of gates in this dock. During stormy weather a bateau could be sheltered or unloaded between the dock and the palisade.

In 1798 there were fears of an Indian uprising (which proved to be unfounded), and Russell had a blockhouse, as later described, constructed at the east end of the town, west of the Parliament Buildings.

By 1799 the military buildings included round-log huts on both sides of Garrison Creek, a blockhouse on the east side, a wooden powder magazine on the west side, a two-storey storehouse for Indian treaty presents, and the blockhouse at the east end of the town. There were also two squared-log and clapboarded buildings for storage, and a guardhouse on Gibraltar Point on the Peninsula.

In 1800, under the administration of Lieutenant-General Peter Hunter, a governor's residence was constructed on the west side of the creek, within the area of what is now called Fort York. It was called the Government House.

A report made in 1802 lists the military buildings, which comprised magazine, carriage and engine shed, provision storehouses, and Indian and Commissary Storehouses. It also lists a guardhouse with an officer's room and a black hole adjoining. There was one blockhouse at the Garrison, one in the town and log huts for men and for hospital and canteen. These buildings accommodated 224 officers and men. In this year the log huts on the west side of the creek were condemned and ordered to be demolished. Many readers will find it necessary to revise their impression of the location of the Garrison during the first American attack in 1813, for most of it was on the east side of Garrison Creek, and not in the location of the present restoration called Fort York.

As there was no actual fort, batteries of various types were built from time to time at the Garrison and along the shore to the west, for it was expected that if an American attack came the landing would be west of the Garrison. A young lad who later wrote a description of the attack said, "We had a small battery at the Garrison, another at the Government House, a short distance farther up the lake, and a third about half a mile beyond it, in the same direction." The one at the Garrison was two six-pound cannon in the ravine behind a sod work near the blockhouse. One of these, or a smaller cannon in this location was fired every day at twelve o'clock noon. The next was the Government House Battery, and it almost touched the building. This had two twelve-pound cannon. It was this battery which resounded with royal salutes upon the arrival and departure of the Lieutenant-Governor and upon the opening and closing of Parliament. About four hundred yards west was the "Half Moon" earthwork which had no cannon and the fourth, about another four hundred yards west, was the "Western Battery," at the foot of the present Strachan Avenue, which this writer referred to. This battery mounted eighteen-pound cannon.

The gun platform on the peninsula was intended by Simcoe to be a fortification fifty-eight feet square, with powder magazine and store-rooms, with a barracks of squared timber on the second level. His engineer estimated the cost at nearly eight hundred pounds exclusive of labour, which would be supplied by the army. As mentioned, this proved too expensive for Dorchester and a substitute was erected.

This work as actually built was merely a boxlike platform of squared logs to mount a cannon. The flat roof was also squared timber, and roof and walls had mortar to make the structure more or less waterproof. A sketch in the Robertson Collection shows the ends of horizontal timbers notched into the wall at five-foot and ten-foot levels, for strength, and these are shown spaced several feet apart. There was a low access door under the first level of ties. With only five feet headroom under this first level the interior could not have been used for any purpose but storage.

This platform mounted a twenty-four-pound cannon on a swivel track or traversing platform, and was probably reached by a ladder or rungs on the exterior. There is no record of this gun platform being used in the attack upon Toronto in 1813. As cannon were in short supply this one was probably moved to the Garrison or used on a naval vessel. This structure was demolished in 1818. There were also barracks in this location, but with the rebuilding of the Garrison, after two attacks, this Peninsula location appears to have been neglected.

The blockhouse mentioned above, which President Russell had constructed on the west bank of the Don River, west of the Parliament Buildings, was for forty-eight men. This defensible guardhouse was destroyed by the Americans in 1813. Early sketches show a crude log-cabin type of building with logs, only partially squared, projecting past intersecting notching at the four corners – little better in construction than the settlers' first temporary log cabin. The second floor of this square building overhung the first floor, and the steeply pitched roof had a "lantern," used as an observation lookout. This location close to the Don River proved to be unfortunate. In 1803, Lieutenant-Colonel Brock mentioned in a letter that the Grenadiers quartered there were falling ill of ague and fever (which was epidemic in town), and within a few days ten of them had to be removed to the Garrison Hospital. Soldiers at the Garrison appear to have virtually escaped the infection.

From eighteen hundred, little was done to the Garrison until Brock, now a major-general, was appointed President and Administrator in October, 1811, during Lieutenant-Governor Gore's absence in England. It was Brock who strengthened the batteries on the shore and constructed the stone powder magazine on the beach, which was blown up by General Sheaffe during the attack upon the town. Brock wished to build a strong fort and naval yard at once, but his superior took the view that the town could be fortified gradually. As the military buildings in Kingston "fell into decay," as his superior expressed it, the arsenal of the province would be transferred to Toronto, for it was at last realized that Kingston was not suitable for the naval centre of the province.

The Governor's residence had been destroyed in the explosion of Brock's magazine, and the only blockhouse at the Garrison and the Don blockhouse had been burnt to the ground. Work was started upon a fort to be located on the west side of the creek. The valley of the creek turned northwest near the lake, so there was a triangle of land between creek and lake. This triangle became the fort, and a dry moat was excavated on the west side. Most of the buildings, including gun platforms, officers' quarters, barracks, and new masonry powder magazine, were erected within this area. The hospital and minor buildings remained in the creek valley. A strong wooden palisade, which was later replaced with earth and stone battlements was constructed at the perimeter.

The fort included a forty-foot square blockhouse about forty feet from the water's edge, and another, forty by sixty, was erected in the centre, and this one was about one hundred and ninety feet from the lake. These two blockhouses were erected in the last few months of 1813. They were constructed of timbers nine and one half inches thick. The squared-log residences of the town had timbers seven to eight inches thick. These blockhouses were defensible barracks for musket fire, not for cannon. This military work was completely finished in 1816. It was restored in 1934 and is now called Fort York.

In 1814 another blockhouse was built on the east bank of Garrison Creek, north of the present Queen Street, and eleven hundred feet from the lake at that time. This one was called the Ravine, or the Gore Vale blockhouse. A third visit by the American fleet was made in August, 1814, but after an exchange of cannon-shot the Americans withdrew.

During this war three earthenwork batteries were constructed at the present junction of King and Queen Streets. Two were on the west side and one was on the east side of the Don River. They were built to guard the Don Bridge. Each mounted a twelve-pound cannon, and a Board of Ordnance map of 1814 described these defences as Tetes du Pont (bridgeheads). The last of these earthworks did not disappear until 1850.

THE ARMED FORCES

In 1810 there were only four thousand British regulars and four thousand Canadian regulars in the whole of Canada. Those in Ontario were at garrisons in Toronto, St. Joseph's Island, Amherstburg, Chippawa, Fort Erie, Fort George and Kingston. Those stationed in Toronto numbered about two hundred and fifty of all ranks. These regiments sent to Canada usually stayed seven years, and did garrison duty for three years in one place.

The rank and file were often better off in the army than in the circumscribed civilian life they had left. In Canada, with little leisure or sport to compensate for the harsh discipline and inactivity, they were often restless. Time hung heavily on their hands during the uneasy peace with the U.S.A., which lasted until 1812. They saw men from their own class becoming landowners, and independent in a short time. Many deserted to the U.S.A., and no questions were asked at the crossing. Desertion was most common among those stationed near the international boundary where, with luck, they could be over the border in a minimum of time.

Early in eighteen hundred six men of the 49th Regiment, stationed at the Toronto Garrison, set out for the American border by crossing the lake to Newark. Brock followed them at midnight with thirteen men in an open boat across the thirty miles of lake, and apprehended them before they reached the border. As there was no state of war they were imprisoned. On another occasion it was not simply desertion but a serious mutiny which threatened Fort George, at Newark, under the harsh discipline of General Sheaffe. Once again, with prompt action, Brock stopped the mutiny before it started, and seven men were tried in Quebec and shot. Brock then assumed command of Fort George, and at once put into practice ideas about discipline which would be approved today. Soldiers were permitted to hunt and fish, and given other privileges. They had something to strive for, also, when Brock arranged for grants of land on the Credit River, and rations and farming tools upon discharge. He wished also, of course, to have as many as possible remain in Ontario to serve in a militia which would be soon required in the coming war with the U.S.A. At this early period Toronto was garrisoned by the Queen's Rangers, the Royal Canadian Volunteers, the 49th and the 41st Regiments and the Royal Newfoundland Regiment. At the outbreak of war their place was taken by the militia, and at this time there were only one thousand four hundred and fifty regulars in the whole of Ontario.

There were also Canadian regulars, known as Provincial corps, and their number increased when war appeared imminent. One of the first Ontario Regiments of regulars was the Queen's Rangers. When Governor Simcoe saw the need for haste in building fortifications and roads, he organized this regiment, which numbered four hundred men. A large number of the officers as well as men were from his old regiment, the Queen's Rangers, or "1st Americans," organized during the American Revolution. Many of the men were carpenters and other tradesmen. When it is mentioned under other headings that the army constructed roads, forts and bridges, in the first years of the settlement of Toronto, it was this regiment that did the work. The forming of the Queen's Rangers also increased settlement by early discharge and grants of land to any member who could find another man to take his place. This regiment was disbanded in 1802. Another regiment of Ontario regulars was the Glengarry Light Infantry Fencibles, which was recruited in the Kingston area. This regiment passed through Toronto on several occasions, and took part in the Battle of Lundy's Lane, in July, 1813. It was disbanded in March, 1814, and all of the three-year men received a bonus of one hundred acres of land, with farming tools and a year's provisions. These provincial regulars also included the Provincial Light Dragoons and the

Artillery Drivers. This last mainly consisted of settlers' sons who supplied their own horses.

One of Simcoe's first acts as Lieutenant-Governor was to pass a militia act, and this he patterned upon the militia system of England. With this act the whole male population of the province between the ages of sixteen and sixty-five became members of the militia. This was virtually conscription. Few in Canada were interested in the army as a career, but both townspeople and settlers were willing to defend their country if the need arose. Quakers, Mennonites, and those of the Dunker sect were excused militia duty upon the payment of an annual fee of twenty shillings in peace time and £5 in war. Exemptions were also granted to civic officials, clergymen, ferrymen, and one miller for each gristmill. This militia act was modified in 1808, and with the new act the governor of the province had the power to march the militia out of the province to go to the assistance of Quebec. The age limit was sixteen to sixty as before, but those over fifty were to be called only in an emergency. The new act authorized captains to call out their companies not less than twice a year for training and inspection. There was an annual muster day as before, and each man was required to bring his own ammunition as well as a musket. These militiamen were not paid.

Those absent from training were required to pay a fine of ten shillings. The money from fines and penalties was used for the purchase of drums, fifes, flags, etc., and small prizes were given at target practice. The annual muster day was on the 4th of June, the birthday of George III.

While this day has often been described as a kind of picnic, in which horse racing appears to have interested the men more than serious drilling, the leaders did not expect to train them. Up until about 1810 at least, the principal purpose was to have them enrolled and ready. The muster day was a fairly good indication of the settlers' attitude toward the defence of their country, and of the number of men who could be raised in each district. In Simcoe's time there was a large proportion of older veterans in the militia, and these could be counted upon to instruct the younger men in an emergency. Up until 1810, however, the number of experienced soldiers decreased.

As previously mentioned, Gore retired to England and Major-General Brock was appointed President and Administrator of the province in October, 1811. It is possible, if not probable, that Ontario would have been conquered by the Americans but for this energetic man. He had the Ontario Parliament vote £5,000 for the training of the provincial militia. With fewer veterans in the militia, real training was imperative. He divided the militia into two classes, embodied and sedentary. The embodied were mostly young men, and two companies called flanking companies from each militia regiment were embodied. The sedentary militia comprised the remainder, and these received little training. In other words, Brock formed a militia of volunteers within the militia who were ready and eager for active service. By 1812, before the outbreak of war, the embodied men were training six days a month, and these flanking companies, or "flankers" as they were called, were given the reserve uniforms of the 41st Regiment of Regulars. They were directly under army authority, which provided rations and equipment, and they were subject to the same pay deductions as the regulars, including income tax.

In Toronto the sons of the upper class were officers in this embodied militia, and in proportion to their numbers the towns provided a greater number of embodied men than did the settlers. This was mainly due to greater patriotism, for many settlers were American in sympathy, but it was also because the settler and his son found it more difficult to leave the clearing.

In the war which followed it was customary to put the militia on parole, if captured, while the regulars, both British and Canadian, when captured, were sent many hundreds of miles to prisons. This parole was virtually a promise never to engage in battle again during the war. It was violated by many, but these parole breakers usually did service away from the lines, for they could be shot if captured.

THE ONTARIO NAVY

There was a provincial core of the British Navy in Ontario in 1810. This unit had been organized at the time of the conquest of Canada, when naval battles were fought between French and British on Lake Ontario. It also served during the American Revolution, taking part in the Battle of Lake Champlain in 1776. Since that time, however, it had degenerated into a branch of the Quartermaster-General's Department for the transportation of stores, and there were fewer than one hundred and fifty men in this branch in 1810. This number was hurriedly increased with the threat of war. Many of its senior officers were too old and the enlisted officers had little experience in navigation or in combat. At the outbreak of the war the British naval squadron on Lake Ontario consisted of the *Royal George* of twenty-four guns, the sixteen-gun *Maria,* the *Prince Regent* of twelve guns which narrowly escaped capture during the attack upon Toronto in 1813, and two small schooners. Another, a frigate to be named the *Sir Isaac Brock,* was being built when the Americans attacked Toronto in 1813. It was burnt in the stocks to prevent it being captured.

Battleships such as the *St. Lawrence* launched in September, 1814, were manned mostly by sailors of the British Navy fresh from Britain. This was probably the first war anywhere in which steam vessels took an active part. The steamboat *Accommodation,* which had been launched by Molson in 1809, was used to transport military stores between Quebec and Montreal.

MILITARY AND NAVAL UNIFORMS

Some artists illustrating books covering the battles of the period have made the error of securing their examples from coloured drawings of the official uniforms of British regiments. In many cases these uniforms were not used in Canada. As an economy measure the uniforms of British regiments were drastically altered after eighteen hundred. No doubt many expected that the old uniform would be brought back after the defeat of Napolean. Before and during this war, however, a revolution had taken place in civilian dress, so that in less than one generation, 1795-1810, the garb of the perfumed dandy was given to his upper servants. The army belatedly followed this simplicity in dress, and the old uniform was never brought back. All of the regiments which took part in the War of 1812, wore the modern uniform, and this consisted of hair cut to conform to the head, long trousers slightly split at the bottom, instead of breeches, and stiff shakes instead of the broadside cocked hats. This shako was a cylindrical stovepipe hat with a small stiff brim in front. It was trimmed in various ways with upright plume, tufts, braided cord and tassels, etc., each regiment having a slightly different design and colour.

Not all British uniforms were the traditional scarlet. The 49th Regiment, or "Green Tigers" as they were called, had a dark green uniform. The Canadian Fencibles also wore a green uniform. Unfortunately there were not enough army uniforms for all of the embodied militia of Ontario. In some battles, in the war which followed, many companies went into action with waistbelts and swords, but only a white arm band added to their civilian dress.

The uniform of the lake navy was blue and white. One described had large yellow buttons stamped with the figure of a beaver, over which was inscribed the word Canada.

SMALL ARMS

The universal firearm of 1810 was the flintlock musket. It was popularly known as the "Brown Bess", and it had an effective range of one hundred and to one hundred and twenty-five yards. This gun was also used by civilians who used shot instead of bullets for hunting small game. Three years before 1810 a Scottish Presbyterian minister obtained a patent upon the detonation principle used today. His invention combined the bullet and the cartridge, so that the gun could be loaded at the breech – not the muzzle. His gun immediately became popular with sportsmen, but was not adopted by the army until about 1840.

This smooth-bore flintlock musket was the standard small arm of Europe, although some rifles, also, were used by the British army in 1810. It was a more personal weapon than the musket, and the American and Canadian settlers who lived by hunting game had had far more practice, and were better shots than the ranks of the British army at the time, for only a meagre amount of ammunition was allowed for target practice.

In the garrisons of Ontario there were also many French muskets, for small arms were in short supply because of the strain on the Ordnance Department due to the war with Napoleon. One Canadian gun expert suggests that the flanking companies of the embodied militia might have used the Baker rifle. This could be true, for the militia, especially the settlers' sons, would have preferred the rifle.

With this musket of 1810, a round paper cartridge of gunpowder was inserted in the muzzle, followed by a small lead ball, and both were forced down the barrel of the musket with a ramrod. This ramrod was a steel rod, about the length of the barrel, and was fastened to the underside of the musket for easy removal. It should also be mentioned that soldiers in the field used this rod to roast their ration of salt meat over a campfire.

Before inserting this cartridge in the muzzle, the soldier bit off the top with his teeth and dropped some powder into the flash pan near the musket trigger. Physical tests for the army required sufficient teeth in the upper and lower jaw to bite this cartridge quickly. Each soldier carried a cartridge box, and the cartridges were shipped from England in wooden kegs. In the hammer of the musket was fixed a piece of flint, which struck a piece of steel near the flash-pan when the trigger was pulled. Pulling the trigger threw up the cover of the pan, and sent a spark into the priming powder causing it to ignite, and this in turn ignited the cartridge and sent the ball down the barrel. "A flash in the pan," an expression still used today, is derived from pulling the trigger and having the priming powder flash without igniting the cartridge. The gunpowder used was black in colour, and a puff of smoke came at each firing. Smokeless powder was not developed until 1888.

The pistol of the period was a miniature musket, including ramrod. Shorter and lighter muskets called carbines and blunderbusses were used by officers and sergeants.

Although Woolwich Arsenal was making thousands of cannon in 1810 there was no mass production of muskets and other small arms by the government. Many were imported from other countries, particularly Germany, or made by private contractors. Finally, in 1812, the British Government took over the factory at Enfield, but private contracts did not end until 1859.

ORDNANCE

There were several kinds of cannon, including guns, carronades, howitzers and mortars in 1810, and each had its special use. They were all muzzle-loaders; the ball was inserted at the end it came out. The rear of the cannon was called the breech. They all had trunions, projecting axles of some kind, cast with the gun and used for mounting. These cannon were of both iron and brass, and the proportion of iron to brass cannon was about equal. Many readers will be surprised at this ratio, for brass cannon are rare today. In the middle of the nineteenth-century brass cannon were going out of use and most of them were sold for scrap, for brass is an expensive metal. For this reason few cannon of this metal now exist.

The gunpowder was encased in a cloth or paper bag, also called a cartridge, and this contained the right amount of powder for the type of ordnance. Cartridge and cannon ball were inserted from the muzzle end of the gun and rammed into place with a wood pole shod with iron. With all of these cannon there was a small round hole at the breech, located over the cartridge. A sharp pointed rod was then inserted in this hole and pressed down to pierce the cartridge. This was then removed and the hole was filled up with priming powder which acted as a fuse, so that the touch of a flame started it burning. The powder in the cloth bag then exploded and expelled the cannon ball. In the war which followed there were many occasions when the gunners ran out of cartridges, and took the gunpowder from the keg and tore up their shirts to make them.

The gun was the most common piece of ordnance, and was made of both iron and brass. The distinction in the name designated a cannon of large bore which fired horizontally or at a low angle, and was used as a field piece and for forts and on naval vessels. The trunions were slightly back of the centre of the gun and usually in the centre of the bore.

The carronade was a shorter and lighter cannon than the gun, and they were all made of iron. This cannon had a loop cast on the underside back of the centre, and also a loop at the breech and instead of trunions. Their range was not as great as that of guns, but their lighter weight gave them certain advantages, for they were more mobile and were a practical cannon for naval vessels.

The howitzer was also a lighter and shorter cannon, with trunions slightly back of the centre. These were all made of brass, and were designed for both horizontal and high-angle fire.

The mortar was a short stubby cannon of very large bore, for high angle fire only, and was used for dropping ball or shot into a fort from above at short range. They were principally for siege work. The metal was usually iron and the trunions were at the breech.

The carriages, or mountings for cannon used in Canada were usually of wood, and for field cannon they had two wooden wheels with iron rims. The trunions, only, were attached to the carriage with metal straps so that the barrel could be raised or lowered. Iron carriages were necessary in hot climates where insects and moisture would destroy wood. Wood was preferred to iron for carriages, however, for a reason which had nothing to do with economy. If the iron carriage was damaged by gunfire it could not be repaired, but the wood carriage could be mended in the field. Also, the impact of a cannon ball could break the iron carriage into shrapnel and injure the gunners. In fact, although iron carriages were used they were considered a peacetime mounting, and a wood carriage was also supplied for use in action. Very few of the original wood carriages remain, but ordance engineers have left us sufficiently detailed drawings to reproduce them with reasonable accuracy. Wood for the carriages was mainly oak.

Generally, there was garrison and field artillery. The first had heavier mountings than the field which, of course, were designed for mobility. The cannon for ships, with few exceptions, were the same as those used for forts. Fort gun carriages had wood mountings and in 1800 the iron traversing platform was introduced with which the cannon could be quickly turned. This platform may be seen in the restored Fort York.

The ammunition for all of these cannon was a solid cast iron ball of various diameters. This ball had the greatest range of any ammunition, and was often heated in a shot oven, which was an iron box on wheels burning charcoal. The heating of the ball, of course, was to set on fire wooden forts or ships. Chain and bar shot, in which two balls were connected by a chain or a bar, were also used, especially in the navy where they could tear rigging and sails. Canister shot were small iron balls enclosed in a round sheet iron container.

Artillerymen were furnished with necessary gun tools, including rammers, sponges, wadhooks, handspikes, etc., for cleaning the gun, ramming the cartridge and the ball into place and removing bits of the cartridge left in the breech.

PART TWO

The
Buildings

The
John Ross Robertson
Collection

The reader who had seen sketches of artifacts and buildings of early Toronto may be curious regarding the authenticity of those included in this chapter. He may have seen one or more drawings of the same building which show considerable variation. Which is correct? I am indebted to those in charge of the John Ross Robertson Collection at the Toronto Public Library, for the following explanation of the origin of some of the drawings of early Toronto buildings:

At one time, the *Toronto Evening Telegram* had as its editor and owner a very amazing man who foresaw the loss of much of Toronto's source history, unless it was collected and preserved. This man, Mr. John Ross Robertson (1841-1918), spent a lifetime, along with his duties as editor and author, seeking out and purchasing original paintings and drawings pertaining to Ontario and Toronto history. In many cases the artist for these original drawings had not mastered perspective. To modern man, who is confronted with correct perspective in every magazine and newspaper, the work of some of these artists has an unreal quality – which did not exist in 1810 or any other period. Sometimes, also, their architectural detail is not in accord with the buildings they sketched or painted.

Mr. Robertson also had an illustrated newspaper column, much of which he personally wrote, pertaining to the history of the city. This column was edited and bound in six volumes, entitled *Landmarks of Toronto.*

In many cases no drawing of the building referred to by a contemporary writer existed. Mr. Robertson, interviewed elderly people to secure any information he could. Sometimes an old man recalled that a certain building was clapboarded, that it had four shuttered windows on each floor of the front elevation, etc. The oldest of these recollections could go back only to the eighteen thirties, when Toronto had plank sidewalks. Robertson then had his newspaper artist draw a sketch of the building from the old man's description.

Some of these pen and ink newspaper drawings were made by two well-known artists, Mr. Owen Staples and Mr. F. V. Poole. These two artists also painted in watercolour and oil for Mr. Robertson's private

51

collection. They often used an early amateur sketch, perhaps drawn by a Garrison officer, as a basis for their work. These two artists, and also the newspaper artists, thought it best to illustrate the buildings as they looked to the old man mentioned above. They did not show them as they appeared when built – or in 1810. Many of these drawings showed plank sidewalks, which were not in use until 1835. They created an artist's impression, rather than an accurate delineation of the building. The appearance and the architectural detail of these drawings is often not in accord with existing contemporary Ontario buildings, or those in the eastern U.S.A. They reflect the world of 1895-1900 – not the world of 1810.

As an architect interested in the period, the writer has made measured drawings of some Ontario buildings, and owns bulletins of the University of Toronto School of Architecture of student measuring, made under the direction of Mr. Eric R. Arthur. The writer has also made notes of materials and methods of construction used at the period, and has a collection of measured drawings of American colonial buildings.

Most of Toronto's carpenter architects came from the U.S.A. as Loyalists or later American immigrants. It seems reasonable to assume they would have constructed the same type of building with the same details in Toronto as those being built in other parts of the province. While some of the detail in the illustrations is conjecture, based upon contemporary buildings, I am confident that these drawings present a fairly accurate picture of 1810.

CHAPTER 1

The Buildings

Toronto was a frontier, and it was only seventeen years old in 1810. The buildings were not as sophisticated, nor as architecturally correct as those in Montreal, and the two Ontario towns of Newark and Kingston. First class brick residences, however, such as the Grange, and Justice Campbell's and Bishop Strachan's residences were constructed around

1820, but the public buildings of Toronto did not compare with those of older Canadian cities until the middle of the century.

The buildings in Ontario at the turn of the century reflected the poverty of the immigrants – not the progress of the times. Those in Toronto with sufficient income as civil servants, however, were well able to bypass the primitive settlers' cabins and the trademen's buildings associated with the period.

The plan of the Government House, near the Garrison, was for a residence of twenty-one rooms and was drawn on this plan ninety by one hundred and thirty feet in size. Several residences for Government officials were designed by a German architect, as later mentioned, and carpenters for some of them were brought from the United States.

The houses built before 1810 showed a great variety of basic forms and this made Toronto at this time very unlike many towns on the Atlantic seaboard, in Quebec or the eastern U.S.A., where all buildings in one area were of a similar pattern. The new town was thirty miles by water from Newark, and came into existence without any regional architectural tradition. There was no guild of carpenters to dictate the plan or the appearance, and the owners requested features reminiscent in some way of those with which they were familiar, or they simply told the master carpenter what they wanted. Some of the features they requested were not in the Georgian tradition of architecture.

In the haste to secure protection for the first winter, a dwelling was often erected which was enlarged by the addition of wings the following or several years later. The elevations of some small buildings were made too "busy" because the owner, or the builder, had underestimated the rigours of the climate and later found it necessary to add a projecting vestibule. Many had an additional door and steps added later, so that rooms could be rented as stores or offices.

No professional architects came with the settlers and civil servants to Toronto. Knowledge of "civil" architecture was not lacking among talented and ambitious workmen. In the older societies of England and the U.S.A. the young carpenter progressed through the stages of apprentice and journeyman, to finally achieve the title of master carpenter. A great part of his training was in what today would be called architectural design. To pass from apprentice to master it was necessary to devote many evenings studying the works of Vitruvius, Palladio, Sir Christopher Wren, etc. These also included textbooks such as Gibbs *Book of Architecture* (1728), Batty Langley's *Builders' Jewel* and *Builders' Chestbook* (1746), Campbell's *Vitruvius Britannicus*, and American books such as, *The Country Builders' Assistant* (1797), and the *American Builders' Companion* (1805), by Asher Benjamin. These two books with detailed plans and instructions for builders considerably influenced the design of homes in the eastern U.S.A. following the War of Independence. All of these skilled carpenters were familiar with the five orders of architecture, and those from the Maritimes and the U.S.A. knew how to adapt the classic tradition to wood buildings.

While it has been said that those trained in the system could be depended upon for careful workmanship, but not for innovation, this was not due to lack of talent but to conviction. The charming eighteenth and early nineteenth century towns of the eastern United States, with their simple and similar outlines of mass, could not have come into being with uncontrolled ingenuity. It was also the day of the gentleman architect in England, and some owners insisted upon exercising their talents – sometimes with unfortunate results. Maryville Lodge, described in this chapter, is a good example.

The first buildings of the town were log cabins, squared-log houses, squared-log construction faced with clapboarding, with plastered interior, and frame construction. Brick was used for only two buildings, which included the Parliament Buildings, constructed in 1797, and Quetton St. George's store and residence, constructed in 1807. Although the first frame house was erected as early as 1795, squared-log buildings faced with clapboard on the exterior and plastered on the interior continued to be built for some years because it was a cheaper construction.

There were fourteen round-log houses, eleven one-storey and twenty-seven two-storey squared-log houses, and fifty-five one-storey frame houses. The reader may be puzzled regarding this classification of round- and squared-log houses. Some writers in the past have either misunderstood these classifications, or have assumed the reader was aware of the difference. A great number of American artists, also, have misunderstood these terms, and have painted scenes of early American life showing log cabins, when in reality the homes they depicted were squared-log houses. One American writer devoted an entire book to correct the myth of the log cabin as the birthplace of many well-known Americans.

The log cabin of Ontario and the eastern U.S.A. was never regarded as anything but a temporary dwelling. It was either demolished or used as an outbuilding when the squared log or frame house was built. It was never plastered on the interior or covered with clapboarding. This cabin was constructed of round logs, sometimes without the bark removed, about eight inches in diameter. At the ends of each log, which was the full length or width of the cabin, a cut-out or notch was made at the top and the underside. In fitting the corners of this cabin together the end logs were half a log below or above the side logs. The ends projected about one foot past this notching. This projection past the corners of the cabin was simply to retain the notching, and if not projected the log walls would fall apart. One inch or more was left between the logs and this gave the moss or clay or mortar fill on one side anchorage to the other. Round logs were occasionally dovetailed at the corners, but this was not typical.

In this first log cabin to house the family until a squared-log house was erected, the floor was often simply earth, but with a large stone hearth around the fireplace. In rural areas the roof of this cabin could be four-foot lengths of cedar bark shingles. Sometimes hollowed-out basswood logs, laid like tile, were used in place of shingles. In Toronto, however, it is probable that in 1810 even cabin roofs had cedar shingles and wood floors. Any handyman who could wield an axe could build this log cabin.

The squared-log house, on the other hand, required an expert axeman familiar with the use of hewing axe, hewing hatchet and adze, to make squared timbers for walls and joists. The roof rafters were not always squared. In this construction the logs were squared to a width of from six and one-half to eight inches, with a height of about twelve inches. This timber was cut from a tree trunk at least sixteen inches in diameter. Squaring each timber took an expert axeman about two hours. As with the cabin construction, the top of each timber on one wall was in the centre of the timbers of the walls adjoining, although in some examples they were at the same level. At the corners of the house the timbers were dovetailed together, as shown in Illustration No. 2. With this dovetailing the corners of the building were then sawn square, giving it a neat appearance. Some of these squared-log buildings are still standing after one hundred and fifty years. A typical squared-log dwelling was a storey and a half in height, and sixteen by twenty feet or more in size, with the top of the wall plate (upon which the roof rafters rested) about thirteen feet six inches above the first floor.

Some larger houses also used this same construction, and clapboarding was nailed to the face, which gave it the same external appearance as the frame house. When clapboarding was used on the exterior the house was plastered and trimmed on the interior. Such houses had cellars with stone walls.

Both the log cabin and the squared-log house, if no cellar was excavated, rested upon a course of stone, usually boulders. The cornerstones were placed on the ground first, and the remainder of the stonework was filled in after the first logs or timbers had been made level. This stone course placed the first logs above grade to prevent rotting. The stone could extend one foot below grade, but seldom more unless a cellar was intended. In modern construction in Toronto, all walls extend a minimum of four feet below grade (more than the deepest frost penetration), to prevent frost placing uneven stresses on the walls which would result in cracks in the masonry. With the log cabin, or squared-log building without a cellar, this was not done. The movement of the structure resulted in cracks in the plaster or clay filling between the logs or timbers, and necessitated an annual fill repair.

The floor of the squared-log house was laid upon log joists whose ends were seated into the sill. The tops were levelled with an adze after being set in place. This floor was one-inch pine boards, up to sixteen inches in width. In both the cabin and the log house the door and the windows were sawn out after the walls were erected, and thick plank was nailed to the sides of the openings. Partitions to divide the floor area were usually pine boards, planed on both sides, and fastened at floor and ceiling. There was usually only one exterior door and this was wide — often three feet six inches or more. Today's entrance doors are only two feet ten inches wide. The widest plank was reserved for the batten doors.

The log house usually had a sleeping attic. It was reached by a dangerously steep winding stair, with sometimes a trap door over it, on the second level, to conserve heat. The second floor joists were exposed for there was no ceiling. These joists were actually beams in modern parlance, about six by nine inches in size, and spaced about thirty-two inches apart. This attic was lighted by a window in each gable end, and these end walls were of boards, not logs.

The cellar walls were eighteen inches thick, and were often boulders from the beach. Because of a hasty mortar job they often dripped water. The headroom under the log beams was sometimes less than sufficient to permit a man to walk upright. Access to the cellar was usually from an exterior covered stairway, of wood or stone from the kitchen, if the house had two doors, or by an exterior stair from grade covered with a pair of sloping, but nearly horizontal, doors a foot above grade. Unlike today, this cellar was lighted by one small window set in an area, for the first floor was less than eighteen inches above grade. Obviously it was used only for storage, and this included apples, potatoes, and kegs and barrels of food and liquor.

Field stone, at this time, was less costly than brick, and was used for cellar walls, and some smoke houses and springhouses. Stone was also used for fireplaces in log cabins and squared-log houses, where it was supported over the wide and high fireplace opening on an oak lintel. This building stone also came from various locations on the lake beach, and was brought to the foot of the town on scows called stone hookers. In the Givins house (1802), the stone was said to have come from as far away as the present city of Hamilton, and the stone for the lighthouse was brought from Queenston.

Brick was being made in the province at Kingston as early as 1794. The brick for the Parliament Buildings was made in Toronto, and it is probable that the brick for Quetton St. George's store, and most of the brick for chimneys and fireplaces in town was made locally also. It was a soft-burned brick, reddish in colour and was usually laid Flemish bond.

Because of the relatively high cost of sash and glass, and the difficulty of framing large openings in log walls, the windows in log dwellings were smaller than those in frame and brick construction. Windows were both side-hinged casements and double-hung, the latter predominating. This latter term indicates two sashes in one window frame; one sash sliding up, and the other down. This double-hung window originated in England at the beginning of the eighteenth century, and gradually supplanted casements as the main windows in buildings. At the time of the settlement of Toronto this double-hung window was standard for practically all types of buildings in England and North America, Quebec excepted.

Casement sashes were still used to a limited extent, particularly in attics at gable ends, and in some dormer windows. Window sash in Ontario was usually made of oak, one and one-eighth to one and one-quarter inches thick. Modern wood sash is one and three-eighths or one and three-quarter inches thick, and is made of pine or spruce. The meeting rails of the top and bottom sash of double-hung windows were not weather-locked and these windows could be drafty on a cold winter day. If the owner wished to spend the money, sashes had counter weights, as today, which permit the sash to remain in any desired position without dropping. These weights were of lead. Sash weights today are of cast iron.

All window glass came from Britain. To insure minimum breakage during transport, in small schooners, bateaux and jolting ox-carts, it was cut at the factory to a standard size, and the sash was made here to suit the glass. The glass size was usually seven by nine inches, and it was packed in straw in a barrel. This one factor of uniform size gave a pleasing scale to the buildings of the period. The glass had a faintly bluish tinge, and was not uniformly transparent due to imperfections in its manufacture. It must be remembered, however, that better glass was being put in windows in England and some parts of the U.S.A., and many colonists here complained that we got the worst.

The panes of glass used in England and the eastern U.S.A. were becoming larger in 1810 and were 12" x 15" and 12" x 18" in size. New buildings in Toronto, also, were changing from twelve lights of glass in each sash to six. As larger glass panes became available, the owner would replace worn-out sash with new sash with larger and fewer panes. In new buildings, also, the windows were becoming larger than formerly.

Later in the nineteenth century the six-light sash became two lights. By the end of the century each upper and lower sash had one pane of glass with no muntins at all, and the shutters were usually omitted. In the comparatively recent revival of Georgian architecture for residences, architects deliberately returned to the six-light sash and used shutters as a stylistic feature, for the wooden double-hung window without muntins or shutters is an ugly window, devoid of charm. Thus, the "Colonial" or "Georgian" house in our own day became an eclecticism and not a logical or esthetically honest building. To a great extent it ignored the freedom and flexibility afforded by modern manufacturing, modern construction, and modern heating and illumination. When architects finally acknowledged these implications, architecture became modern.

Early sketches of Toronto reveal that few windows had shutters in 1810. The omission of this one stylistic feature associated with Colonial architecture might change the reader's whole impression of the appearance of Toronto in 1810. The only window shutter available had two solid wood panels, and this entirely eliminated daylight when closed. Its purpose was to exclude the cold of a winter night, and it was seldom considered necessary in Toronto. The dark painted louvre shutter, contrasting with the white clapboarding is a charming feature of old colonial houses in both Ontario and eastern U.S.A. which has interested tourists for generations. This same shutter, which remained permanently folded against the wall and served no practical purpose, has also been a stylistic feature of modern colonial and Georgian style residences.

The practical shutter, with movable slats, which may still be seen on many old houses in Ontario, is a replacement or an addition to the house and was not in use until some time after 1810. This shutter was actually a light diffuser, for with the shutters closed the amount of sunlight could be controlled by activating a vertical wood rod fastened to each slat so that all slats moved with the rod. When introduced, many home owners had them installed. The modern venetian blind, with metal slats, is now used for this purpose in todays' buildings.

The best houses were in the category of "frame houses." The fifty-five one-storey frame houses in the assessment comprised fifty per cent of the total. Although the log cabins and squared-log houses were constructed with verbal instructions regarding size and location of doors and windows, and type of shingles and fireplace, etc., the frame house was designed and specified, for these frame buildings were far more elaborate than the others, and could vary in cost with the type of construction and interior finish. These were all described in the assessment as one-storey in height, but many had attics, finished or unfinished, with gable end or dormer windows. Some of these houses would be classified today as one and one-half storey.

Some of these frame houses were constructed as additions to existing squared-log houses, and an attempt was made to hide (and make more weatherproof) the original building by covering it with the clapboarding of the frame addition. Later in the century many farmhouses were covered with one course of brick for the same reasons. Included in the category of houses designed and specified were some, both one and two floors, which used squared-log walls faced with clapboarding.

While some of these frame and squared-log houses were planned by master carpenters, the best were designed by professional and amateur architects, for even at this early date there were a few men who could be given this title.

The first architect we will mention was an amateur and, oddly enough, a medical doctor. Dr. W. W. Baldwin had come from Ireland and settled in Toronto in 1802. He was a professional lawyer as well as a doctor, and he even taught school for a short time, as mentioned in Part-3, Chapt. 10. We may presume that he had a larger library of architectural books than most of the master carpenters in town, and became fascinated with his new interest in making architectural drawings with a T square and set square, and dividers and compass on the drafting board. He is not credited with the design of any important buildings until 1824 when, with another architect, he designed the Jail and Courthouse on King Street.

The only man who could be considered a professional architect was also of diversified talents, for he was primarily a fine painter. William Berczy (1748-1813), was born and educated in Germany and was widely travelled. He became agent for a land company and brought a large group of German settlers to New York State. Following a dispute with the company he brought his colony to Ontario and settled them north of Toronto around the village of German Mills. After his company had failed he renewed his interest in painting, and also practised as an architect in Montreal and Quebec. He is considered to be the first artist in Ontario, and a great number of the portraits of public and military men of this period, familiar to every schoolboy, are from his brush.

This frustrated land developer, painter, architect-engineer and writer came to Toronto in the fall of 1794 when he was forty-six years of age, and could be considered a resident until October in 1804. This architect, who won the competition for the design for Montreal's Christ Church Cathedral in 1803, was in Toronto primarily to assist his settlers, for there was little work for an architect in the small community at this time. While here, however, he submitted a design for a stone building for the first church. This was unanimously approved but proved to be too expensive. He then designed a frame building as a substitute, which was constructed, and this is described in Part-3, Chap. 6. His design for the bridge over the Don, built in 1802, is now considered very advanced for its time and his residences were the finest erected up until 1810.

This frame construction was not uniform, for there were no mortgage companies or a building code to enforce conformity. They had studs and joists of sawn lumber, not dressed, for there were no planing mills, and it was not considered necessary to plane by hand such hidden members. Wood to be exposed was planed at the site.

All lumber in the province did not come from sawmills using water-power, for much of it was produced by "pit sawing." A platform was built on the side of a hill – if possible. One sawer stood on this platform and another on the ground, about seven feet below him in a shower of sawdust. They pulled a whipsaw up and down through a log to make plank, studs and beams. In Toronto, at this time, the mills on the Humber and Don supplied sawn lumber, but if something was wanted in a hurry pit sawing was resorted to. The word sawmill in source information must be accepted with reservations, for this word was also used to describe a timber yard. In some parts of the province at this early period, a timber yard could be in business for a few years to supply sawn lumber to settlers, and in these yards it was sawn by hand.

In some of the frame houses in Toronto there was one course of brick, as an insulator, between the studs. The clapboarding nailed to the studs touched this course of brick, for when brick was used the one-inch wood cladding under the clapboarding was usually omitted. In attics this course of brick was sometimes laid on edge, instead of flat, for the two or three feet from the attic floor to the underside of the wall plate supporting the roof rafters.

This clapboarding was not tapered, as today, but was of uniform thickness, sometimes as little as three-eighths of an inch. It was narrow, usually no more than seven inches wide with five or five and one-half inches exposed to the weather.

Some of Toronto's first inhabitants had come from parts of the U.S.A. where the masonry of the fireplace and chimney was exposed on the exterior. In Toronto, however, nearly all fireplaces and chimneys were constructed inside the exterior wall or in the interior of the house. This was to conserve heat. It also permitted a faster and cheaper building for a rough masonry job could be hidden under furring and plaster. Sometimes as many as four fireplaces, in a two-storey house, had flues to one chimney on the roof.

White and yellow pine were the universal woods for both construction and trim, and this wood was painted. In some buildings, such as St. James' Church, the studs were of oak. Oak was used almost exclusively for window sash, and sometimes the whole window frame. Roof shingles were made by sawing large logs into pieces about eighteen inches long, which were then split with the grain with a tool called a frow. In one residence the shingles were 27 inches. The split slabs were then placed upon a "shaving horse" and smoothed and tapered with a sharp edged steel knife with a handle at each end, called a draw knife. As today, cedar was generally used but some were of pine. Some shingles were not laid upon a complete roof deck as today, but on wood boards or strips, spaced apart. It was thought the shingles would rot without exposure to air on the underside.

The first lath was made by sawing lumber one half-inch thick, or less, scoring it and pulling it apart to make slots for a plaster key. Wood lath, as we understand it today, was just coming on the market.

One building, the store and residence of Quetton St. George, was roofed with tin as in Quebec. There were no metal roof gutters or metal rain water pipes to carry the water down to the grade, for the cost of sheet metal was prohibitive. In most buildings the rain water from a portion in the roof splashed into a V-shaped wood trough carrying it to a rain water barrel. Sometimes this wooden gutter was fastened to the wall below the roof. In many cases, however, it was only high enough above the ground to take water to the barrel.

Most entrance doors in frame houses had six wood panels. Doors were never glazed and light for the hall came from a transom or fanlight over the door, or from sidelights; sometimes both. Occasionally there was a narrow window to light the hall on each side of the door. With few exceptions, however, houses with much glass around the entrance door were constructed after 1810. This entrance door was trimmed with a neat wood architrave, and had a wood sill.

The interiors of clapboarded houses were usually painted. Oil paint was used for all woodwork, including floors, dadoes, treads and risers of stairs, etc. The exception was the cherrywood or walnut stair-rail, which was given a natural finish and varnished, and the wide boards of the kitchen floor. This floor was sometimes fastened with wooden dowels, and was scrubbed regularly with a finely powdered sand. The plaster walls above the dadoes of the rooms were generally painted with a home-made water paint, prepared with buttermilk faintly coloured with indigo or red or yellow ochre. A few houses could boast wallpaper in the principal rooms.

Many houses of medium size had a "square plan" with two rooms on each side of a stair hall which extended from the front to the back of the house, with no vestibule. Such a hallway possessed considerable charm, for the garden could be seen through the open door at the back. By 1825, however, this hallway was seldom clear in new houses being erected and in our own day we have taken this space for kitchens, breakfast rooms and first-floor toilets. This "square plan" of 1810 provided nine rooms, including the small second-floor room at the front of the house in the stair hall. This could be the "morning room," where the women did their sewing, cut out silhouettes, painted with brush and canvas, and worked on "samplers." A squared-log house might have its entrance opening directly into a large room that served the purpose of living-room, dining-room and kitchen. It could have a steep open stair, adjacent to the fireplace, to a sleeping attic above. Two small rooms on the first floor served as bedrooms.

No rooms, in 1810, opened into others: there were always partitions and doors between them and these were always single doors. On a cold winter day the whole family could assemble in the parlour with the assurance that the fire would be well tended, and that one room at least would be warm. On such a day the man of the house, to go to his library or his office, would close the parlour door behind him, cross the chilly centre hall, open the library door being careful to close it behind him, and put a fresh log on the fire. The residence of today, with its open planning, would not be possible without central and automatic heating.

Although clothes closets were coming into use in the eastern U.S.A. there were few in Toronto in 1810, except in the large houses built for high-salaried civil servants. Maryville Lodge, constructed in 1797, had six closets on the first floor, two of which were in the owner's office. By about 1830, however, most frame houses in Ontario had some clothes closets, even if not in every bedroom. Later in the century, closets in large houses became larger with the increase of wealth. A friend of the writer's, who bought an eighty-year-old residence on the outskirts of Metropolitan Toronto said he would tell me the number of rooms it contained when he could decide which were closets. With the later introduction of coat-hangers on hanger rods, most closets became shallow, not walk-ins, and came to be included in every bedroom of the lowest-cost house. Until the built-in closet came into general use, however, a movable piece of furniture called a clothespress was used for hanging, and these may still be seen in some rural houses today.

The cellar of the frame house had greater headroom, and often had neatly trimmed wood joists, a dry exterior wall and a stone floor. In size it was any area that the owner or builder considered necessary. Occasionally it extended the whole area of the building, or the main building. Often it was only the size of the kitchen, and was reached by a trapdoor in the floor or by an outside stair for, of course, it was not used for heating. In a fair-sized dwelling it was reached by an inside stair as today. Some hotels and residences had the kitchen in the cellar, and in this case there would be an inside stair and an additional exterior stair to grade.

The kitchen was a large room, and what was called a back kitchen was often added later as an addition to a house constructed before 1810. As families grew in these first houses, we may picture the housewife protesting to her husband that she could keep the kitchen tidy if there was another room behind it for a week's supply of split firewood, kegs and barrels, a place to hang work clothes, and storage for the accumulation of needed but seldom used articles that had increased in number since the house was built. The cellar with its stone floor, or no floor at all, was not a desirable storage area except for food and liquor.

The largest residences in town were built for men in government office who had come from Newark, England, or elsewhere to the new seat of the government of the province. It was not until after the War of 1812 that the commercial expansion of the town started the construction of larger and finer residences, culminating in the "Grange," built in 1818, which finally became the nucleus of the present Art Gallery of Ontario. The first complete stone house was not built until 1824, although some small wings of buildings were stone before 1810.

Some of these residences of 1810, even in the original part of the town, were miniature farms, with all of the appurtenances necessary to supply the owner's table with fresh meat and fowl, milk, vegetables and fruit.

The master carpenter's drawing for the Jarvis house in Newark, built in 1794, illustrates how buildings were designed at this period. It shows two floor plans and the front elevation in ink and wash, at a scale of one-eighth of an inch to one foot. The eight fireplaces, with their semi-circular openings, are drafting symbols, and no hearths or door swings are indicated. The nine windows on the front elevation are simply blackened in, but the fine Georgian entrance is fully drawn. Estimates of labour and materials were also prepared so that the carpenter could submit an exact tender to the client.

JARVIS HOUSE

Erected 1798. See Illustration No. 3.

This residence in Old Town, at the northwest corner of Caroline (Sherbourne), and Duke Street, facing Caroline Street, was built for William Jarvis, a Loyalist officer in the Queen's Rangers. Even before Simcoe arrived at Newark, Jarvis had been appointed by him to be the

Provincial Secretary and Registrar, a position he held until his death in 1818.

This house was built of squared logs covered with clapboarding, and had a fanlight over the entrance door but with no elaborate detailing such as he had at Newark. Jarvis chose squared logs in preference to the more expensive frame construction for the walls because he did not wish to spend much money upon a house he would be forced to sell if the capital was moved to London. The interior, however, had what a contemporary writer described as "a handsome flight of winding stairs." Jarvis's office was the room at the corner of the ground floor. Above his office was a large drawing room for entertaining. This house was thirty by forty-one feet in size and two floors and an attic in height. The lot was two acres in extent, and large enough for barns, roothouses, buildings for sheep, cows and poultry as well as a stable. There were also many fruit trees and a vegetable garden on the property.

RUSSELL ABBEY

Erected 1797. William Berczy, architect. See Illustration No. 6.

This residence was constructed for Administrator Peter Russell, who came to the Thirteen Colonies as a secretary to a British administrator, returned to England after the American Revolution, was appointed Receiver-General of Ontario in 1792, and succeeded Governor Simcoe as administrator in 1796. It was located at the southwest corner of Princess and Palace (Front Street), in Old Town. Russell's house was built in 1797, and replaced one which was destroyed by fire during construction. His house was described by the people of Toronto as, "elegant and pretentious." He was a bachelor and lived in this house with his half-sister Elizabeth, a spinster.

It was a frame building and we are told it was roofed with shingles twenty-seven inches long. Modern shingles are exposed four to five inches to the weather, but the Russell house shingles must have been exposed ten inches. The dry lumber for the construction of the house came from Newark, and the carpenters from the U.S.A. This house was fifty feet in width. The cost, including the ornamental fence, was over £1,000. Typical of the houses constructed during this period, it was later enlarged with wings at the rear, and this made it an H-shaped plan.

After the administrator's death in 1808, Elizabeth was entertaining a group of young people. One of them remarked that the gathering reminded him of a similar one described in a currently popular novel entitled *The Children of the Abbey*. This caught the fancy of the young guests, and thereafter they referred to Miss Russell's house as the Abbey, or Russell Abbey. The name was not descriptive for the building was contemporary Georgian – not Gothic.

The writer has taken some liberties with the only sketch of the building by Henry Scadding, for the large panes of window glass in his drawing were not being used in 1810.

JUSTICE POWELL'S HOUSE
Erected 1800. See Illustration No. 5.

This residence was constructed for the Hon. William Dummer Powell, born in Boston, Mass., in 1775. Powell was educated in England and Holland, and later called to the bar in Boston. He became a puisne judge in Ontario in 1794, and in 1816 was Chief Justice of the province.

This house was clapboard on frame, and was built in front of a squared-log clapboarded house as an addition. While most sources give the date of this building as 1800, there is some doubt that it presented the appearance shown in the sketch until a later date.

It would have few duplicates in Ontario, for the plan of the new building was U-shaped, with a double-deck veranda between the wings of the "U." No doubt, this was another example of the owner telling the master-carpenter what he wanted, for the veranda makes it very unlike traditional houses. We may surmise that Powell wished to capitalize on the magnificent view across the bay to the "'Island," for the house was on the north side of the present Front Street, in New Town, on the site of the present Royal York Hotel.

GIVINS HOUSE
Erected 1802, and demolished in 1891. William Berczy, architect. See Illustration No. 4.

Major James Givins came to Canada as a young man and worked as a clerk for the North-West Fur Company. He obtained a commission in the army, was aide-de-camp to Governor Simcoe, and in 1797 was appointed Indian agent at Toronto. He had this house built on his one-hundred-acre park lot north of Queen Street, in the vicinity of the present Givins and Dundas Street.

There is no doubt that one section of this house was designed by Berczy, and it is probable that he designed both. Excellent photographs of the front section still remain, for it was not demolished until 1891. These photographs of the front of the house show a one-floor dwelling with the floor about four feet above grade, with wide wooden steps to an imposing portico, and entrance door with full height sidelights. Large cellar windows are shown in the stone foundation walls. This front portion contained only two rooms. Three sketches of the rear, drawn some time later, show a one-and-one-half-storey dwelling with the first floor only one step above grade. There is no doubt that one section of this house was constructed some time after the other. It is evident that the front is the later construction, for the back portion with its floor only one step above grade would not have been built as an addition. We may presume that the owner wanted a properly lighted and dry cellar when the addition was made, even if this resulted in a "split level." This front addition was certainly built before 1813, for wounded soldiers were carried into these two front rooms. It could have been constructed a short time after the rear section, and Berczy could have been architect for both. The rear view of the house is shown.

GOVERNMENT HOUSE
Erected 1800. See Illustration No. 8.

During the governorship of Peter Hunter a residence was constructed for the home of the King's representative in Ontario. It was located within the area of the present "Fort York," and was on the west side of Garrison Creek. It was one storey in height with a low-pitched roof. The building was of frame construction with clapboarding on the exterior. This was another U-shaped plan, with the front elevation at the bottom of the "U," facing the town. The building was extremely dull in appearance, and as mechanical in plan as an army barracks.

Captain Robert Pilkington, of the Royal Engineers, who was on Simcoe's staff from 1793 to 1796, is given credit for the design. He returned to England in 1803, and later became Inspector-General of Fortifications. His plan shows a building about ninety feet wide, with a dimension from the front to the ends of the wings of about one hundred and thirty feet. It shows open corridors on north and south sides to serve cross corridors giving access to rooms. Fourteen fireplaces for heating, not including kitchen, and a total of seven chimneys to serve them, are shown on Pilkington's plan.

However, this appears to be another plan not followed, for George William's British Ordnance map of the Garrison, dated November, 1813, shows the site of the Government House, burned May 1st, and it is indicated on this plan nearly square. It is also shown square on a contemporary watercolour sketch. This would reduce the number of rooms to ten, including the large kitchen.

The first occupant was Hunter, and the building served as the official residence of the Lieutenant-Governor until the American attack upon Toronto in 1813, when it was wrecked in the explosion of the magazine of the Garrison.

MARYVILLE LODGE
Erected 1797. See Illustration Nos. 9 and 10.

The owner of this house was the Honourable D. W. Smith, the surveyor-general, who came to Toronto with Simcoe and retired to England in 1804. This man had been an army officer, a lawyer and a member of the Executive Council. He was the author of a book about Ontario and was created a baronet in 1821. Smith owned a great deal of land in the province; one source says twenty-thousand acres.

While a few of the buildings of 1810 lasted long enough to permit excellent photographs of them to be taken, Maryville Lodge, the most extensive house and grounds in 1810, was soon demolished with the expansion of downtown Toronto. Complete plans have been preserved, but in this case they were made not to build the house but to sell it, for Smith took these plans to England in an attempt to dispose of the house to his successor, Mr. C. B. Wyatt. This house was located at the eastern limit of the town at the northeast corner of King and Ontario Streets.

It is probable that Smith was his own architect, for he was a land surveyor and, of course, a draftsman. Some of the plans show excellent draftsmanship but, as executives usually do not have the technical ability of some in their employ, it is likely that the planning of the house and out-buildings was the joint effort of Mr. Smith and one of his assistants. The elevation of the house, however, does not properly indicate the Georgian detail which, no doubt, was skilfully executed by the master carpenter. We must remember that Smith and his assistants were surveyors, not master carpenters.

The four end divisions shown on the plan were exactly the same in size. Any one of them could have been the squared-log house, sixteen feet six inches by twenty feet, six inches, he purchased with the property. The original house probably became the drawing-room, for the location of the fireplace is typical for squared-log houses. Plans in the Smith papers show a cellar under the area in the location of the stair, and extending half the length of the parlour. There was also a stair from cellar to grade with a "yard" door. This cellar contained wine cellar, bottle racks and a "dairy."

The plan of the second floor reveals that the four bedrooms occupied the area of the stair section, and office, hall and drawing room. The parlour and study areas had flat, or nearly flat, roofs. The room over the hall was lighted by one small circular window. In attempting to save money by building his house around an existing squared-log building, Mr. Smith probably realized too late that the massing of the exterior could never be acceptable. In the plans he had prepared to take back to England only the west elevation is shown.

All four rooms of the second floor had fireplaces except the east room, which was heated by a stove. There were a total of five clothes closets on this floor. These rooms, with their sloping ceilings, were no better than the attics of squared-log houses, except that they were lined with plank.

The house, except for the original section, was frame construction, and according to a letter from the building superintendent, was clapboarded and lined with beaded random plank, not plaster. This letter also mentioned that the space between the studs was to be filled with broken brick as an insulator. A drawing prepared by one of Smith's assistants, however, shows horizontal boards on the exterior, a foot or more in width, which throws some doubt on the clapboarding. Only the house is mentioned as having been painted yellow (when white was standard for frame houses), and it was known in town as the "Yellow House."

Smith gradually increased the number of outbuildings, as shown on the area perspective, and these included a stable with thirteen stalls, coachhouse, wagon shed, store and mill, and buildings for servants, sheep and poultry. Even a blacksmith's shop is shown at the end of the garden. An elaborate pigeon-loft was also included.

CHAPTER 2

Heating,
Lighting and
Plumbing

With the exception of the few box stoves, all buildings in Toronto in 1810 were heated with fireplaces. The kitchen stove was also a fireplace, although sheet-metal ovens, turning spits and reflectors for use in the fireplace, were coming into use. The kitchen fireplace usually had one or more "ovens," consisting of small-diameter recesses in the masonry beside the fireplace opening. The fuel was cordwood, up to four feet in length. This wood was usually purchased from men who had secured the cutting rights on standing timber on the outskirts, and cut and delivered their wood to customers in town. Pine knots, which the householder's children collected in a basket, supplied a bright light in the fireplace.

Hot embers, covered with ashes, were always left at night in the kitchen fireplace to start a new fire, in the morning, for there were no matches. The first matches, if such they could be called, were simply pieces of stick dipped into melted sulphur, and these were lighted by placing them in contact with live coals or candle flame. The first real matches were made with phosphorus and ignited by friction but these were not invented until 1827. If the fire was completely out, and flint and tinder could not produce combustion because of dampness, the householder or the young son or daughter of the family visited a neighbour and carried back a pot of live fireplace ashes or a lighted candle. Some used an old flintlock musket. A combustible material, such as punk or a shred of cloth, was placed in the flash pan. When the trigger was pulled sparks from the flint flew into the pan and caused ignition. This punk was a dried-out fungus found on decaying wood, and a boxful of various ignition materials was always kept ready for use. Occasionally the Indian method of a bow twirling a pointed stick, or even a sun-glass was used to ignite tinder.

Some of the larger houses had small fireplaces in second-floor bedrooms, as well as first-floor rooms. Sleeping rooms were seldom brought to modern bedroom temperature, and it was not unusual for the water to freeze in the jugs in bedrooms. To prepare for bed on cold nights a warming pan was placed between the sheets for a few minutes and then the ashes were returned to the fireplace. These were similar in shape to frying pans, and had hinged brass lids and long wood handles. Our ancestors did not expect much heat in bedrooms, although they did not open their windows at night. Even in August, bedroom windows were tightly closed as a precaution against "lake fever," a mild form of malaria.

Most people could afford some kind of andirons, or firedogs, for their fireplaces. Some of these were made by the local blacksmith, but being relatively small in size they were also imported from the U.S.A. or from Britain. These were usually square bars of wrought iron, turned down at the back to support logs about four inches above the hearth. The fronts were often brass castings in pleasing classic designs, and some of these andirons, because of their chaste elegance could pass unnoticed in any fireplace today.

The cast-iron stove for heating came into use in Toronto about 1805. These first stoves were made in Three Rivers, Quebec. They were made of cast-iron plates and rested upon cast iron legs at the corners. The faces of the plates were covered with classic ornament in low relief. These stoves could be taken apart in the spring and stored. They were usually placed upon the hearth. Fireplace openings were higher than today, and did not have dampers, so that a tin stovepipe could be led directly into the flue. As they were expensive only a relatively few people could afford them. Box stoves were seldom used in second-floor bedrooms, for they would make the room too hot for sleeping, and there was danger of fire, which sometimes occurred from overheating or careless installation. A town regulation of 1808 ordered that stovepipes be led into chimneys, and not through the roof or side walls. It was not long after 1810, when these stoves were increasingly used for offices and stores, that the practice was adopted of constructing brick chimneys on the external walls of frame buildings on wood platforms, near the ceiling, supported upon wood brackets. The writer has seen such a bracketed chimney on a building being demolished on Queen Street, west of Bay Street, as late as 1940.

People also carried temporary heat around with them. Live embers from the fireplace were placed in tiny boxes called foot-warmers. One such box had three-quarter-turned spindles at the corners and wire mesh in the two panels at the top. The heating material was in a copper or tin box inside. Other warmers were slabs of soapstone with iron handles, and sometimes ordinary fieldstones were used in sleighs. Some warmers were taken to church, and the churches of the period had box pews to conserve the heat from these warmers and eliminate cold drafts from the door.

In winter the blazing logs in the fireplace usually provided enough light, and when reading, the chair was moved close to the hearth. Other times, however, candles were necessary to light the room, and there was a great variety of fixtures to hold them made from pewter, cast and wrought iron, brass, tin and silver. These included candlesticks of many kinds, candelabra, wall brackets and scones with tin reflectors, hanging ceiling fixtures, etc.

Although we could assume that in 1810 all households in Toronto possessed candlemoulds, there were probably some who made their candles in the old-fashioned way. With this method about six inches of boiling water was placed in a pot. Tallow was then poured into the pot and remained on the surface of the water. The purpose of the water was to raise the tallow, so that a whole potful was not required to make a dozen candles.

Five or six wicks, purchased from the store as candlewick, were suspended from a stick with more than enough space between them for completed candles. These wicks were slowly dipped into the pot and lifted out again with a coating of tallow. As soon as it congealed they were dipped again and again until the resulting candle was of the proper diameter. These, of course, took longer to make and were not as smooth as those made in moulds, but they burned just as brightly. Tallow was the fat of oxen or sheep, while wax candles were made from refined beeswax, and it was not until about 1850 that paraffin wax came on the market. Most of the candles used in Toronto in 1810 were tallow.

The candlemould had a single or double row of slightly-tapered tin tubes, about ten inches in height, for half a dozen or a dozen candles to be made with one pour. With these moulds, candle wicks were pulled through a small hole at the bottom pointed and knotted below it. At the top the wicks were tied to a stick above the mould. The hot liquid tallow was then poured into the mould. After making several dozen candles the householder placed them on a shelf for two days before taking them out of the mould and trimming off the six inches of wick at the bottom. As they improved with age, tallow candles were not used, if possible, until two months after they were made.

Every household had one or more candle snuffers, and these were similar to scissors. The candle flame could be extinguished without touching it, and the scissors trimmed the charred wick. Many, of course, would prefer the quick closing of thumb and finger on the wick, by which many people today extinguish their dining-room table candles. In the winter the flame to light the candle was taken from the fireplace with a tallow-coated reed or twig.

For outdoor use, to carry to the stable or visit a friend in the darkness, there were a great variety of lamps suspended from a metal band or heavy wire loop. These were made of tin, soldered where necessary, and usually had glass on three sides. They had perforations in their sloping tops for vents. The glass was removable for cleaning, and it lowered into slots at the corners of the face. The cheapest of these lamps was called a stable lantern. It was a tin cylinder with a cone-shaped top secured to a large ring of heavy wire. This stable lantern had no glass. The light came through hundreds of punched holes in the metal, and these were not uniformly spaced but formed a simple pattern.

The candle with its fixtures and lanterns was a feature of the life of the period, along with open fireplaces, and horses and oxen for conveyance. Such expressions as, "he is not fit to hold a candle to him," "the game is not worth the candle," and "burning the candle at both ends," slipped into the speech of everyone. The first refers to "link-boys," who were ushers in theatres and other places of amusement in England, and led patrons to their seat holding a lighted candle. The second could refer to continuing a card game when the interest would not compensate for the cost of another candle; the third, overdoing work or play. It is interesting to note that the second Covent Garden Theatre in London was using 270 candles at each performance in 1810, so we may assume that it was an almost universal light source.

Little needs to be said about plumbing, for it was non-existent, and the first trunk sewer was not laid until 1835. Drinking water was obtained from carters who delivered from door to door, or the householder went to the nearest creek. The kitchen had a "dry sink," and this was simply a woodbox on legs to hold the wash pan and the soiled dishes. The water from this sink drained into a bucket on the floor.

A bath was taken in the kitchen in a wood stave or metal tub, and it was sometimes a standup bath if the tub was not large enough. A mahogany portable bidet is mentioned as one of the items to be auctioned from Holyrood House in 1811, and this was a small bathtub. The owner of this residence was wealthy, however, and there were probably few others in Toronto.

The privy was usually close to the house, instead of in the more sanitary but more obvious location at the back of the lot, as in Ontario villages and summer resorts today. Germs were little known and contagion was not understood. Because of the small number of wells, however, there was little infection from this source. Generally, only the young men used the privy. Young children, women and older men used receptacles in bedrooms.

CHAPTER 3

Interiors and Furnishings

There were, of course, no interior decorators in 1810. Indeed, most people would have been astonished if it was suggested that someone should design their interiors, and there were no suites of furniture, such as the complete furniture for a dining-room or a bedroom in the same style and craftsmanship purchased together. Although there were double floors of wide boards in some houses, this was because of the shrinkage of the first layer. There was no "hardwood flooring" of narrow three-eighths-inch tongue-and-grooved oak and no parquet flooring, which is today the standard wood flooring in apartment houses to lay directly on concrete floor slabs. The negatives also included linoleum and tile floors, cut stone and marble mantels, plate glass and plate glass mirrors, plywood, walls, acoustical tile ceilings and Venetian blinds. There were no bathrooms, very few built-in clothes closets and, of course no central heating or running water, nor gas or electricity for lighting and cooking.

By our standards, practically all of the furniture was odd pieces. Much of it was "second hand," purchased at the auction sales in homes or hotels. It was made of different kinds of wood with dissimilar finishes, and no furniture was upholstered except the occasional imported chair or sofa. Furniture is rarely mentioned in the advertisements by the stores, and this may have been made locally. Some houses had a prized piece of mahogany or walnut furniture which the owner had brought from the U.S.A. for there was no importation of fine furniture from England, at this date, by the stores.

It is probable that the British Government paid for the transportation of furniture owned by top civil servants in Ontario. From the list of furnishings to be auctioned from Holyrood House, in 1811, it would appear that William Firth, the Attorney-General, lacked for nothing he would have in his home in England. The list includes such items as "drawing-room sofa on castors, with brown Holland and chintz covers," complete law library, cut glass, Pembroke tables, pianoforte inlaid with satinwood, and cast-iron pots lined with white metal.

The houses of Toronto were furnished for comfort and the quantity of furniture and utensils was adequate. The three most necessary pieces were the chest, table and chairs, and a bed, and many settlers around the town had little else with which to start housekeeping. Because it could be so easily cut and planed, pine was the wood used for much of the furniture made in town, although chairs were usually of hardwood. Pine was used for chests, tables, chests of drawers, cradles, and some chairs and beds. Pine furniture was usually finished natural, but was later painted when the finish became soiled. As there were few vestibules in houses, a high-backed bench, with a hinged seat for storage, was placed near the door or the fireplace and served the purpose of draft screen.

The bedrooms contained single and double beds called "four-posters." The bedposts, usually three feet six inches in height, were of three-and-one-half-inch-square pine or hardwood, turned on a lathe. Some had cross spindles at the top of the posts, front and back, and had a board with shaped ends between cross spindle and bed frame. This bed had no springs, or spring mattress. The predecessor of the modern bedspring was cord lacing, advertised by the stores as "bed cord," and it was spaced about eight inches in each direction across the bed frame. This bed cord stretched and sagged with use and had to be regularly tightened by re-lacing. One person took a wrench, for the purpose, and drew the rope tightly through each hole in the bed frame. Another, working with the first, used a hammer and a wood pin at each rope insertion in the frame to hold the cord tight until it was taken across the frame to a hole on the opposite side. With some beds the cord was taken across the top of the bed frame and looped around wood pins on the underside. This tight lacing adjusted to the reclining sleeper. Over this cord lacing was placed a hair mattress, or more often a thick feather-filled tick of goose feathers, or a straw-filled one in a modest home.

The trundle bed, which had been a feature of colonial times in the U.S.A., was still used in Ontario and Toronto in 1810. To save space in small houses with large families, the bed frame contained a large drawer at the floor, and this was pulled out at night to form a bed for young children.

One room in a fairly large house had a bed with corner posts high enough to support a canopy of cloth, with a valance of cloth or lace – sometimes elaborately tied with bows or ribbon at the corners. This bed could have side curtains. The tick, or double tick of this bed was sometimes so high above the floor that movable steps were required to climb in and out. Bedsheets were cotton or linen, and there was usually a seam down the centre, for loom widths were limited. Pillows were filled with feathers, and had cotton pillow cases as today. The blankets were of wool. As cloth was relatively expensive, a patchwork quilt was "elegant" enough for beds in any home.

Each bedroom had a washstand. This could be simply a small pine table to hold a china or tin bowl and a water pitcher; or it could be something more elaborate with turned legs, a splashboard at the back, two drawers, and a large hole in the top to make the basin rim level with the table-top, like our bathroom countertop basins today. The water pitcher rested in this basin, and one of the chores of the housewife or her servant was to empty a slop pail and keep the pitcher filled.

Every bedroom had a chest of some kind, with a hinged lid and iron or brass handles at each end. The sides and the lid were of one pine board, without jointing. The corners of this chest were dovetailed, similar to the corners of squared-log houses. Sometimes there was a cradle in this bedroom. It could be made of natural finished pine, and it rested upon two cross rockers. One-third of the length of the cradle sometimes had a wooden top over the baby's head.

The bedroom could also contain a trunk, which was often a strong wooden box covered with pigskin or deerskin, and ornamented with iron or brass upholsterer's nails. It usually had a convex-shaped lid and the long sides sloped inward to the floor. Some trunks were formidable-appearing boxes reminiscent of money chests. Most women had several hat boxes of stiff leather called "bandboxes," or "bonnet-boxes." The suitcase of the period was a "portmanteau," of many shapes and sizes but usually made of leather.

This room contained a chest of drawers, in natural finished pine or possibly an imported dresser of finely finished wood, originally imported from the Old Country or brought with the family from the U.S.A. On this dresser was a "looking-glass" in a small wooden frame. A finely made "sampler" frame could also rest on this dresser along with combs and brushes, etc. If it was a girl's room the doors of the clothespress might have been left open to reveal brightly coloured and white garments, and perhaps a pair of riding-boots on the floor and a riding-jacket on a chair. A few pictures and perhaps a "sampler" hung on the walls.

The chairs were much the same as those in the parlour and might be natural finished or painted. The wide pine boards of the floor were painted, and often in a bright colour such as pumpkin, which formed a colourful background for the small homemade rugs.

One of the rooms on the second floor could be the library, with open shelving for calf-bound books, and perhaps a globe on the floor. Father could also own a telescope and even a microscope. He had his writing-desk, which the family dared not use, and perhaps an old musket hung over the fireplace. There were no furniture stores, but joiners or furniture craftsmen could have for sale in their shops a few pieces which they had made while waiting for customers' orders. If father wanted a desk, he either bought it at auction or gave the order to a joiner in his shop. At this time furniture craftsmen appear to have regarded writing-desks as a challenge. One from the period was similar to a dresser in appearance when closed. Below the top drawer a bottom-hinged vertical door dropped down to a horizontal position to form the writing surface. This was supported from above by ingenious upright wooden slides at each side of the desk, and these came out when the writing surface was dropped. Large quarter-circle brass rings, moving in brass slots, then held the writing surface to the bottom of the wooden slides. When the writer had finished he simply lifted the edge of the writing surface and the slides retreated into the desk.

As desks were usually made to a customer's order, he might request a hidden compartment for storage of documents, such as his will. These secret compartments in desks formed the basis of many Victorian novels, where the lost will was found by the hero just before the family were evicted from their home.

In prosperous families each member could have his or her own portable writing-case, usually of thin wood, and this could be carried to the parlour or the kitchen fire when bedrooms were too cold. At this time thousands of letters were written which were not delivered by mail carriers. In an age before telephones, a hastily scribbled note, an invitation, or a love letter could be taken by the servant to the house of a friend.

In many houses, that we would describe as a storey-and-a-half, a portion of the second floor was often left unfinished. This empty area, without heat, could have a gable end or a dormer window, but was unplastered. Access to this area was sometimes through a bedroom door, and it gradually became a storage area. Sometimes it was used for weaving, for the bulky loom of the period was too large for a habitable room. This weaving was not always a necessity, but a woman who had no interest in reading, for example, could weave as a hobby.

We may now go downstairs to the first floor. There were few open-string, natural finished staircases with turned balusters in Toronto in 1810 except in the houses owned by high-ranking civil servants. This stair was usually of painted pine, with closed strings, although the handrail was always finished natural and made of walnut, cherrywood or oak. This hall on the first floor contained an umbrella-stand, coat-hooks on a wall board, and a mirror or looking-glass in a frame, with perhaps a grandfather clock or even an eight-day clock on the wall.

The parlour might be the same size as the other rooms on the first floor. This was the show room and the "living-room" in moderate-sized houses. It contained the best furniture. There were a few oil paintings in gilt frames on the walls, with daughter's sampler, a professional silhouette of a member of the family, or a friend, and perhaps a miniature painting in oil of mother as a girl, which father had brought from the U.S.A. or from England.

Few families had upholstered sofas, and usually only the seat and the back were padded. Most chairs were of wood, with and without seat cushions. Chair-making was a specialized branch of furniture-making by hand, and in 1802, the first chairmaker, Daniel Tiers, set up in business in Toronto. He advertised in the *Gazette* that he would make armed chairs, settees, fan-back and brace-back chairs. Rocking-chairs are not listed, although they were extensively used at this time. His advertisement mentioned that he shortly expected a quantity of different paints to "finish his chairs in the best manner." Tiers imported some chairs from Montreal. Many of these were no more elaborate than those we describe as "kitchen" chairs today, but others had turned legs and spindles, with elaborately shaped cut-out wood for the backs. Some seats were of moulded wood and others had basket-weave wood. These were called "rush-bottomed chairs." These chairs were used for every room in the house.

A comparatively wealthy family might own a pianoforte, which was usually a rectangular box on four legs. It had four or five octaves, compared with seven in modern pianos. It had a pleasing but tinny sound by modern standards. The pianoforte was the first instrument which could play *piano* (soft) and *forte* (loud). These pianofortes came from the U.S.A. or from England, for they were not made in Toronto until 1847.

In lighter moments the family could group around the pianoforte and sing "Love in a Tub," or "Jemmy Riley," and become serious enough to sing "Hearts of Oak," or "'The British Grenadiers." Father could assist daughter with his flute. Very few in town, however, could play any classical music.

The muslin curtains on the windows were cross-draped, and sometimes there were overdrapes on thick wooden curtain rods. The window-blinds, of white or green, were of washable cotton, with a light wooden stick sewn into the bottom edge. They rolled up from the bottom and buttoned at half or full opening, for blinds on rollers containing coil springs did not come until years later. Prosperous families could have an imported rug on the floor, but these rugs were small by modern standards.

On the wide mantel shelf were candlesticks, snuffer, tinder-box, mantel-clock and perhaps a book from the lending library which had been founded in 1810. Around the fireplace were the best tongs, bellows, brooms and other necessary fireplace equipment, in the house. This parlour fireplace also contained a crane to hold a kettle, so that water could be boiling for an informal cup of tea without leaving the guest and going to the kitchen.

The dining-room could have a pine table covered with a dark-coloured baize cloth to the floor, which was removed for dining upon the bare table, or it could contain a finely finished hardwood table. The chairs could all be of the same design but were not necessarily purchased with the table. The sideboard, unless it was imported furniture, was a chest of drawers, with open shelving over it to hold the family silverware or pewter, and some fine china. As glass was relatively expensive, and as the quality available was imperfect, it was used very little for china cupboards made in town.

The scullery or kitchen was a large room – often larger than the parlour. It contained a wide, open fireplace, with one or more bake-ovens in the brick masonry. Sometimes there was a deep recess on the other side for firewood. In this fireplace was a swinging arm securely fastened to one side called a crane, and this was used to hold hooks, which in turn held the large iron rings fastened to the pots. All cooking-pots had these half-circle iron rings for hanging to the pothooks and all pans had long handles to protect their users from the fire. During the preparation of the meal the wide and deep stone hearth was covered with pots and pans ready for the fire, or left there to keep warm after cooking. A large pine table was used for preparing food, and there were other smaller tables with food dishes waiting to be filled and taken to the dining-room. All of these dishes had covers to keep cooked food hot while other food was being prepared. Two or three kinds of meat, fish or fowl were usually served at one meal. The wife, with a servant, slave or daughter assisting, worked much harder to prepare a meal than a modern housewife working alone today.

Perishable food, such as fresh meat, butter and milk, was stored in a springhouse, if the family owned one, or in the cellar, and some families had a smokehouse for curing meat. Most meat, however, was salted, and was taken out of a barrel in the cellar. The salt was thoroughly washed off before cooking.

There were many accessories on the market to assist the housewife in cooking with an open fireplace, but most people in Toronto could not afford them. These included ingenious turning spits suspended from the mantel-shelf which revolved by a clockwork mechanism, tin reflectors, and double tin roasters.

After the meal the dishes were washed in a dishpan on the table, or in a "dry sink." Open shelving, and shelving with doors, stood upon the floor at the walls. No kitchen cupboards were "built in," as today. These shelves held large jars of cookies, preserves in bottles or jars, pickles, as well as flour, sugar, salt and other staples. Other shelving held china, pewter, candlesticks and candlemoulds, candles, lanterns, footwarmers, water-pitchers, washbasins, wooden ladles, coffee and pepper grinders, etc. Frying-pans and pots with long handles and warmingpans for beds had rings at the ends of the handles and these were hung on the wall.

In a large house there could be a doorbell, in addition to the knocker, and the bell was on the inside of the door or on the wall, connected with pull wires. Sometimes there could be an additional bell in the kitchen, for with a fire on the hearth and closed doors the main bell might not be heard.

PART THREE

Daily Life

A levelling process was taking place in the U.S.A., and to a lesser degree in Canada, which was viewed as a symptom of deterioration by visiting Europeans. They had expected to see the rigid society of Europe reproduced in America. They did not realize that land ownership was the basic reason for the difference between American and European society.

Most of the land in Europe was owned by a tiny percentage of the population and a large proportion of the people were servants. In America, cheap land available to all increased the percentage of land owners and decreased the percentage of servants and those employed by others compared with Europe. The immigrants, if they were men, could secure land for themselves, and these were men who in most instances could never have become landowners in Europe. If they were women they could become the wives of men who secured it. As the wife of a settler, this immigrant woman could not be hired by others as a servant. The settler and his wife worked harder than servants but they were independent. This new status enlarged their horizon and gave them resourcefulness and self-respect.

In sparsely-settled communities, this man was called upon to serve in politics and upon school boards – offices which were practically closed to him in Europe. He also found himself a participant and even an organizer, instead of merely a worshipper in the church, for the Christian Church was being built by its members. If he found he was not suited for farming, there were business opportunities in fast-growing towns and villages where only a small capital investment was required.

In contrast to those of her sex in Europe, the new American woman became a social entity. The husband, preoccupied with acquiring wealth (and with few or no servants), was more likely to leave the raising of the children to the wife. The mother then became a greater influence upon the children than the father. The male children could not then look upon women as inferior. Fewer women than men ventured into pioneer settlements. They became prizes for the men who treated them as equals. This is the origin of the much discussed American woman.

The factor of cheap land, available to all, put a higher value upon the "hired man." This man was saving his money for a "stake" to buy land, or perhaps he lacked initiative and preferred to work for another. He was often a good wood-chopper and could handle the farm chores as well as his master. In sparsely-settled areas he was a companion, rather than a servant. Those who had been born in America seldom forced this man to sit at a "second table." There appeared to be no justification for it and it could be an insult which might result in the loss of a valued assistant. Often this man married his employer's daughter and bought a farm of his own up the road. Europeans, with quick judgment, described this settler and his hired man as "felons of one table," and fancied they saw a great deterioration of manners in America. Thus we see cheap land as the major factor in the breakdown of the rigid class distinction of the Old World.

The weather was another factor in moulding the character of the North American, particularly if he came from England. He came from a climate which puts a brake upon nervous energy, a land where the earth is always green and never turns a forbidding face. These men came to America where the seasons change dramatically, where trees turn from yellow to scarlet in a single frosty night, where the earth becomes gray and hard and covered with snow, with only the coniferous trees remaining green to remind them that summer was here and would come again. Imperceptibly it changed the immigrants – and their sons were no longer Europeans.

In the seventeen nineties, the men who came to Canada from the U.S.A. as Loyalists brought with them a progressive spirit of democracy. This self-reliance, however, was not encouraged to any extent beyond that stage for, of course, Canada was a colony and the example of the American Revolution was fresh in the minds of British statesmen. These Loyalists brought with them ideas of individual freedom, independence of spirit and participation in government, as well as intense loyalty to the Crown. Their coming to Canada hastened the rise of democratic institutions, such as the town meeting and the Legislative Assembly.

While it is true that because of an accident of history, Ontario was virtually empty during the period when the Eastern U.S.A. was becoming economically self-sufficient, and hence had gained many generations in the population race, the handicap of colonial rule retarded the development of Ontario and Canada by not permitting legislation in the best interests of the majority. Majority rule in the United States was making it apparent to the world that greater freedom and representative government were conducive to initiative, and that prosperity for the average man produced even greater wealth for those already rich.

The spirit of these Loyalists and American settlers was countered and checked by those in authority in Ontario, reared in the social system of the Old World, who controlled Canada's destiny from the Colonial Office in London. British rule in Canada was not oppressive or tyrannical. It was intended to be fair and just but, of course, it was colonial rule. The original form of government embodied in the Constitutional Act was designed by Englishmen in England – not by Canadians in Canada. It was framed to restrict initiative, not to encourage it.

In the year 1810 over ninety per cent of the inhabitants of Europe and America were engaged in agriculture. Consequently the opinions of farmers and settlers were the opinions of most of the population. If Canada had become an independent nation in 1810 we may assume its statutes would have reflected more of the ideas of this majority.

These stumbling blocks to the progress of Ontario were finally removed but not soon enough to offset the initial handicap of competition for population with the U.S.A. when settlement was predominantly rural.

In reading the following pages, which give the daily life of the people under twenty-five headings, this colonial status should be kept in mind. The reader should also remember that Toronto was unique among all of the towns of comparable size in North America. No other small town contained so many government office-holders and civil servants; no other town, set in a forest, had so much luxury for a small elite.

CHAPTER 1

Sights, Sounds, Scents

Sights, sounds, scents, no one took particular notice of them. They were a part of the daily life of Toronto in 1810. The period may come alive, however, better when they are recalled.

The sun shone in Toronto as in the countryside today for the fireplace chimneys and the trifling amount of industry did not create enough dust to obscure it. Occasionally a fog rolled in from the lake but the air was so clear that the glow in the sky at night from the burning of the town of Newark in 1813 could be plainly seen by the hundreds of curious people who came to the beach to watch. From Queenston Heights the cliffs of Scarborough and the buildings of Toronto could be seen across the blue waters of Lake Ontario.

The white sails of schooners and small craft sparkled in the sunshine upon the bay, or became dark shadows at dusk on the gray water. For a few days at the end of October fresh fallen leaves made a golden carpet.

Fireplaces made an intense ruddy glow but left shadows and darkness in the corners of rooms. The soft yellow light from candles seemed very precious. It scarcely touched the walls and moved gently with the slightest draft. Neighbours' houses were swallowed up in blackness, or there was a faint glow on the washable cotton blinds of the windows.

It was a period in the climate cycle of lower temperatures and more snow than today. Lake Erie was usually frozen over from shore to shore and Lake Ontario as far as the eye could see. The blanket of snow in the town remained white until the thaws of spring made it dusty and gray. Roofs near chimneys had melting snow, even in zero weather, for they were not insulated. There were some days when the smoke from hundreds of chimneys rose as straight as tree trunks and made a magic forest in the sky.

The people of Toronto heard the sounds of nature every day. They caught the chirping of crickets and the sustained beeeeeeep of toads under their front stoop. In summer they were plagued with the buzzing of flies and mosquitoes, which bred in the dead and motionless waters at the mouth of the Don River. It was often necessary to make bonfires in front of houses so that the smoke would prevent their entrance. From their houses and gardens they heard the barking of dogs and the mewing of their cat at the front door. They heard the heavy thump of horses' hooves past their windows as one of the family rode into the stable behind the house. Out on the street, horses trotted by on the hard earth of autumn, or neighed at hitching posts on the business streets.

Slow-moving oxen lowed as they pulled their carts, and the wheels made a sucking sound in the spring mud on the road. One often heard the mooing of cows, the grunting of pigs and the bleating of sheep. Every day roosters crowed at dawn and every summer night one heard the croaking of thousands of frogs in the river marshes. Some nights one heard the harsh wail of the prowling wolf, the sharp bark of the fox, the growl of a bear and the scream of the lynx. As the settlers lay in their beds in silent darkness they listened to the calls of the great owls in the pine forest on the edge of the town.

They heard the cheerful and exciting tingle of doorbells and the startling but friendly thud, thud, of door knockers. Footsteps in houses sounded on the wide floor-boards without carpet. From the kitchen could be heard the turning of the coffee grinder, the sharpening of knives, the lifting of pot lids and dish lids and the frying of meat.

There was no closed hunting. Nearly every day the people of Toronto heard shots from hunters' firearms. Birds were so plentiful that they were shot for sport rather than for food. One diarist mentions shooting wood-peckers out of his bedroom window. Then there were the exciting times, which always came unexpectedly, when for several days firearms of every description roared from dawn to dusk, shooting at the millions of wild pigeons flying over the town.

They heard what a contemporary writer described as the rich musical sounds of the Indian language when redmen passed through the town, or sold their fish, basketware or moccasins at the market or from door to door. Every day they heard the distant cannon roar of the twelve o'clock gun from the Garrison, a mile away from the town. The church bell was suspended from a wooden platform on the ground beside the building and its musical clang-clang could be heard in every home. Sails flapped loudly at the docks when raised or lowered in the wind, and a long tin horn was blown to announce the arrival and departure of vessels.

Sleigh-bells made a pleasant jingle, and in the cold winter stillness the thump of the axe could be heard at the shrinking woodpile. They shivered in their homes in sub-zero temperatures and heard the unpleasant hissing sound of iron-shod sleigh runners. Sometimes they heard the wrenching crash of an ice-burdened tree limb. On mild winter days they heard the dripping of icicles on their roof. Pedestrians' feet made a tinkling cracking sound when false ice broke on the footpaths.

The people of Toronto could smell the fresh breezes off the lake, but sometimes on a hot summer night the air would be permeated with the odour of fish from the beach at the foot of Princess Street. The resin of the pine trees, the horsey smell from the stable at the rear of the houses on a hot July day, the appetizing smell of freshly ripened fruit, the smell of tanbark and the not very savoury smell of hides from the tannery, the pleasant fragrance of flowers, and of burning leaves in autumn – all of these sights, sounds and scents were the background of life in Toronto in 1810.

The People

The reader's attention has been directed to the fact that land within reach of all upset the rigid pattern of life which Europeans brought with them to America. These immigrants found they could not make a living renting land, for even the servants which some of them brought with them obtained land for themselves and left their masters to begin a life of their own. This fundamental difference between Europe and America diminished the contrast between the gentleman and the labourer. He was in the same boat with all, for it was his own skill, his own character and personality, as well as his willingness to work, which could raise him above his fellows.

In 1810 in Toronto, the class distinction of England, which would have disappeared more quickly if Canada had been free, was to a great extent artificially maintained because of colonial status.

In 1810, the people of Toronto were living in a town seventeen years old. The population, if we take the average of the assessment figures for 1809 and 1811, was 630. About 13.5 per cent of this number were servants, including those employed by merchants, tradesmen and hotel owners. There were some negroes, both freemen and slaves, and a few French Canadians. A portion of the population were disbanded British soldiers, for they could obtain their release without returning to Britain. Along with the British, there was also a sprinkling of other nationalities, including American immigrants, Germans, and Loyalists.

No Indians actually lived in Toronto, although there were always a few, in the mild weather, living in their wigwams on the "Island," where the fresh breezes from the lake were supposed to have curative value for those recovering from illness.

Because of the young age of Toronto, all adults had come from somewhere else. The population at this time was constantly changing. The influx of new residents, and the movement of families to their park lots, farms, and country-houses on the outskirts, created a situation whereby the township was rapidly increasing in population, but the town did not show much increase until after the War of 1812. The war with France, and the danger of capture on the high seas, made settlement in Canada a real risk which not many incurred. At this time the immigration to Canada from Europe was probably less than one thousand per year.

The Loyalists in Ontario had usually spent most of their lives in America. They were intensely loyal to the Crown, but often had little in common with the newcomers from Britain, and they were inherently more democratic than those who formed the ruling class in the province. Later provincial history, including the activities of the so-called "Family Compact" and the Rebellion of 1837, becomes clearer when we realize that the province was not ruled by the Loyalists of 1783 or their descendants. The Family Compact members, in most cases, came to Toronto and Ontario after the Loyalist period. They came from New Brunswick, from Nova Scotia and from Great Britain. The Loyalist in Toronto or in the province was more likely to be a tradesman or settler than a man of wealth, or a high-ranking civil servant. Many were illiterate. The Ontario Loyalists had less money than those who settled in the Maritimes. They were given less government support and less cash compensation.

The later American immigrants who followed the Loyalists, were also more likely to be tradesmen or settlers. These Americans had selected Canada for their home simply because of cheap land. They preferred to gamble their future in Ontario rather than take the long journey to the comparatively lawless and Indian-ridden western frontier where cheap land could be obtained. Land in Ontario was worth about one-quarter as much as similar land in New York State. Little national spirit had as yet developed in the new United States of America and these immigrants considered themselves citizens of a state, rather than citizens of a country. To those leaving their home states of New York or Pennsylvania, their own far west was more foreign to them than Ontario. After coming here, some of them found they had no taste for farming, sold their land grants and drifted to the towns and villages to become workmen or tradesmen. The Toronto of today is often described as an American city, but this cannot be said for the town of 1810, for most of the inhabitants were from Britain or eastern Canada.

In 1810 the three social classes of people had brought their status with them from other parts of Canada, the U.S.A., and from Britain. Even the most Tory of the Loyalists had come from a society less highly organized than in Britain, where a high value had been placed upon individual initiative and achievement. Other newcomers had come from the lower class of Britain; some from the same class had spent a year or two in Canada before coming to Toronto, and had tasted the free air of America long enough to own some land and a house of some kind; still others came from the middle or from the upper class in Britain. Some from Britain included army officers. Then there was the Lieutenant-

Governor, from a high segment of society in Britain. In addition, there were those of the black race, both slaves and free men, who were not considered to belong to any class.

We must remember that Canada was a colony of Britain, and immigrants, particularly the English, took their class structure with them to Canada. This included the humblest workman, as well as top civil servants of the government of Ontario. However, as many of these people had breathed the free air of America for years before coming to Toronto to live, there had been a subtle change in their outlook. They could not now accept and live by the standards of England. Many were grateful for the liberal society in which they lived in Toronto.

By 1810 social strata were becoming evident. As Toronto had all the elements of an English provincial town, social classes were emerging, and life was very different from that of the actual settlers in the province. Each social group in Toronto had its own diversions and social life. In some cases they overlapped; in others they did not. Because of the isolation, and the petty jealousy caused by the patronage system, the ruling class was divided into cliques and factions, and gossip was often malicious.

The middle class English brought with them an outlook upon life quite different from those who had lived for a generation or more in America. English periodicals were available at the library and the stores in Toronto. The women's fiction magazines, particularly, reveal the outlook of the period. These stories are cold and lacking in emotion. Their writers perceived no drama in the events transpiring around them, which subsequently provided some of the greatest novelists with their material. Gardens, in these stories, are a choice setting, but nature is raw and uninteresting. Religion is a mode, rather than a deep faith. There are few references to outdoor amusements and no mention of the nursery. These stories of 1810 had wit and puns but no humour.

Police court records of the period reveal there was much ill-will shown by individuals toward one another. Many fist fights took place in the streets among citizens of all classes and two duels were fought. There was also a great amount of jealousy, and jostling for position, particularly among the upper class, so that life in Toronto at this time was very different from life among the settlers of the province, where lifelong friendships developed during the hard and gruelling period of establishing a home in the wilderness, which could not be done without the assistance of neighbours.

Toronto was a garrison town as well as the capital of the province. The highest-ranking officers were entertained in Toronto homes, and they in turn reciprocated in the officers' mess at the Garrison. The Lieutenant-

Governor lived in Toronto in a Government-owned residence on the grounds of the Garrison. During the winter the House of Assembly was in session, and this brought representatives to Parliament from as far away as Cornwall to the east and Amherstburg to the west. There was a large group of civil servants, and some professional men, such as lawyers and doctors. The Governor, top civil servants and officers represented authority, and those citizens who had houses with servants vied with one another in entertaining.

Class distinction, although less rigid than in England, was maintained by these people. This civilian group of about twenty families constituted the upper class. They all had at least one servant; one family had five, including negro slaves and free negroes. They required a fair-sized house, a carriage of some kind, and riding horses as well as carriage horses. Social life for them was fairly complicated, for they competed with one another to put on as good a show as possible. Before telephones, more letters circulated between friends. Some of these reveal jealousy and attempts to impress.

The top twenty families had the most education. They were active socially but usually paid fines rather than accept a town office. Most of them were civil servants and their work was not arduous. Government employees of the time worked seven hours a day, from ten A.M. to three o'clock, and then from five P.M. to seven. The men in top positions usually had their offices in their own homes, for which the province paid rent. We may presume that even when the clerks were kept strictly to these hours, the "boss" found much time for gossip and visiting. A call upon another civil servant, with wine and conversation, could easily take far more time than the business justified.

These twenty families were intensely loyal, conservative in politics, and distrustful of the United States. Some of them corresponded regularly with friends or relatives in that country, for while they regarded the government with suspicion their dislike was not personal. They were the first to purchase pews in the only church. Their sons sometimes went to school in England, or took a trip to Europe to round out their education. Their daughters occasionally attended boarding schools in Quebec, where there were schools for girls. It was an age of little social conscience, and there was no income tax in Canada for civilians. These men were, no doubt, more friendly to their servants and to their employers than their counterparts in England, for the North American employee-employer relationship was already operating at this early period because of high wages.

In exile from the fashionable middle-class society of England, they attempted to transplant it to Toronto. But being more than three months from that country, they tended to cling to the habits and fashions in vogue when they had left. They had, however, lost contact with trends which were making England a rapidly changing land. They, more than the classes beneath them, tended to cling to outmoded dress, and powdered hair, after it was out of style in England. Like the traditional planters of the southern U.S.A., most of them attempted to live in a style befitting their position as leading citizens. With the higher wages paid to servants, and the cost of living higher in general than in England, they were tempted to spend more than they earned. Of course they hoped that the thousands of acres of wild land which most of them owned would increase in value. This was wishful thinking, however, for they could see that it was not rising, and sometimes a cleared farm did not fetch more than virgin land. It was not until the great immigration after the war that land values began to steadily increase.

Perhaps "prominent citizens" have been given too much importance in history, but they are usually the ones who have left the records and have played the greatest part in moulding the political and social life of their era. The middle class, if such they may be called, formed a much larger group than the twenty families. They were minor civil servants, storekeepers, surveyors, building contractors, doctors, and business men such as Jesse Ketchum who purchased the tan yard in 1812 and became prosperous. The reader will not be surprised to learn that this man is probably better known today than any member of the twenty families we have described as the upper class. Another man, also, who could not qualify for upper-class listing in 1810, was the well-known John Strachan, rector of St. James, whose funeral in 1867 was the largest ever held in Toronto to that date.

The remainder of the people may be considered a third class. This group consisted of skilled tradesmen, such as carpenters and bricklayers, minor tradesmen, tailors, furniture makers, and unskilled labourers and servants. Most of these people were uneducated and many were illiterate. In 1804, the Rev. O'Kill Stuart, the second rector of Toronto, stated in a letter: "The labouring class consists almost wholly of disbanded soldiers, whose manner of life has been ill-calculated either to improve or preserve their morals." No doubt he was prejudiced, but while the British army produced brave and disciplined men, no vocational training was given to fit them for civilian life. As discharged soldiers most of them were totally unfit for skilled occupation and a large percentage drank to excess.

There is no doubt that there was a greater uncertainty to life in 1810: the struggle for existence started at an earlier age, and most people worked longer hours. A greater number ended their days in poverty, if not on charity. To many people the past – and 1810 is far enough in the past to appear relatively tranquil – is too far back to be compared with the present. There is no doubt, however, there were many frustrations for the average man in an age when opportunity was unfairly distributed. This sense of frustration was, no doubt, greater than in England. A new perspective had been forced upon those who came to Canada, and they never again would be able to accept the rigid class distinction of the old land as a fact of life.

Because of the number of Loyalists and American settlers in the province, many phrases and expressions became the common speech of all. The American-born brought with them the institution of Thanksgiving Day. They gave us the expression "Indian summer." The Indians left the Puritans alone in the winter. Often in late October a spell of warm weather, however, brought on an Indian attack. Merchandise in Toronto was sold in "stores," not in shops as in England. Pie more often contained pumpkin or fruit than meat or fowl. Workmen spoke of the "boss," instead of the master. These American-born brought with them New York currency, school sections, and school spellers. Ontario was being covered with split rail fences, as in the U.S.A. Indeed, it was a split rail fence that was placed around St. James' Church in 1810. They also brought with them the town meeting, which was given legality in 1793.

As in England, the educated of the British born were fond of Latin phrases. We have few records of their slang, or figures of speech, for these were seldom used in writing. We do know, however, that "elegant" was an overworked word of the period. It could describe a dress, a social evening, the railing of a stair, or almost anything that needed a superlative. A mild shock or set-back threw them "into a bustle." One woman describing a friend's life said, "Her couch had not been strewed with roses." A boss could warn an employee not to work in a "slap-dash manner." One young man said he was having a military coat made and would "sport" an epaulet. Simcoe called the name Toronto "outlandish." "Female" was not just a statistical word as today.

Those from England must have brought much of the slang with them, which included, "thingumbob" (if you did not remember the name of the object you were describing); "a piece of goods" (a woman or girl); "fiddlesticks" (an exclamation); "he stinks" (both literal and figurative); "foisting" something on another; "humbugging" (deceiving); "churchyard skin" (consumption); "brave" (praise); "smart" (describing something fashionable). The American immigrants used such slang as, "calculate" and "reckon" (to suppose), "slick" (fast), "critur" (animal of some kind) "sleeful" (skilful), etc.

These people have bequeathed to us many street names, such as Gorevale and Strachan Avenues, Jarvis, Baldwin, Givins, Simcoe Streets, and Danforth Road; and have given their names to buildings, such as Jesse Ketchum School, all named after men who walked the footpaths and rode their horses on the rutted and often muddy streets of Toronto in 1810.

In considering the society of Toronto at this period; it must be mentioned that William Pitt made an effort to establish a Canadian aristocracy, and that Governor Simcoe was also in favour of such a policy. All educated people in Toronto were aware they must take a stand upon a question that was agitating both Britain and Canada at this period. The issue was described in various ways, but the substance concerned was who and what group should have authority. The first seeds of democracy appeared to many as a symptom of social deterioration and moral decay, which must be checked. Toronto's "best people" held this view. Those who did not agree with them were often described as rascals, creatures, demagogues – and even rebels.

CHAPTER 3

Dress

By 1810 in Britain there was less difference than formerly in the style of dress worn by the upper class and that of the average person. The distinction was now achieved by niceties of style, clothing materials and tailoring. The revolution in dress which had come about during the war between France and Great Britain was now over, and the clothes for the men and women in 1810 were for the modern society that the political and social revolutions of the immediate past had created. So quickly did the social outlook in England and France change that in less than one generation, 1795-1810, the garb of the perfumed dandy was given to his footman.

Women's clothing in every age has accented some part of her anatomy. In 1810 it was the bosom. Boned stays (corsets), of whalebone or steel went out about 1790, although still worn by some older women.

Young women wore unboned stays continuously throughout this period. Boned stays again became high fashion in 1809 and quickly spread throughout Europe. It is probable, however, that this new boned corset did not reach its full popularity in Toronto until 1811, for communications were slow and merchants received only one stock of new dresses per year. There were always new visitors from Europe who brought the latest fashions with them, but the whole of Canada received less than one thousand immigrants from Europe each year, and a large percentage of these would be men.

The silhouette was straight and slim, but with a very high waist, and stays were necessary to maintain it. This high waist lasted until about 1820. With young women the corset was a waist girdle, tightly laced at the back, so that the bosom came into prominence, evenly if modestly covered with the dress.

The neckline was wide, and for daytime dress it was filled with a tucker or kerchief. The sleeves were short for "dress-up," but very long, extending to the fingers, for street wear. Most dresses buttoned down the front, but the chemise dress, which slipped over the head, was also in style. Ball dresses were trained, but this was disappearing in 1810. Dresses touched the shoes which had rounded toes and were without heels. Perhaps this was to make the men taller. The poke bonnet, of which there was an infinite variety, added a mystery to the face and shawls of cashmere, from India, were an indispensable part of the ensemble. But the most characteristic article of apparel during the period was the pelisse for outdoor wear, and it was a kind of overdress, rather than a light coat. It buttoned down the front but usually only one or two buttons at the neckline were actually fastened, so that the dress under it was revealed when the wearer was seated. The pelisse was usually nine inches shorter than the dress, and was often a vivid colour, such as scarlet. Winter coats were form fitting with tight waists and with puffed sleeves at the shoulder. Beaver hats were often worn in winter.

The hair was short and curled. It was becoming longer in 1810. The average woman in Toronto paid regular visits to the hairdresser, or one of the family curled her hair. The first "ladies and gentlemen's hairdresser" opened for business in 1802. Soaps which claimed to whiten the skin were popular. Although complexions were more natural than today, rouge and "pomade for colouring the lips" were used.

The women of the working class in England and settlers' wives in Ontario wore a much simpler and more sombre attire and our rural women wore cotton and homespun dresses to the neck, and plain poke bonnets and shawls.

The men in Toronto in 1810 were clean shaven, but with sideburns reaching to the bottom of the lobe of the ear. The hair was curled over the forehead, and was sometimes as thick as that of the young woman he courted.

The most important change in male attire had been the discarding of "small clothes" (knee breeches), and the adoption of pantaloons and trousers. The first pantaloons simply extended to below the knee, but by 1810 were close fitting and buttoned from knee to ankle to fit into the high boots of the period called "top boots" which had a top of buff or white leather. These pantaloons, which were braided up the side seams, were also worn with shoes which, unlike women's, had heels. The trousers, originally the dress of the sailor, and pantaloons usually had straps at the bottom to go under the instep of the shoe. Suspenders were worn with all three leg coverings. Pantaloons and trousers were of a lighter cloth and were lighter in colour than the top coat, and were made of cotton, linen, linsey woolsey and even a knitted material.

For formal wear breeches were still worn, and in 1810 many old men in Toronto had not yet adopted pantaloons or trousers. Most men wore pantaloons, especially for riding. Trousers, which were introduced in 1807 in England, were worn in Toronto by only a few relatively fashionable young men. The front fly for trousers and pantaloons did not come out until 1825, and was not in general use until 1840.

Shirts were pleated down the front and had a soft collar. The sleeves had soft, full cuffs at the wrist. Pantaloons and waistcoats, or trousers and waistcoats were not usually purchased together. These coats buttoned down to the waist, and from there cut back to a tail reaching to above the knees. A brightly coloured and patterned double-breasted vest was worn over the shirt, and a wide neckcloth completed the ensemble. This was often voluminous, and could be coloured, or black or white. By 1810 the crown of the top hat was becoming tapered, making it smaller at the top. The brim on the new hat was narrow and curved down at front and back. The overcoat often had overlapping capes, similar to the coachman's coat of England, and had a high collar.

As men rode horses primarily for transportation, there was no special riding dress, and pantaloons and top boots made a satisfactory riding habit. Although women rode side-saddle, there was no relaxation in the tight and the high-waisted clothing of the day. A special dress was required as a riding habit, and this had a very full skirt, for freedom of movement, and a jaunty hat which might simply be a crown trimmed with an ostrich feather. This "habit" could be worn as casual street wear.

Children's clothing was adult clothing in miniature, but was not as formal, and aprons were worn by little boys as well as young girls.

This was the dress of the people of Toronto in 1810. A young man of the town, visiting in England, says in a letter to his parents: "I have got an entire new suit of clothes in the London cut, very different from the York," (Toronto). The Loyalists and American emigrants had come from a country where the norm was hard work for all; where only a few wealthy idlers sought to maintain their social position by the quality and the cut of their clothes. Those from the Maritimes had become used to a less stylish cut; and most of the people of Toronto had never worn fashionable clothing. Women's dresses were made by dressmakers or by one of the family, and although the stores regularly advertised hats, bonnets, slippers and shoes, dresses are seldom mentioned.

However, there was nothing "pioneer" about the dress of the men and women in Toronto in 1810. Indeed, many travellers commented that some of the stores were as good as those in London. They stocked such items as Irish linens, plain and fancy muslins, velvet ribbons, ostrich feathers, long silk gloves, black and white silk stockings, fine silk mitts, elegant silk shawls, India satins, lace handkerchiefs, London beaver bonnets, Imperial chip bonnets, silk and cotton umbrellas, etc. This is part of a long list of articles of dress for women advertised in the York *Gazette* as having arrived from England by way of New York. The stores also stocked a great variety of dressmaking supplies, including laces, ribbons and feathers as well as needles and thread. Being far from the style source, however, some older men and women continued to wear the dress of a generation past.

Upon coming to live in Toronto, women accepted the custom of wearing coarse knitted socks over their shoes in winter. Rigid adherence to the dress of England was modified by the summer temperature and dress was more casual. A man might wear a lumberman's shirt while gardening, and he left off his waistcoat and his vest more often than in the old land. Indian moccasins were worn as house slippers.

CHAPTER 4

The Coming War
with the U.S.A.

In 1810, war with the United States was expected by the people of Toronto. The conflict came with the American declaration of war against Great Britain, June 18, 1812.

The first seeds of this war were sown at the Continental congress of 1774-75, when invitations were sent to Canada to join the Thirteen Colonies in their revolt against Britain. These offers were refused and American invasions of Canada were repulsed. After this War of Independence Americans began to look upon Canadians as vassals of Britain who lacked the spirit and courage to follow their example.

The War of Independence terminated with the peace of 1783. From that date, and for twenty-eight years before 1812, the new United States of America was attempting the difficult task of forming a union of peoples of widely divergent standards and aspirations. A national senti-ment had to be created from a vacuum for a nation born in a war. A past and a heritage were necessary to bind the separate states into a nation. Britain had been the enemy and France the friend. At all public gatherings for the inauguration of new projects and for celebrations of various kinds the theme of the oratory was the victory of the colonists against the tyranny of the mother country and the friendship of France. Every schoolboy orator repeated this thesis, so that by the early eighteen hundreds it had become the catalyst for unifications.

The second reason for the war was a simple one, also. While the peoples of Europe had lived in the same house and on the same land for generations, conditions in America fostered a constant movement westward. At this time there was distress among New England farmers. They wished to leave their rocky acres and head west, for the alternative was whole families working in the new cotton mills for starvation wages.

The "West" around eighteen hundred, was Pennsylvania, Ohio, Kentucky and Tennessee, and the basin of the Mississippi was fast becoming a separate country with its trade outlets at its mouth through Spanish ports, and not by land to the east. There were a million people in this area which Britain had attempted to close to settlers by the proclamation of 1763. With the conquest of Spain by France, Louisiana became French, and in 1802 the port of New Orleans was closed to

American commerce. This vast Louisiana territory of nearly one million square miles extended west from the Mississippi to the Rocky Mountains, and from Texas to the Canadian Border. President Jefferson realized that the settlers would provoke war with France to open New Orleans, so with a stroke of genius offered fifteen million dollars for Louisiana to Napoleon at a time when he badly needed money to finance his conquests. It has been said that the War of 1812 started in Napoleon's bathtub where he announced his intention of selling the territory.

Louisiana became another frontier and another sieve in the westward march of migration. At each sieve, from east to west, there had been a screening of the thoughtful, the cultured and the learned. At the last frontier there was an absence of all architecture, handicraft and higher learning. Material success and local leadership were the only goals. Oratory, rather than literature, emerged as the inspiration. Aggressiveness, self-assertion and self-satisfaction at conquering the wilderness were the qualities of the frontiersmen, and also that of their leaders, for in what was then the most democratic area on earth the leaders were but a mirror of the people.

In the House of Representatives in 1812 the total vote of these western states of Ohio, Kentucky, Tennessee and Pennsylvania was 27 to 2 for war with Britain, although the total vote of the seventeen states was 79 to 49. The state of New York, whose population was mainly in the East, voted 11 to 3 against this war.

By 1810 the oratory had had its effect upon the masses and upon the new breed of statesmen which the revolution had created with the broadened franchise. Government by the people was an innovation, and it is no wonder that in their satisfaction with their own mode of government their judgment became warped, particularly if they lived in the new West. They saw the people of Canada, including the Loyalists, as servile men under the heel of despots, waiting to be liberated. Most of the enthusiasm for attacking Canada came from those farthest away, from the south and from the "War Hawks" of the new western states, who shouted that Canada could be conquered in six weeks. In 1811, Dr. Eustis, the United States secretary of war, said: "We can take Canada without soldiers; we have only to send officers into the province and the people disaffected toward their own government, will rally round our standard."

Henry Clay said on the floor of Congress: "It is absurd to suppose we will not succeed in our enterprise against the enemy's provinces."

By 1810 free or cheap land, within the grasp of the average man became farther away from the East than ever before, and news drifted back to the East of the lawlessness in the new west and the trouble with hostile Indians. The relatively tranquil and sparsely-settled Ontario was far nearer to those in the East and appeared to many to be more desirable. During the war which followed maps were found in the possession of American prisoners showing land in Ontario to be given to American volunteers after victory had been won.

The conservative outlook of the people of Canada and Toronto in particular tended to make them view the liberalism of the U.S.A. as a symptom of deterioration. In 1810 Canadians looked upon the U.S.A. with the same distrust and disapproval as that country now looks upon Russia.

Those in Toronto were resentful of the savage attacks made in the American press against Great Britain. They distrusted the motives of a people who professed to be admirers of atheistic France. Feeling ran higher in Toronto than in England, for the hostility of the U.S.A. to that country aroused only a shrug of the shoulders from the hard-pressed British who had had no personal dealings with either Americans or Canadian colonists.

For many in Toronto the feeling against the U.S.A. was personal. With the Loyalists it was the inevitable reaction of a people who still felt the sting of being driven out of their own homes, and who had an ideal conception of the mother country thousands of miles away. Many of these Loyalists still used the word "rebels" in speaking of Americans. With the remainder of the townspeople who had come from Britain, or from the east coast of Canada, the feeling was not as personal as that of the Loyalists, but most in Toronto disapproved of them collectively. This, however, did not prevent them from having relatives and friends in the U.S.A. whom they occasionally visited and wrote to.

In 1807 a roar of indignation arose in the U.S.A., which was heard in Toronto, when the British frigate *Leopard* fired upon the American frigate *Chesapeake* and took off four crewmen, presumably deserters from the Royal Navy. From the time of that incident to 1810 it seemed to those in Toronto that war would come very soon.

Events in Europe and the U.S.A. were watched with interest, and American newspapers were eagerly read and passed on to others. They heard gossip that certain American settlers around Toronto openly talked of union with the U.S.A. Even the most loyal of those in Toronto were impatient with the delay in making the Garrison into a fort, for there was only one blockhouse and some gun batteries.

But generally there was optimism. It was not based upon cold reasoning from known facts. Rather, it was founded upon emotion, and boundless confidence in the mother country. After 1810 this confidence was stimulated by the presence of General Brock, who assumed his post as Lieutenant-Governor in October, 1811. It was due to the spirit and energy of this remarkable man, later killed in action at Queenston Heights, that Ontario was able to take the initiative at the outset of the war which followed in 1812.

CHAPTER 5

Government

Toronto's present system of municipal government had its inception in the second session of the first provincial parliament at Niagara in 1793, when a statute was passed which made town meetings legal. The first town meeting in Toronto was in 1797.

This Ontario statute merely legalized the holding of such town meetings which the United Empire Loyalist settlers had held in the townships of Sidney, Adolphustown, and elsewhere, as early as 1791. Such meetings were unlawful until the new legislation, but these settlers from the American colonies had been accustomed to this degree of democratic civic government, and saw no reason why they should not have it in the British colony of their adoption.

These town meetings to elect men to fill town offices and to pass prudential laws encroached upon the authority of the justice in session, appointed by the Crown, whose decrees sometimes dealt with matters over which the town meeting had assumed jurisdiction. These meetings displeased Governor Simcoe. They were New World and suspiciously democratic. The freedom they represented had aided in creating an atmosphere of rebellion in the American colonies. However, he was too sensible a man to make an issue of the matter, for it was the very Loyalists who had fought to uphold the British rule in the American colonies who wanted town meetings in Ontario.

The original conception of colonial government was to have towns and townships entirely governed by officers appointed by the Crown. The creation of townships had been intended only as a means of granting land to settlers. The management of local affairs in each township was the responsibility of the District Court of General Quarter Sessions, composed of magistrates or justices of the peace appointed by the Lieutenant-Governor. A premature bill to adopt the elective principle in municipal affairs had been killed. With the legalizing of the town meeting, however, the whole conception of town and rural government began to change. Powers of local government were later transferred to "Boards of Police," who were annually elected, and Toronto's present system began in the year 1834.

Although the town meeting was a small start toward democracy on a local scale, the actual control was still in the hands of these salaried Crown-appointed magistrates in 1810.

The Ontario statute of 1793 classified as a town the type of settlement we now designate a township. All civic offices in 1810 were for the Township of York, including Toronto. The statute provided that if a township had thirty or more resident householders, the two Crown-appointed justices of the peace (magistrates) of the district could instruct the Crown-appointed high constable to call a public meeting the first Monday in March to elect town officers, and it was the high constable who was in charge of the meeting. Thus was inaugurated the foundation of government in each district, and the first step toward local democratic government in Ontario.

These town officers performed the duties of paid civic employees who eventually supplanted them. We must except fire fighting, which was on a volunteer basis until the year 1874. They did not perform the duties of later mayor, controllers and aldermen, for municipal government did not come until the act of Incorporation in 1834. They were paid a token salary or no salary at all. Their work, however, was only part time and much of it could be done in the evening. The system permitted civic duties to be performed at little expense, and there was no alternative for there was insufficient taxable wealth to provide salaried full-time civic employees. Because there was no reward, all townspeople except those of the upper class, considered it to be their civic duty, and it put them in the forefront as leading citizens. Those of the upper class invariably paid fines in lieu of serving.

The annual town meeting was held in any hall convenient for the purpose, for there was no civic building. In 1800 and 1802 it was held in Playter's Hotel, in 1807 in Gilbert's Tavern. One meeting was held in St. James' Church before the structure was completed. In 1810 it was in Stoyell's Inn. These annual town meetings were held on the first Monday in March, and lasted from eleven in the morning until about one o'clock.

All of these buildings were small in size so it is probable that less than one hundred attended. Many must have brought their own chairs;

probably many others stood in the room or in the hallway, with some on the street – just to be there to catch some of the excitement.

The meetings were very informal, comparable to the annual meeting of a small modern church. The high constable announced the office to be filled and nominations were made by the assembled townspeople. A vote was taken, probably with a show of hands, and the man who received the most votes was chosen for the office. Many were elected and appointed who were absent from the meeting. If agreeable to the man elected, he could hold some town office year after year. If not acceptable to him, however, he could not be elected again until three years after his last term of office. Once a man had refused office and paid a fine, the elective principle was abandoned. The magistrate then suggested another and the high constable served this new man with a notice. If he refused to act he was fined £2. In many cases the fine paid by the first man was given to the one who accepted the office willingly.

Much time was consumed in listening to speeches by voluble citizens who had a grievance to air, or who simply wanted to talk and be listened to. The town meeting's scope in passing laws was limited, to say the least. It voted and passed only upon "Prudential Laws," which regulated such minor matters as the height and construction of fences, the extermination of weeds, and the control of animals running at large.

These town offices in 1810 included clerk of the town and township, assessors, collector, overseers of the highways and roads (they also acted as fence-viewers at this date) pound-keeper, and town wardens. During the War of 1812 the office of billet-master was added, and his duty was to find lodgings in hotels and private homes for convalescent soldiers.

The list of town officials begins with the High Constable, and this man was appointed by justices of the peace or magistrates. In 1810 ten others in Toronto and four in the township were also appointed to serve under him. These men were appointed, not elected, and paid a fine if they did not accept the office. They had no uniforms, and, of course, did not patrol the streets. They acted only when called upon to do so by the magistrates, or in an emergency. It must have taken considerable courage for these men to make arrests of desperate men who sometimes faced banishment (deportation) or the gallows, for they had no training.

The Clerk of the Town was required to bring up to date the list of inhabitants. This included newborn infants and newcomers. He also corrected the list by the deletion of those who had died or moved away. It appears that it was not thought necessary to include the marital status at this date, and we can now only guess at the number who were married.

The duties of the two assessors, as the word implies, was to assess property, and it was upon their valuation that the township tax was levied. All householders were divided into ten classes for taxation. This grouping was based upon real and personal property, which ranged from £50-100 in the first class to £500-550 in the tenth. Taxes were very low for there was little public service, and the highest tax was only £1. 5s. There was also an excused list of those whose property was assessed at less than £50, and these men paid only two shillings. The assessment list was given to the magistrates and a copy was posted in some public place. We may well imagine these assessors' friends and neighbours kidding them about their power to increase or decrease their taxes, and making sly remarks about their valuation of their own property. We may also conjecture the mixed feelings of those who paid the two shillings.

The Collector, of course, collected the tax based upon the assessment. In an age of little cash, it must have taken several visits to some households to collect this money, and he could, according to law, require a sale of the assessed owner's goods to collect this tax. Such an expedient was probably seldom resorted to. There was also a Treasurer, an appointed employee, whose salary was three per cent of the tax collected. This tax money was intended to defray the cost of building a jail, courthouse, and bridges in the township.

The Overseers of the Highways and Roads also acted as Fence-viewers in 1810, but this became two offices at a later date. Each of these men was allotted a certain area of the township for his inspection and it was his duty to supervise the road work done by owners whose property fronted upon township roads, or on streets in Toronto. This road work involved making a level surface, draining with ditches where necessary, and the removal of stumps and large stones. No gravel was laid at this time, but probably some conscientious owners did lay some gravel if it was readily available. In some locations owners often had to construct corduroy roads, which consisted of laying logs at right angles to the road over swampy ground, and filling the spaces between the logs with earth or gravel. Road work was often indifferently carried out and the courts were usually lenient with this neglect. If the property owner persistently neglected his road work, the Overseer brought him before the Court of Quarter Sessions to be fined. From 1800 to 1830, in Toronto, the sentence for drunkenness in Toronto was the removal of one stump from the streets. This town and township road work is not to be confused with provincial roads built under contract or by the regular army, or later toll roads constructed by joint stock companies. As fence-viewers the Overseers checked the height and construction of fences. They had to notify owners if their fences extended over the road allowance and order their relocation, if necessary.

To the modern city dweller, a pound is a place where stray dogs are kept until claimed by their owners. In 1810 dogs are not mentioned and it was the duty of the two poundkeepers to gather up all cattle, sheep, and hogs that trespassed upon another's land – if the land was properly fenced in, we should add. They also had to impound any uncastrated horse more than one year old, running at large. The owner had to pay twenty shillings to get his horse back from the pound, half of this sum going to the poundkeepers. The pound was simply a small fenced-in pasture, and there were several of these pounds on unsold lots in 1810. What was called pound-breach was the removal of impounded animals without permission, and there was a heavy fine for this misdemeanour.

The last town officers were the two wardens. These men had more prestige than any of the others, and less work to do. One of these town wardens was the churchwarden, selected by the minister, who automatically became a town warden. The other was elected at the town meeting. These men represented the township in the legal sense.

The nucleus of our present judicial system was already in operation in 1810, with Courts of Common Pleas, having both civil and criminal jurisdiction. The council and judges were selected from wealthy citizens. Appeal was to the Lieutenant-Governor. The management of local affairs in each district was the responsibility of the "District Court of General Quarter Sessions of the Peace," and this court was presided over by justices of the peace or magistrates appointed by the Lieutenant-Governor. This system was familiar to the Loyalists of the province for it had been in force before the American Revolution.

Trifling matters, such as assault and drunkenness, which today would be the business of a magistrate's court, were tried at the Quarter Sessions Court, of which there were two sessions in 1810. This court had a "Grand Inquest" (grand jury), consisting of twenty men. The grand jury of today has seven. It also made recommendations, which became law, pertaining to selling liquor on the Sabbath, burning garbage, and the burning of the shavings of cabinetmakers at certain hours of specified days. In addition to the Quarter Sessions, there was a Court of the King's Bench, and a Court of Appeal. These three courts were held in the Parliament Buildings in 1810, for no court building had been constructed.

In the fabric of the provincial government were numerous offices, including Attorney-General, Surveyor-General, Solicitor, Chief Justice, gaolers, bailiffs and coroners.

The government of the province aroused more interest and excitement than local politics, and as Toronto was the capital, and had the Parliament Buildings it was the political centre.

In 1810, most educated and wealthy people, even in the New World, believed the masses should be governed by the few. Most of the inhabitants of Toronto were Anglicans. The King ruled by divine right, and submission to King and Government were Christian duties. Some of this divinity would, of course, have brushed off on titled families, and the preservation of the established order was part of the Anglican faith, even if not actually stated. Democracy was the anti-Christ to many of the Anglican persuasion, and the French Revolution appeared to have verified this interpretation.

This cherished belief, that the mass should be governed by the few, had one flaw that was becoming more apparent as more and more social changes followed the industrial revolution. Was it possible for the few to be unbiased and unprejudiced? And most important – how were the few to be selected? Previously the selection had largely been through accident of birth. With the acquisition of wealth from industrialization, rather than from land rent, a new wealthy class was emerging in England which could buy titles and social distinction. With the exploitation of the large new factory and mine worker class it was becoming increasingly evident that the few were governing for their own benefit, and for the first time their right to do so was being questioned in Britain. Already, in that country, the House of Commons (although elected upon a limited franchise) was becoming more powerful because of the control of the country's finances, and the unjust system was beginning to be corrected.

In Ontario there were no actual exploiters and exploited, but the new outlook upon government had reached the colonies, particularly when there were five thousand Loyalists and many other thousands of recent immigrants from the U.S.A. who had been used to a broader share in government, and did not hold to this Anglican Church view.

The Constitutional Act provided that a governor for all the colonies, and a lieutenant-governor for each province would be sent from Britain to represent the King. It may not have been intended that his power would actually be greater than that of the British Monarch. All the other lawmakers were to be Canadians.

At the top was the Executive Council, of five men, approved by the Governor to assist him in his administration. In Peter Russell's administration these Council members were given five thousand acres of land. These men were approved, rather than selected, by the Governor for he usually came to the New World or to Ontario a stranger. Next came the Legislative Council of ten men in 1810. Only five or six of this body regularly attended the meetings. They were also approved by the Governor, upon the advice of the Executive Council. The same men were appointed to both bodies at different times, and upon a member's death or resignation a new man was appointed who had the same outlook upon government as his predecessor.

The second house was the Assembly of twenty-five members in 1810, and its members were elected by popular vote. These Assembly members came to the Legislature in Toronto from as far away as Cornwall to the east and Amherstburg to the west. For the duration of Parliament they stayed at Toronto hotels. Many stayed at Mrs. Johnson's boarding house which had accommodation for twenty guests. These out of town Assemblymen were paid ten shillings per day during the sitting of the house, while resident Assembly members did not receive any remuneration.

Although this constitution appeared to follow closely that of Britain, it actually did not. The elected Assembly had no power to force their measures on the statute books. They passed laws in their own house which could be rejected, within two years, by the Governor, the Executive Council, and the Imperial Parliament in Britain.

In practice, the Executive Council's decisions were accepted by the Governor, for he was a short-term official who usually had little first-hand knowledge of Canadian conditions. Members of this body sometimes visited the Colonial Secretary in Britain to present its recommendations. As the Governor received his orders from this Colonial Secretary, and he was from the British ruling class, both his views and those of the Executive Council were in harmony. The Legislative Council, whose members were appointed for life upon the recommendation of the Executive Council, were supposed to take their orders from the Governor, but this appears to have been a formality. The Governors of the province were often only pawns in the game between the Colonial Office in London and the Executive Council.

Both of these appointed bodies were usually in complete agreement. They felt they were protecting the infant colony from the hated democracy of the American republic, and thus preventing the loss of Canada to the U.S.A. by conquest or future assimilation. In each vetoed bill of the Assembly, they were convinced they were saving their country from "anarchy and innovation."

Although there was periodic frustration in the Assembly early in the century, the election of 1808 was quiet with personal rather than group dissatisfaction. Even at this early date, however, the seeds of the so-called Family Compact were germinating to provoke trouble in the future.

Even in Tory Britain the reformers in the Assembly received support. Here we see an example of the innate sense of justice of a whole nation.

During this period, after 1814, the reformers sometimes went over the heads of the Governor, the Council and the Colonial Office, direct to the Imperial Parliament, with remarkable success.

Toronto, along with the counties of Durham and Simcoe, constituted the East Riding of York. The town did not have a member of its own until 1821. The polling station, or husting as it was called, was in Toronto, and voters from the entire riding came to the town to register their votes for the Assembly in the provincial elections. This voting lasted a whole week in most rural areas of the province, and three days or more in Toronto. There had been a session of Parliament at Newark in 1796. By the following year the new Parliament Buildings were ready, and then on June 1st, the first Parliament sat at Toronto for a session that lasted eight weeks. The first election in Toronto was in 1800: other elections were in 1804, 1808 and 1812. Three by-elections were also held during this period.

This was the day of the "open vote" and men publicly and audibly voted for the candidate of their choice. The secret ballot of today did not come until 1874 in provincial elections and in 1867 in Toronto municipal elections. This open voting seemed reasonable at the time it was used; for in an age when many could not read or write, all those who congregated to watch the proceedings knew that John Smith had voted, for they heard him pronounce the name of the candidate of his choice. The open vote was also an assurance that such registry could not be falsified, and, no doubt, candidates delegated someone to check such audible votes, for they could not personally be at the hustings continuously for three days.

The grave weakness of the open vote, however, was that the individual voter could be intimidated by threat of punishment, and an employer could too easily influence his staff to vote as he did himself. It created an atmosphere of emotion and prejudice, not to mention drunkenness that lasted for three days in Toronto and a week in most of the province.

In an age of no organized sport or the diversions and entertainment we take for granted today, a provincial election could be the most fascinating event of the whole year. At one of them an enterprising showman exhibited a monkey in a cage, in one of the hotels, and charged a shilling. Large crowds congregated around the voting platform of rough boards set up outdoors. In 1808 the hustings was between the houses of Parliament. The voter walked up the half dozen steps to the platform and said, "I vote for so-and-so," in a loud clear voice, or perhaps a timid one, depending upon the popularity of the candidate he had selected, and the amount of liquor he had consumed.

The regulations stipulated that voting should continue as long as not more than an hour elapsed between single votes. Friends of candidates held back voters, so this would not occur, until the very last voter had been gathered in. Candidates supplied free refreshments and liquor. In 1808, one candidate spent the sum of £200 on "Electioneering," which if translated into modern money, cost him $5,000. In 1812 one candidate spent double this amount. Many voters kept postponing registering their vote until they had exhausted the hospitality of the candidate. Then, perhaps in a befuddled condition, they were persuaded to vote for another.

Political parties had not yet arisen in the province, and all candidates assured the electors that they did not represent any party. There was antipathy toward the extravagant party politics of the U.S.A. which, no doubt, accounted for this attitude. Each candidate appealed to the electorate as an individual, with his own platform, such as popular education, control of the House of Assembly over expenditure, etc. The large block of Quakers and Mennonites in the riding usually voted for the opposition candidate, who was not popular in Toronto, for the protestations of loyalty, and the maintaining of the *status quo* did not strike a responsive chord in this group.

Drunken election brawls frequently occurred, and there were fist fights between partisans and a great deal of horseplay attending the exciting period of the election. After the votes were counted, the succesful candidate's supporters marched triumphantly through the streets to a splendid dinner in one of the hotels.

It was in the following year (1811) that the election of judges to Parliament was not considered to be in the best interest of the province and was abolished. Officers of the government had offices in their own homes, for which the government paid rent, and it was not until the third parliament buildings were erected in 1832 that adequate office space for government departments was available.

As early as 1810, many people were "disgusted" with politics, and one contemporary writer says "instead of sitting down cordially together to form regulations for the public good," he found the government disposed to "calculate their measures as much with a view to patronage and private endowment as the prosperity of the colony."

CHAPTER 6

Religion and the
Clergy Reserves

Eighteen hundred and ten was an age of intense belief, and men ardently believed in class distinction, in their political creed and in their church. We are startled by the vigour of the language used in 1810 to denounce another faith, a political party or a nation. The world was much smaller, and men knew less, so they would be more dogmatic about it. To a great degree they believed that the last word had been spoken, so they were opposed to "anarchy," and "innovation," and democracy.

Religion in England and in Canada was inseparable from politics, because the conditions of the age compelled it to be. As the dominant faction promoted the idea that only a select group (and they themselves were the selectors) was entitled to rule, they also believed that the church they favoured should have authority in the state for, of course, they believed in authority. As the first assumption was being questioned in 1810, it was inevitable that the second should be also. Thus in Ontario, a British colony, we see the struggle for separation of church and state, coincident with the progress toward democracy. It is doubtful if this parallel was understood at the time. Some in Toronto who favoured steps toward democracy were dismayed that the authority of the Anglican church was being questioned. Both of these issues were emerging in Toronto in 1810, and to an even greater degree in the province, and they were beginning to arouse the bitter resentments which culminated in the Rebellion of 1837.

The Anglican clergyman in Toronto in 1810 was the Rev. George O'Kill Stuart, who was to accept a pastorate in Kingston the following year. He was St. James' second rector, and was a graduate of Harvard and a Loyalist, who also taught the Home District School. Dr. Strachan, the man who succeeded him, was not a Loyalist, but came directly from Britain. Later to become bishop, he was from Aberdeen, Scotland, and was born in 1778. Trained as a teacher, he was invited to come to Canada to head a college which Governor Simcoe intended to establish in Toronto. When he arrived in Canada, however, he found that Simcoe had been appointed to San Domingo, and his college scheme had been abandoned. Strachan settled in Kingston, and earned his living as a tutor. Three years later, in 1804, he decided upon the church as a career and took holy orders. He was appointed to the mission church at Cornwall, where he also started a boys' school. Many of his pupils were from Toronto, for his school was the best in the province.

After the passing of Ontario's first educational act in 1807, authorizing District Grammar Schools, there were many in Toronto who desired a school of the high calibre of Strachan's. The opportunity came when Dr. Stuart decided to live in Kingston. Strachan was offered the rectory of the Toronto St. James' Church and the new school. In addition, he was to be given the chaplaincy of the troops, at a salary of £150 per year. This man argued that union of church and state was not for the aim of making the church political, but for the purpose of making the state religious. Yet it was power for himself, primarily, that he wanted. Upon first coming to America, and finding that he was not required to head a college, he wrote to a friend in Scotland about his plans and added: "If I do not think I can easily succeed, I shall recross the Atlantic and try my fortunes in Britain." Fortune favoured him, however, and he stayed in Canada. His interpretation of the Constitutional Act regarding the so-called Clergy Reserves, and his association with, and leadership in the "Family Compact" contributed more than did the efforts of any single individual to the unrest and resentment in the province which eventually culminated in the Rebellion of 1837.

Dr. Strachan was a small man, five feet six inches in height, but compactly built and erect. His voice and appearance revealed unusual firmness and determination, and he thoroughly believed in the rule of the many by the few. He was convinced that education should be a by-product of the established church. He was given to describing ideas and writing as sophistry if it did not concur with his own opinion. He believed, that he was the trustee of all moral and religious truth, and to compromise in dealing with others was tantamount to making concessions to the devil. There was no Christian humility, however, in his character, and with the aid of his wife's money, he lived in better style than anyone in early Toronto.

After the British conquest of Canada, the Quebec Act of 1774 permitted the French in Canada to retain their church. In order to counterbalance the influence of the Roman Catholic Church in Quebec, and to promote loyalty to Britain, it was decided to create a strong Protestant church in Ontario by giving it state aid. No taxes were exacted to support this new church, as in England. Such an expedient would have been useless, for there was not enough wealth in the new province to tax. A long range plan to support this church which appeared reasonable, and even brilliant, in theory, was devised by British statesmen.

They decided that one-seventh of all Crown Lands would be set aside for this purpose and rented until sold. Such an increasing revenue, they assumed, would gradually make a Canadian Protestant state church self-supporting with no expense to the taxpayers of the province, or in England. On paper, a township was divided into forty-two 200-acre farm lots, the dimensions of which were in the proportion of one to five. Each end of these lots fronted upon a road. Six of the forty-two lots were reserved as Crown Lands, and another six lots as Clergy Reserves. The remaining 30 lots in each township were offered for sale to settlers. These Clergy Reserve lots in Ontario totalled 2,200,000 acres.

By 1810 the reserved lands were already causing dissatisfaction in the province, and by 1817 outright agitation for a change began. The vitality and prosperity of the U.S.A. was arousing jealousy in Ontario. This was especially true of the settlers, rather than of those in Toronto who were making their living from trade or government office. These settlers were asking why the reserved lands were not sold, instead of rented, or if the land must be rented, why were they not in large blocks, instead of being interspersed in land sold for settlement? In newly-opened regions there would be great advantage in having farms contiguous, roads would more easily be kept open in winter, drainage, ditching and road building could be more easily done, fewer farms would be surrounded with the tall trees of the reserved land, shading the settler's cleared land and housing predatory animals, and settlers would also be closer together for mutual assistance.

These reserved lands became barriers to combined action of settlers for school and local improvements, by separating them from each other, and in addition, raised the cost of such improvements in a given area.

The reason for incorporating Reserved land with land sold for settlement, was, of course, to raise its value by the labour of the surrounding settlers. If these Clergy Reserves had actually been rented to settlers, as anticipated, there would have been little complaint, but no immigrant had any desire to spend the best years of his life clearing the forest on land he did not own when land could be purchased for a small sum. One writer of the period claimed that not one acre of land had been rented by 1810.

Then there was the added dissatisfaction regarding the title to these church lands. The Constitutional Act merely stated, "For the support of the Protestant Clergy." Both Simcoe and the framers of the Act, no doubt, intended it to mean the established Church of England, and perhaps Scotland, for Canada was acquired after 1707 when Great Britain had two established churches. (The Crown validated this later interpretation in 1817). On the other hand, these framers could not know that these denominations in Ontario would be challenged by the dissenting churches of American immigrants after the War of 1812, so that by 1840 the Anglicans would constitute less than ten per cent of the population of the province.

With an actual representative government, the Clergy Reserves problem would have been solved as soon as it became evident that such reserves were not in the best interest of the majority of the people of the province. But democracy was yet to come. In 1810, practically all of the Family Compact members were Anglicans. They also made up most of the membership of the Executive Council and the Legislative Council. Under Dr. Strachan's autocratic leadership these lands were held long past the time when it became evident that they should be shared with other denominations or returned to the state. In effect, these Clergy Reserves were retarding the development of the province and making the U.S.A. more attractive to prospective settlers.

Of course, not all of the people of Toronto in 1810 were Anglicans. Many from England, as well as from the U.S.A., were of other faiths, but their numbers were so small that they were not yet able to build their own churches. Some of other faiths, including a few Catholics, attended St. James; others conducted services of their own in homes and in taverns. While the mention of a tavern to hold a religious service may arouse a smile with modern readers, such buildings were the only ones with a room large enough for a public meeting of any sort. And it was not until some years later that drink ceased to be respectable to an increasing percentage of the population. Members of these minority groups were sustained in their faith by occasional visits from itinerant "saddlebag" preachers from the U.S.A. whose field was the whole province.

A site for a Catholic church had been granted by the Crown in 1806, and the following year a church was organized and a chalice and vestments were purchased. Being few in number the members were dependent upon the services of priests travelling from Quebec to the predominantly Catholic settlement on the Detroit River, and it was not until 1826 that they had a church building in Toronto. The first Methodist chapel in Toronto was built in 1818; the first Presbyterian, called John Knox Church, was built in 1822; and the first Baptist church was constructed about 1832.

Bible societies had their beginnings in England before 1800, for the revival started by the Wesleys had awakened an interest in reading the Scriptures. The first such society in Ontario, called the Bible and Prayer Book Society, was established by Anglicans in 1817.

As early as 1800, officialdom in Toronto was hearing rumours of a secret society being formed in Montreal, ostensibly to oppose Catholicism, but "whose real purpose was to overthrow the government." It was organized by Irishmen and was called the Orange Society. However, it does not appear that the Glorious Twelfth was celebrated in Toronto until 1822.

Taking the province as a whole, it is doubtful if more than twenty-five per cent were regular church-goers. In 1817, one writer stated that, "at maturity, about one half are professors of religion." It should be noted, however, that in the pioneer state of society there were few church buildings to attend, and only a few travelling evangelists to call meetings together. Because of the absence of colleges and universities, Ontario escaped trends which in England (except in the evangelical churches) were making religion philosophical and abstract.

In the U.S.A. after the Revolution, religion was in a state of decline for a decade. One American writer stated in 1789, that only three or four students at Princeton made any pretensions to piety. In every American college deism was popular. In 1804, Lyman Beecher, the American divine, stated "Irreligion has become in all parts of our land alarmingly prevalent. The name of God is blasphemed; the Bible denounced; the sabbath profaned; the public worship of God is neglected."[5] No doubt he was an alarmist, but his statement cannot be ignored.

The Loyalists in Canada escaped this inevitable reaction to the upheaval of a revolution. The religious faith of Loyalist Anglicans was sustained by their loyalty. "Fear God and honour the King" had real meaning for them.

Within a short time after the Revolution, however, the American sect churches were championing the uncompromising ethics of Jesus to "preach the gospel to the poor" and were recalling the Christian Church to its mission. In 1810 the settlement of the middle-western U.S.A. was by a people who have been described as the first Americans. They were being saved from paganism by the efforts of evangelists who followed the new frontier settlers on horseback to provide religion and conversion in log cabins and at camp meetings. These itinerant preachers came to Ontario, also, so that practically all of the travelling preachers in Ontario were missionaries of American churches, of the Methodists, Presbyterians, Quakers, Dutch Reformed, Baptists, etc., and their salaries were paid by American missionary societies.

The evangelical movements which combated agnosticism on the frontiers of the U.S.A. were slower in getting started in Ontario because of the lack of a strong dissenting church to support them. The schismatic faiths in Ontario, particularly Methodism, were held up to scorn and ridicule by many Anglicans in Toronto. Methodist preachers were often considered ignorant and hypocritical. They were also suspected of being political spies, for with war with the U.S.A. a possibility, their interest in spreading the gospel in a British colony appeared insincere. The first "camp meeting" in Ontario was in 1805, at Hay Bay, near Belleville, but as yet there was no general revival of religion.

In Toronto, with its preponderance of military officers and civil servants, going to church was the loyal and the socially acceptable thing to do. Money to build St. James was raised by subscription, with the donation of the Lieutenant-Governor topping the list. The sale of pews needed little promotion. Taprooms were closed during the periods of church service, and at least one man, Jesse Ketchum, endeavoured to stop Sunday skating on the Bay. We should also mention, however, that this man later joined the Methodists when they built their chapel.

The only church building in Toronto in 1810 was St. James, an unpainted clapboarded structure standing alone on a six-acre lot in a partially-cleared pine forest. The property was bounded by King Street to the south, Church on the west and Jarvis on the east, the site of the present St. James Cathedral. The lot was granted by the Crown in 1797. The church was built in 1807, and altered and enlarged in 1818 when a small steeple was added as a bell tower. A third St. James, of masonry construction, in the Renaissance style of architecture, was erected in 1831, and a fourth in the same style in 1840. Both of these buildings were destroyed by fire. The present building in the Gothic style was built in 1850. The original building was a simple carpenter-built structure, comparable to the residences and business buildings. Forty by fifty feet in size it had its axis east-west. It was erected by soldiers of the Garrison, by order of General Sheaffe, and these men raised the frames, put in the oak windows and sash and covered the exterior with clapboarding. The interior was plastered. The credit for the design, which may have entailed drawings on only one sheet of paper, was given to William Berczy, the first architect mentioned in the history of Toronto.

The double rows of windows on each side indicate that it was intended to add galleries to three sides, for this form was typical of the period. This was not done at the time the church was erected, although a gallery at the rear, with benches for visitors and soldiers of the Garrison was added in 1810. The seating, including the gallery, was about 250. The building was four box pews in width, and had a wide centre aisle and two additional aisles, six and one-half feet from the exterior walls, so that the side pews extended from aisle to wall. There were eighteen single and fourteen double pews. They were described as box pews, for they were enclosed with thin wood partitions, about forty-two inches in height, enclosing seating for four or eight persons.

The pulpit, on the left of the congregation, installed in 1808, was the gift of Governor Gore. His wife donated the bell, which was hung on a temporary cradle outside the building. In 1810 there was a large congregation in the morning. What was called "evening church" was held in the afternoon, but this service was sparsely attended. There is no record of any music in the service until 1819.

CHAPTER 7

Birth, Marriage, and Death

The first white child born in Toronto was John Graves Simcoe Wright in 1794 (although one source claims J. Cameron in 1798) and this birth took place 173 years after the birth of the first white child in Canada. His father was a retired soldier of the Queen's Rangers, and the name the parent selected for his child indicates that he held his commanding officer in high regard. By 1812 this child had grown to become a young man in the Canadian Militia, and took part in the capture of Fort Detroit under General Brock.

Unless serious illness attended the birth, the few resident doctors were not usually in the picture, and the mother was attended by a midwife in 1810. For many years there was a sign over the door of a modest clapboarded house on Duchess Street which read, "Isabella Bennett, midwife from Glasgow." She would not always be called, of course, for some families felt quite capable of rendering such service without her assistance.

The child was baptized as soon as possible after birth by Dr. Stuart, the rector of St. James, or if Catholic the parents sometimes waited for the visit of a priest travelling from Quebec to the French-Canadian settlement on the Detroit River.

Godparents were usually appointed, and this was important when there was no state aid and no organized charity, for it assured the parents that their children, if orphaned, would be looked after. It also strengthened the future social position of the children to have close relatives, or family friends, as godparents, feel an obligation toward them.

While we usually assume that families are smaller today than formerly, the census of 1809 reveals some surprising facts. Although a few families were large, one family having eleven children, the average number per family was not high. This census of 1809, no doubt, served the purpose intended, but it leaves a lot to the imagination today for it does not reveal the number of men and women who were married. There were 195 men, 162 women, and 137 male and 83 female children, a total of 577. The greater number of adult males need not surprise us for there is always a higher proportion of men in new settlements than in older communities. There would be fewer older people, also. We do not know the age limit of those described as children, but even if we guess that only one hundred women were married, and the other sixty-two were looking for husbands, or were spinsters or widows, the number of children per family would be less than 3.78.

Courtship in Toronto was much the same as in England. The presence of a church, the Lieutenant-Governor, and high ranking army officers, civil servants and professional men, and a Masonic lodge, created an atmosphere of respectability. Young people, particularly those of the twenty families, lived the same town life as in England and the eastern U.S.A. With servants and with leisure, they had the opportunity to meet one another at the church, whist parties, balls, picnics and sleigh rides, not to mention the Garrison, where the right people could pay their shot and have cakes and wine in the officers' mess on visiting days. A young girl in 1810 could even decide that she did not want any of the suitors available, for there were other towns, Niagara, Kingston, Montreal, and even Boston, where friends and relatives were able to provide them. But this seldom happened, for in a less complex society than today the population was large enough for the selection of a mate. It is doubtful if young people today make a better one. Before permission to court was given, we may asume many polite and earnest conversations, flirtation and mystery between the sexes at each social opportunity, until the young man was sure of his own mind and his chance of success.

These young people were not Puritans. Their religious faith did not put a halo around courtship. But they were not vicious, and there was no large servant class, or distinctly lower class, as in England, to play around with before marriage to one of their own rank, and the smallness of the town made dalliance hazardous. Besides, they married young. There was no long training for professional or business careers, so there was no reason for delay, especially when the girl had usually finished her education at fifteen.

The opinion of many English visitors of Toronto women of this period must be taken with a grain of salt, for they often described them as sallow and unhealthy looking because their skin was not the same as that which these visitors had always accepted as normal. At this time a young Toronto visitor to the old land was astonished at the universally ruddy complexions of the English. Both complexions, of course, were normal for the climate. The neck goitre in women these visitors sometimes mentioned was real, however, but was probably no more prevalent in 1810 than it was fifty years ago.

Marriage licences were issued by the King's printer and wedding announcements were often printed in the *York Gazette*. Sometimes the editor added something of his own to the bare announcement, such as: "This matrimonial connection of the amiable parties we think replete with, and wish it productive of, the most perfect happiness."

The wedding ceremony was preceded by the compulsory publication of banns, which was simply a notice of intent. This consisted of announcements from the pulpit on three successive Sundays, with a notice upon the door or the wall of the church. Although the origin of banns has often been told it needs to be restated for our picture of 1810, for even in marriage we see an importation from England of a kind of game law, originally intended for the benefit of the titled and the rich.

Fifty-seven years before 1810, the members of the British parliament dropped their discussions of treaties and commerce long enough to pass a bill requiring banns to be called upon three successive Sundays before a couple could marry. It was ostensibly to protect the morals of the nation, and to put an end to the notorious "Fleet Marriages." Before this bill a scandalous condition had existed around the London docks. Only the clergy, of course, could perform the ceremony, and a brisk trade had been going on in this district with disreputable clergymen hawking the marriage ceremony to drunken sailors and their female companions. "Would you like to be married, Sir?" called these clergymen or their touts in the streets. Acting, also, as marriage brokers, they told single men of widows with money and young girls without. The fleet marriage was confined to the lower class and was tolerated.

When fashionable London society, however, discovered the Fleet Marriage, and began to slip away to have the knot tied at the London docks, the titled and rich saw their sons and daughters tempted to marry in haste out of their class, and determined to put a stop to the practice. Hence, in 1753, the publication of banns, delaying the wedding ceremony, became one of our institutions. While it was progressive legislation, it was not inspired by religion or respectability, but simply to maintain the *status quo*.

Marriages were solemnized in the morning; indeed if the knot was tied at any other time it was not legal. The ceremony was performed at St. James, or at the home of the bride.

Our picture of marriage in 1810 would not be complete without mention of those settlers outside the town, who lived on isolated clearings, and here we find little to compare with rural folk in England, or the settled eastern U.S.A. They or their parents had come from Britain, or south of the border and the young people had been reared as settlers' children, with all that implied. With little education, and little contact with town life, the young men were often shy and gawky, and these negative traits made them the quicker to find a mate. There was little dalliance. Young people went steady with and married the first one of the opposite sex who awakened the mating instinct. Sunday night was for courting, and even the most strict parents took this for granted. It should be mentioned that in Ontario there is no record of bundling, or anything resembling that much-discussed custom of the early eastern U.S.A.

A yoke of oxen, a few sheep, the indispensable cow, with a bed, a table and some chairs, in addition to fifty acres of land, a few of which were cleared – these were the young man's contribution. The bride's offering was linen and bedding, and as much as sixty yards of linen was woven at one bee for her benefit.

Although this settler's marriage was typical where there was a church in the district, there was a large proportion of couples in the province who were living together in 1810 without being married, simply because there was no one to perform the ceremony. They were married upon arrival of the saddlebag preacher, or when a church was erected. In one township there was said to have been three hundred such couples.

Then there were many others in the province who had left their wives in England, and intended to send for them as soon as everything was ready. Many underestimated the back-breaking toil and the long hours necessary to become a farmer in the bush without capital, and they were not equal to it. There were women nearer, who understood conditions and would not be critical. Many took these women as their mistresses. The arrival of the real wife, however, usually displaced the substitute.

At the time of the founding of Toronto, one of the most important issues in the province was the legalizing of marriages that had been performed by army officers, and even army surgeons, because of the scarcity of ministers. Such couples were worried about the legality, as well as the sanctity of their marriage, and of the possible stigma that might affect their children. At their request, an act was passed in 1793 to permit such couples to appear before a magistrate and obtain a marriage certificate. This act of Parliament also gave ministers of the Church of England the sole right to perform the ceremony. It provided, however, that if no clergyman lived within eighteen miles, a couple could be married by a justice of the peace, using the Church of England form of service. This act aroused strong antagonism among the settlers, for less than one-tenth of the population of the province by 1840 were of that persuasion. Some couples even took the long journey to the U.S.A. so they could be married by a minister of the denomination of their choice. This act was altered in 1798 to permit Church of Scotland, Calvinists and Lutheran ministers to perform the ceremony. Even this grudging concession limited the ceremony to couples where at least one had been a member of such congregations for a minimum of six months. The petition of the Methodists was refused. It was not until 1830 that they and the Baptists and Congregationalists, and other Christian denominations were allowed to perform marriages.

The practice of Charivariing or serenading the newly-married couple, which originated among the French-Canadian settlers in Quebec, was also prevalent in Ontario. It was practised in Toronto as exuberantly as in the backwoods, and we have a record of a couple being serenaded upon three consecutive nights, climaxing with overthrowing the haystack of the bride's father.

Originally this charivariing was limited to marriages thought to be unequal, such as between an old man and a young woman; or when the marriage took place within too short a time after the death of the former husband or wife. Sometimes it was done to remind the happy couple that they had invited too few people to the wedding, or simply because it was a good way to get in on the fun.

After the wedding the happy couple were usually at the home of the bride, for they did not go on honeymoons. Young men, sometimes disguised or with masks, sometimes not, assembled at the house after dark and serenaded the newly-married couple with guns, horns, drums, kettles, whistles, cowbells, tin pans, and anything that would make discordant sounds. It was useless for the couple to resent it. They were usually prepared for such an event, and after listening to the din with forced smiles, they invited the noisemakers into the house. Most of the guests had to sit on the floor, and there was considerable good-natured horseplay and baiting of the groom who was forced to make a speech. Refreshments were served, and the evening often turned into a sing-song. It was a harmless enough custom, but sometimes it ended in a drunken brawl. If such was expected, the newly-married couple could snuff out all of the candles in the house, or not actually be present. .

When a death occurred in Toronto in 1810, one of the relatives made it his business to call upon everyone who might be interested in attending the funeral and visiting the bereaved. Although there were a few burial-plots on the grounds of private residences, most people, including the few Catholics, were interred in the churchyard of St. James. Toronto had no hearse and no undertaker. The first undertaker was John Ross who took charge of General Brock's body after the Battle of Queenston Heights, in 1812, and it was this responsibility that prompted him to become a professional undertaker.

The coffin was made to order by a carpenter, after he had taken, or had been given the measurements of the deceased. It was usually of pine or basswood, stained with lampblack, sometimes varnished, and it had plain wrought iron handles. Occasionally cherrywood or oak was used to make coffins. The service was conducted at the home of the deceased the day following death. A body was seldom kept over the second day for obvious reasons, and a contemporary writer refers to the "ghastly face of the dead." This, of course, was taken for granted, and the curiosity of the mourners to take a last look at the face of the loved one cannot be considered morbid, for they were motivated by the same sentiments as those who visit our funeral parlours today. After the service at the home, the coffin lid was nailed down and it was carried upon men's shoulders along the street from the house to the churchyard. These walking processions were described as solemn and impressive, but they must have been rather pitiful when there were only a few mourners trudging through the mud of the street on a rainy day.

Sometimes the coffin was transported to the churchyard in an open wagon, or on a sleigh in winter. In such cases the bells were removed from both horse and sleigh. The grave was ready; it had been dug by the sexton for a fee of $2.00. The minister said a few words at the grave and after the interment the relatives retired to the home of the deceased for refreshments, and the will, if any, was read.

Masonic funerals were described as impressive, with the master of the lodge delivering an oration, after which a procession, headed by the clergyman, went through the streets to St. James' churchyard.

Readers may be surprised to find that inquests into deaths were conducted at this early period. After a drowning in the Don River in 1802, the coroner summoned twelve citizens for the inquest, and they reported accidental death, as the victim was assumed to have gone into the river to bathe.

Gravestones were flat slabs of stone, often cut in a simple outline at the top, terminating with a half circle, which framed a full circle of carving. This carved circle was one of a few standard designs. It could be an urn, a weeping willow, or a hand with a finger pointing upward. The inscription on the stone was extremely matter-of-fact and brief, such as, "Sacred to the Memory of John Jones who Died April 6, 1810, Aged 58 years." Roman letters with an occasional line of italicized letters were used. Frequently the carver miscalculated the spread of his letters and found it necessary to reduce their size, or crowd them at the end of a line. These gravestones were expensive. At this time Toronto did not have any masons with the skill or interest to make gravestones, so they were brought from Newark or Kingston. More graves than not were marked with a simple wooden cross. Sometimes a white painted picket fence enclosed the plot.

At this time there were few rural churches, and most Ontario settlers buried their dead on their own land. Many had coffins ready to avoid the delay in constructing one, or someone in the family worked all night to make it.

Wearing black clothes as mourning for the dead was the custom in 1810, and this could mean a whole wardrobe of black for many months, sometimes for years, depending upon the temperament of the bereaved. Even young children were put into mourning. Some mourning was an impersonal formality, and had little to do with grief. Mrs. Simcoe writes in her diary in 1794, "The news was received of the death of the Queen of France (Marie Antoinette). Orders given out for mourning, in which everybody appeared this evening, and the dance was postponed."[6]

CHAPTER 8

Food and Drinking

In Ontario, a great variety of food was served in the homes and hotels of such towns as Toronto, Kingston and Niagara. At improvised hotels and in the settlers' cabins, however, the variety was so limited that during some months the traveller might have only bread, cheese and a tea substitute set before him. He was advised to take his own provisions and utensils, especially when travelling by bateau. These included a provision basket containing a cold round of beef, tin plates and drinking cups, tea, sugar, biscuits and "about a gallon of brandy."

In Toronto, although game and fish was all around them, salt beef and salt pork were still the staple meat diet a great part of the year. One traveller was astonished to find that a brace of partridges for sale in the stores cost as much as in London, and that very little game was for sale at all. The settlers had no time for hunting except for their own table. The townspeople hunted for sport and for their own use, but not for sale.

There was an abundance of food, but because of the colder climate, there was not much fresh meat in the towns. Settlers' barns were small and drafty and could hold only a small number of cattle. The scarcity of fodder, before turnips were grown, necessitated their slaughter and preservation in brine before winter. For this reason there was much less fresh milk and butter than today. Cheese took its place. Sometimes the adults got the butter while the children had to be satisfied with ham gravy. Vegetables were often scarce, even in season. However the first settlers planted orchards and most Toronto gardens had fruit trees so that there was an abundance of plums, peaches, pears and apples. Even watermelons were grown in the Niagara district.

Fish, generally caught by the Indians, were sold at the market and from door to door. Salmon were so plentiful in the Humber River in the spawning season that they were caught by hand and thrown into wagons driven into the shallow water. Most people in Toronto could afford tea and coffee, or cocoa occasionally, if not regularly. Many settlers, however, were forced to depend upon tea substitutes. The most popular was hemlock tea, which many people could not drink, even with cream and sugar.

The food advertised for sale in the stores included the same luxuries and spices sold in eastern U.S.A. and in England, including nutmeg, pepper, pimento, pickled oysters, lemon juice, raisins, prunes, and many other delicacies. Market day in Toronto was every Saturday and the law stated that the stores could not sell meat, poultry, fish, or butter, eggs or vegetables between 6 A.M. and 4 P.M. on that day.

The time for meals varied with class and occupation. While the settlers arose at daybreak, government officials and clerks worked from ten in the morning until three, and then from five to seven o'clock. The dinner was at four. Many families must have followed their example.

Army barrack fare was a standard, monotonous diet, occasionally varied with fresh fish or fowl. It consisted of salt pork, bully beef, potatoes, pea soup, biscuits and bread and cheese. Rations of rum, brandy or whiskey were given every day.

The Indians, because of their lack of cooking facilities, dined chiefly on stews. Everything, including corn, pumpkin, wild rice and vegetables went into the pot. They varied this diet with wild honey, maple syrup, wild fruits and nuts. As with wild animals, instinct guided them to take herbs of various kinds and they were remarkably healthy except when exposed to white men's diseases.

Practically all adults drank to some extent in 1810. This attitude toward alcoholic beverages in Toronto coincided with that in England and the U.S.A. It continued until about 1830 when the first temperance societies were formed.

Although the settlers around Toronto drank whiskey, we find that the gentlemen of Toronto more often confined their drinking to rum, gin, brandy and wines. Beer was drunk principally by low income groups and soldiers from the Garrison. Although they were given a daily ration of hard liquor in their own mess, they could not afford to drink it when they passed an hour or two with men of the ranks in the hotels in town.

Drinking more closely followed the pattern in England than that of the frontiers of the U.S.A., where whiskey was often the only drink available. European travellers were often shocked at the amount of hard liquor consumed in America – instead of the light wines and beer of Europe. In pioneer areas of America, a relatively large capital outlay was required to build a brewery. It was slow and expensive to transport the equipment to the site. As a freight charge, light wines or beer, in kegs or bottles, weighed as much as more expensive and more intoxicating beverages. Whiskey could also be made by amateurs in pioneer areas, with homemade equipment. North American drinking habits may be said to be based upon this one factor.

Whiskey, in Ontario sold for twenty-five to fifty cents a gallon and was not taxed. Many people kept it in an open jug upon the dinner table. At barn raisings in Ontario it was usually drunk to excess. There were often fights —sometimes a death. In a period when strength was an admirable quality, one powerful young man at a barn raising accepted a wager that he could drink a pailful of liquor at one sitting. He won his bet but staggered to a fence and died. The method of building barns by volunteer labour was gradually abandoned when the cost of food and drink for the workers and drones exceeded the expense for professional carpenters.

Drinking was respectable, however, and it was not uncommon for men to become dead drunk and to be carried home by their friends. The best families drank wine at their meals. One diarist in Toronto records that he took one hundred and three empty bottles out of his cellar to be washed. Most households kept a keg or two of hard liquor and many bottles of wine. Every age has its own cocktails. In 1810 they were, "gin slings," "rum slings," "sour punches," "syrup punches," and "whiskey punches."

CHAPTER 9

Social Life
and Recreation

In 1810, in Toronto, the individual was usually a participant in recreation. Even a horse-race at the Island or a fox-chase on the Bay often had more participants than spectators. The individual received his satisfaction first-hand. He felt the tug of reins of his own horse, and the exhilaration of racing against others. He chased the fox, speared the fish, sailed the boat and flew the kite.

One English visitor to both the United States and Canada, at this time, stated that he never saw schoolboys playing at any games whatsoever. He reported that, "cricket, foot-ball, quoits, etc., appear to be utterly unknown," and remarked upon "the total want of all those games and sports that obtained for our country the appellation of Merry England." He was, of course referring to organized sport. A new country has to wait for an environment conducive to sport requiring organization and discipline for, in English-speaking America, civilization was not simply transplanted. These English sports were gradually accepted during the nineteenth century. At the same time, however, America was developing sports of her own, and baseball soon eclipsed cricket in popularity.

One diarist, who might be considered just below the twenty families in social position, has given us a very good idea of how a young bachelor spent his leisure time. In the heat of summer, he went for a swim in the Bay every morning. He owned an Indian canoe and a sailing boat. Indeed, he mentions in his diary that a young lady is repairing the sails. He raced his horse on the Island, and fox-hunted on the ice of the Bay in winter. He hunted game for sport and cast his own bullets. He even made a whip handle. This young man danced at balls, played billiards, dined at the Garrison mess, spent many evenings playing cards and gambling a few shillings, attended theatrical performances and puppet shows, and, in general, appears to have had "a good time."

At this early period, winter was the time for recreation in rural Ontario, for much of the settlers' work could not be performed when the ground was frozen. This was also true in Toronto. The lake-shipping season was shorter than today. Carrying by sleigh, until the War of 1812, was minimum, for stores endeavoured to have sufficient stock to carry them through until spring navigation. Transportation by water was far cheaper than by land.

The winter sports for those in Toronto included fishing, which was done through a hole in the ice of the Bay, hunting, fox-hunting, sleigh-riding and skating. A captive fox was let loose in the centre of the Bay, and hounds and huntsmen, and feminine spectators in sleighs, all joined in the sport of killing the fox. Hunting fowl and animals was done at all seasons of the year. The extent of it depended a great deal upon the quality of the meat in any season, for there were no game laws. There were no packs of hounds in America, as in England. Dogs were used, but the hunters did not follow them on horseback, as in the old land. The hunters were posted at stations in the forest to shoot the deer as it passed.

For sleigh-riding or carioling, as it was called, the women riders pulled coarse wool stockings over their shoes, and wore wool or leather and wool gloves. These sleighs were often lined with bright-coloured cloth or bearskin, and buffalo robes covered the driver. Sometimes a farmer's sleigh, with straw, buffalo robes, and blankets for warmth, was filled with young people for a sleigh ride on one of the roads leading out of town. Spills were expected, and to be overturned in the snow added to the fun.

Skating, which originated in Holland, appears to have been limited to the male sex at this time. The skates were of wood, with iron runners, and had leather straps to fasten them to the wearer's boots. Then the early spring, with its maple syrup time, brought adults and children into the settler's bush for a "sugaring off."

Warm weather, brought sailing on the bay. Many owned small sailing craft, rowboats, and canoes which were purchased from Indians. Not all were the traditional birchbark, for the bark of the elm was occasionally used. Friends and whole families went on picnics. A favourite picnic location was the mouth of the Humber River, which was travelled by boat or canoe from the Bay shore. Sometimes the picnic was in the valley of the Don River, or at the Island, which was reached by boat, or by land, over the floating bridges at the mouth of the Don and the inlet to the north of it.

Many went in bathing, but the number who could swim would be small compared with the present. Few women either swam or bathed outdoors. The word bathing suit is never mentioned, so we must assume that the few women who swam wore abbreviated clothing which, of course, would make swimming more of a chore than a recreation.

Fishing was a favourite sport for men, and even Indians often fished for the sport alone. During the spawning season in the fall, ten- to twenty-pound salmon were speared in the Don and Humber Rivers.

These salmon were so plentiful that settlers often drove their wagons into the shallow river bed, and filled them by lifting out the salmon with their hands.

As early as 1807 a law was passed prohibiting the use of nets to catch them. These salmon apparently came from the Atlantic ocean, although there is some difference of opinion on this. They spawned in all rivers and streams flowing into the St. Lawrence and into Lake Ontario, but, of course, never got into the other Great Lakes, as they were stopped by the falls of Niagara. In proportion to the size of these spawning rivers, these salmon were as plentiful as on the west coast today. Other fish, also, were in abundance, including salmon trout, sturgeon and maskinonge, pickerel, whitefish and herring, and smaller fish such as perch, bass, and sunfish. At night, both Indians and whites speared fish in the Bay with jacklights of burning pine knots in metal pots on top of wood or iron poles.

Most of the men, at this time, owned firearms of some description, and supplied their own tables with small game or fowl. There was little conscience regarding shooting small animals or birds simply for sport, without retrieving them, for being so plentiful they were regarded as pests. Some thought that robins made good eating, and many other songbirds went into the pot. Occasionally wolves came to the outskirts of the town and killed sheep, and even bears were sometimes seen on the streets. To kill these marauders was a duty, and a bounty was given by the Government for wolf scalps. A few men owned duelling pistols, which they periodically took out of the case and cleaned. Such weapons were a status symbol for some people, similar to silver plate on the sideboard.

Horse racing was popular, although not organized to any extent. The first race track in the province was probably the one at Niagara, in the early seventeen nineties, where there were three days of racing, with purses up to twenty guineas. Even the rider's dress was specified in the newspaper advertisement for the races. In Toronto there was no regular race track in 1810, but there was a favourite straight run on the Island. At this location there were pine and black poplar trees, up to two feet in diameter, but virtually no underbrush; horses could be viewed for the entire run. As many as twelve riders took part in a single race. It was a sign of affluence, and the sporting thing, to own a stopwatch to clock racing time. Many small bets were laid, but gambling never became the mania it was in England at this time.

Women as well as men rode horseback. They did not ride astride but used the side-saddle which placed both legs on the left side of the horse. Nice women would have been horrified at the idea of riding "man fashion." The left side, of course, is the side of the road in England. This women's saddle was not used all over Europe in 1810 for one writer of the period mentioned that there was no such thing as a woman's saddle in Italy. The side-saddle in Toronto riding clubs was all but abandoned for many years. Visiting women riders from England and some clubs in the eastern U.S.A. maintained some interest in Toronto in the side-saddle and there now appears to be an actual revival of its popularity.

Men did not usually wear special breeches for riding, but women always wore a riding-habit, with full skirt, special jacket and a hat which sometimes sported an ostrich plume. They could wear this habit as a casual dress on the street.

Weddings, the Market, Church attendance, the sight of prisoners in the stocks, and occasional public hangings were all part of the social life of the period. Shivarees permitted the young people to give vent to their primitive instincts. The tough element in the town often stripped to the waist for their rough-and-tumble fights. No gentlemanly instincts were displayed, and the participants often tried to injure one another, and even gouged out an opponent's eye, or bit off an ear, if not separated in time. Flying kites was also an outdoor recreation for both men and boys. Men of the working class played a kind of ball game on the streets. Firefighting too may be considered recreation, for all the firemen were volunteers and thrilled with excitement when the church bell rang for a fire.

Gardening was a favourite pastime for many people, particularly when it could be the only way of obtaining certain vegetables and fruits. Some arranged their gardens, both vegetable and floral, in formal plans reminiscent of those in England.

A recreation which came unheralded to Toronto at intervals was pigeon shooting. Dr. W. M. Dunlop, a doctor with the British army, who spent a great part of his life in Canada, wrote in one of his books:

> Everyone who has been in America has described the interminable flocks of wild pigeons, so I shall not trouble my readers on that score. Some two summers ago, a stream of them took it into their heads to fly over York (Toronto); and for three or four days the town resounded with one continual roll of firing, as if a skirmish were going on in the streets, – every gun, pistol, musket, blunderbuss and fire-arm of whatever description, was put into requisition. The constable and police magistrates were on the alert, and offenders without number, were pulled up – among whom were honourable members of the executive and Legislative Councils, crown lawyers, respectable staid citizens, and last of all, the sheriff of the county;

till at last it was found that pigeons flying within easy shot, were a temptation too strong for human virtue to withstand, and so the contest was given up, and a sporting jubilee proclaimed to all in sundry.[7]

In 1810 these graceful, fast-flying birds existed in astonishing numbers. There were several main flocks, each containing from one billion to two billion birds. Stragglers, in flocks of thousands to millions, brought the total to about five billion. The whole of North America, east of the Rocky Mountains, from the Gulf of Mexico to Hudson's Bay, was their hunting ground. They were not migratory, and the great flocks roamed in all seasons over forest and prairie to feed upon beechnuts, acorns, chestnuts, wild berries, wild rice, and farmers' grain.

They were considered pests, and although the breasts were often eaten, or salted down, a far greater number of birds were shot and not retrieved. The phenomenon described by Dr. Dunlop, when one of the great flocks suddenly darkened the sky, and took three days to pass over Toronto, brought every person into the street.

Today we see a rapid change from one new style of dancing to another, which is indicative of our changing world. Dancing was never static, but was always in evolution. Although dances in 1810 were called minuets, cotillions, quadrilles, and Scottish and Irish reels, they were tending toward alteration. Emigrants to America brought their dances with them, and probably the only dances created here were the Paul Jones and square dances, which developed after 1810 in rural districts.

Both Britain and the New World danced the same way at the same period. In 1819, an English visitor to rural Virginia stated that, "an Englishman, particularly if a young one, might well think his travel to be all a dream, and that he was still in a Boroughmonger country. Always the same tunes, and dances, same manners, same dress . . ."[8]

Although the Governor had a ball in 1810, there were no "assemblies" that season. What were described as party balls were held in private homes, where the guest list was restricted. Dances often began at "early candle light" and continued after a hearty supper until dawn. In 1810 all dancing in Ontario was to the music of an army band of predominantly wind instruments, or the violin, or fiddle, sometimes augmented with a tambourine. In garrison towns like Toronto, a regimental band could usually be secured for dances. In the backwoods at this time, all dance music would be from one violin, occasionally two.

What we now designate classical music was seldom, if ever, played as it was written by the composer, for the only instruments in use were violins, flutes, clarinets and the bassoon, and these were played solo, or perhaps two together. The first organ was in the second St. James of 1830, which was destroyed by fire in 1839. Because of their lack of familiarity with music, many objected to an organ in a church.

At least one social club existed in Toronto, and its purpose was to entertain young people at moderate cost. In a letter of 1810 the writer describes how fifteen families shared the expense of renting a house half a mile from town, once a fortnight, for the purpose of dining and dancing. Each family took a cold plate and a bottle of wine, and the young people danced to the music of fife and drum. The fife was a simple reed instrument used with military bands. It is doubtful if young people today would be satisfied with such a "dance orchestra."

The town occasionally saw a puppet show. Groups of amateur actors, and sometimes officers of the Garrison, contrived to enact plays with few props, makeshift scenery and homemade costumes. Comedies were usually selected, and even Sheridan's *School for Scandal* was attempted. Female parts were often taken by men. The first club for civilian amateur actors, however, was not formed until 1824. At this time professional plays were seldom performed without the addition of a one-act play, usually a farce, or a recitation.

Many so-called theatrical performances by professionals were merely a collection of unrelated acts, like the vaudeville of the recent past. One advertisement in the *York Gazette* of 1810 announced a "theatrical performance" to be performed at Mr. Miller's Assembly Room "formerly the Toronto Coffee House." The list of acts included "philosophical, mathematical and curious experiments, songs and recitations, ventriloquism and singing, accompanied by a violin." Tickets were to be had at the place of performance. Front seats were "half a dollar and back seats half price."

One week later a second performance was advertised by the same cast, but with "new songs and recitations." In this advertisement, the readers are assured they may be under "no apprehension of accidents by the future giving way of the Gallery, it having been secured under the direction of an obliging Gentleman." At another time an advertisement in the *Gazette* announced that the Comedians from Montreal were to perform the Reverend Mr. Home's celebrated "Tragedy of Douglas," or "The Nobel Shepherd," with a cast of seven. This poetic drama was written in 1756, so it was hardly recent dramatic fare. In addition to this play a comic farce was included, with the same seven actors, and with a recitation between the play and the farce. The following year an "entertainment of various curiosities" was advertised to take place in O'Keefe's Assembly Room.

Books, plays and poetry were read aloud in the family group.

Newspapers were also read to others and a man who was fortunate enough to borrow an American newspaper had an attentive audience, for the threat of war with the U.S.A. interested everyone.

The mess at the Garrison took the place of a club, but for only a limited number of people. It was an officers' mess and the civilians welcomed were only those who, in the opinion of the mess, were on the same class level as officers. This must have taken some subtle screening, for in a new town it would sometimes be difficult to judge. After a civilian was sure he was welcome he would drop in with a male or female friend, or with his family, for dinner, or for cakes and wine which were served almost every evening. He, of course, paid for the refreshment. A regimental band often played in this mess, so we may assume there was often dancing by a few couples. At special functions of the mess, invitations were issued in the form of cards, which were delivered in town by an officer's batman.

The assessment list for 1810 mentions only one billiard table for the whole town, and it is easy to surmise the reason. In 1810 the Legislature set a duty on billiard tables of £40 Halifax currency. This duty would be the equivalent of about $1,600 today. There was also at least one at the Garrison, for officers.

Most women did sewing of some kind, and girls were taught to use the needle at an early age. Young ladies of the upper class had time to make "samplers," and these may be seen today in Canadian museums. A sampler was a piece of sewn or embroidered work done by girls for practice, and was often an artistic expression. Some of them depicted rural scenes, and their work was considered good enough to frame and hang upon the parlour or bedroom wall. As cloth was relatively expensive, discarded pieces were made into bed quilts, called patchwork quilts, and these, if of pleasing pattern, were considered fashionable enough for any home.

Cards were played, of course, and whist, a game for four players, was very popular. Some were addicted to the game and played several times a week. Backgammon, a game played on a marked board, with draughtlike pieces, governed by the casting of dice, was also a favourite game for two players. Chess permitted two male friends to spend an evening together, and enjoy companionship and wine, without the necessity of talking all evening.

The reader may have seen a silhouette, also called a profile, which is a curiosity today. Before cameras, and with few artists available to paint portraits or miniatures, a great number of people made use of amateur or professional silhouette artists. Sometimes this silhouette was of the whole figure, but usually head and shoulders only. It was, of course, in profile to show characteristic features. Although amateurs made them for each other, there was great excitement when a travelling professional, usually an American, came to town and advertised in the *Gazette*. One of them charged six shillings, glazed and framed. The artist usually made four copies of one silhouette, and kept one as a sample of his work. These were simply cut-outs of black paper, mounted on "pasteboard." This profile likeness would be hung on the wall, or placed on the mantelpiece or given to an admiring suitor.

Nearly everyone drank in 1810 and a man did not lose face if his friends had to carry him home from a party. Smoking was also prevalent, and one source states that duty was paid upon 100,000 pounds of manufactured tobacco imported into Ontario in 1810. This registered amount could be easily doubled or tripled, for smuggling, even by respectable people, was very prevalent at this period all over the world. Clay pipes could be purchased at hotels as well as stores, and cigars were also smoked. Snuff was also used in 1810 and even some women used it. A few women, particularly old ones, smoked pipes in the privacy of their homes.

We must include auction sales as entertainment, for, as mentioned elsewhere, all people attended them. They anticipated such a sale when someone died or moved away, for it could be their only opportunity to purchase some coveted luxury item, or simply furniture to use. There was no stigma attached to used furniture, neither were there any antiques in the sense we now use the word. These auctions were held in hotels, in the dining-room or the barroom, or in the house.

Fraternal societies were in existence in Toronto in 1810. The first was the Masons, who had a lodge in Niagara as early as 1792, and shortly after in Toronto. A St. Patrick's Society and a St. Andrew's Society were formed early in the century. A St. George's Society was founded in the early twenties. These societies held an annual dinner to honour the birth of their patron saint. An Orange order celebration is recorded as early as 1822.

At this time Toronto was closely tied to Europe, rather than to the U.S.A. and events there were celebrated. As mentioned elsewhere, Mrs. Simcoe did not hold her ball when the news reached Niagara that Marie Antoinette had been guillotined. Word was received in Toronto on January 3, 1799, of Nelson's victory at Aboukir Bay, six months previously. Citizens donated cordwood for a large bonfire at the Garrison, and candles were lit in the windows of nearly every house. Feeling was so strong that one man who refused to burn candles had his windows broken. In 1801 the British victory over the Danes in Copenhagen Roads was celebrated with the guns of the Garrison firing, and with bonfires all over the town. On January 20, 1806, the guns fired a salute for Nelson's victory at Trafalgar, which had taken place October 21, three months before. The birthday of George III, June 4, which, strange to say, was hardly thought of in England, was celebrated as a holiday in Toronto. This date was also a holiday during the short reigns of George IV and William IV. Upon the ascension to the throne of Queen Victoria, her birthday, May 24th, took its place. In 1809 a ball was given to honour the birthday of the wife of George III. There appears to be no record, however, of any celebration in Toronto for the Battle of Waterloo in 1815.

Christmas day was observed, as in England, with a special dinner, and with houses decorated with wintergreen and cranberry branches, for there was no holly or mistletoe. After church service there was much visiting between relatives and friends, with more than the usual amount of drinking. On this day there was an exchange of gifts, with sleighing, skating and horse-racing on the ice of the Bay. The Scottish exchanged their presents on New Year's Day.

Christmas cards were not in use until later in the century, for it was the German consort of Queen Victoria who enriched the traditional English and Canadian Christmas with a more extensive exchange of gifts, decorated Christmas tree, and toys for children.

Two years later, on the 15th day of December, 1812, the Loyal and Patriotic Society of Upper Canada was formed to provide relief for families of men in the militia. It also provided financial assistance for wounded veterans, and its members knitted socks and made shirts and underwear for the soldiers all during the war. Over one thousand pounds was immediately subscribed.

CHAPTER 10

Education

Toronto's present Board of Education was not formed until 1847, when there were 1,221 pupils in the city's fifteen one-roomed schools. Most of these buildings were rented. The parents contributed in fees a little less than half the cost of their children's education. School attendance was not compulsory, and fees charged denied education to many. After some deliberation by this board, it was decided in 1851 that teachers would receive a fixed salary from the city, and that the pupils would not pay for their tuition.

In 1810, thirty-seven years before the forming of the Board of Education, there was but one publicly-owned school in Toronto. The education, however, was limited to children whose parents could pay the $16.00 per year tuition fee, (eight days' wages for a skilled workman), for although the school was subsidized by the provincial government, fees were charged also. This school, founded in 1807, was one of eight that provincial legislation had provided in the province. The one in Toronto was called the Home District School, and was described as a grammar (secondary) school, although its students ranged from six to nineteen years of age. It was co-educational. The teacher was the Rev. Dr. O'Kill Stuart, a Harvard graduate, who had been rector of St. James' Church from 1801, and had also tutored private pupils since that time. The students were children of government officials, and a few merchants and tradesmen. This first public schoolhouse, if such it may be called, was a low stone building, later covered with clapboarding, an extension to Dr. Stuart's own residence, at the southeast corner of King and George Streets. This school lasted until the year 1813.

These schools provided by the province were secondary schools for senior pupils (even though some children attended). Primary schools to feed these authorized schools were not provided, which may appear to be a strange omission. But the answer, no doubt, is to be found in the state of the times. Those who had money endeavoured to make their proprietary rights secure, and the existing parliamentary system enabled them to put their own interpretation upon the legislation of 1807.

The poor who could afford only an elementary education for their children, and so would have no use for the secondary school, were being taxed to support a school for the sole benefit of those parents who could well afford to pay for education. As one petition to the Legislature expressed it: "The Government casts money into the lap of the rich who are sufficiently able without public assistance to support a school in every way equal to the ones established by law." It was not until 1817 that this unfair school act was emended.[9]

What was probably the first school in Toronto was opened in 1798, five years after the town was founded, and when the first white child born in the town was four years old. In this private school the subjects taught were reading, writing, arithmetic and English grammar. It was kept by thirty-seven-year-old William Cooper, from England, who later became a tavern keeper and an auctioneer, as well as the builder of a sawmill and a gristmill on the Humber River. He owned the wharf at the foot of Church Street, and later claimed to have built the first house in Toronto. One of Cooper's pupils was the son of a slave, the slave's owner being the benefactor. Cooper conducted this school until 1801, and then a Levi Willard operated it for a short time.

In 1802, Dr. William Warren Baldwin, born in Ireland and a graduate of Edinburgh University, advertised in the *Upper Canada Gazette and Oracle* as follows: "Understanding that some of the gentlemen of this town have expressed much anxiety for the establishment of a classical school, begs leave to inform the public, that he intends on Monday the third day of January next to open a school, in which he will instruct twelve boys in Writing, Reading, the Classics and Arithmetic . . ." The inclusion of "the classics" made this a secondary school. This school was terminated in about five years when the Doctor's medical and legal practice absorbed his full time.

The third did not come until 1805 when parents, who had grown tired of waiting for a government school, united to hire Alexander Carson to teach their children. The subjects taught were limited to reading, writing, grammar and arithmetic. Although the maximum number of pupils was supposed not to exceed twenty-five, it is doubtful if it ever reached this figure. Then about this time a Mrs. Dudley conducted a short-lived school for girls, and in 1808 a Baron de Diemar advertised that he would conduct a French school.

An advertisement in the *Gazette* in September, 1810, reveals that Mr. Charles M'Donnel planned to open a night school in addition to the day school he had been keeping since June. This night school was for "apprentices and others who cannot conveniently attend in the day time for study." The evening scholars were expected to furnish a pound of candles per month during the winter. This school operated for about five months. Still another private school advertised in October, 1810, by a William Barber, lasted only a short time also.

Music was not overlooked by those with ambition to be teachers. An advertisement in 1810 announced that Joseph Abbott intended to open a school in the principles of church music and stated: "Music – vocal or instrumental – is universally considered as an elegant accomplishment, not more interesting than useful to the profession. The said Abbot flatters himself he will be able to give satisfaction to all those who may be inclined to encourage him, by teaching it in the most expeditious manner, and according to most approved standard of modern times." This school was apparently not successful, for two years later Mr. Abbot obtained a licence to keep a tavern. A "Penmanship School" was advertised in the *Gazette* the following year.

The attitude toward education for girls is revealed in a school advertisement which describes the instruction thus: "All that is necessary for their sex is to appear decently and be useful in the world and in all that concerns housekeeping."

The wealthy families of Toronto sent their children to school in Quebec, New York and even to England. They also sent their boys to a school in Cornwall, on the St. Lawrence River, as later mentioned. It takes little analysis, however, to realize that with the small number of students in school in 1810, and before, compared with the total population, many young people received little or no formal education. Many were taught the rudiments of reading, writing and arithmetic by their parents or family friends. Diaries, and personal and business letters reveal that a large percentage of the population were poor spellers, and their sentence construction often makes for hard reading. Some could only make their mark as a signature on a legal document.

Although there were some Catholics in Toronto in 1810, they did not have a school of their own until 1839-40. A few Protestants attended this school. Up until the building of their own school these Toronto Catholics attended Protestant schools or went to Quebec. As some of them attended St. James' Church in 1810, it is probable they did not feel as strongly regarding separatism as do those of today, and were satisfied to have their children educated with Protestants.

All of those short-lived schools of early Toronto were kept in private homes, and even in taverns. It was not until after the War of 1812 that a genuine school bulding was constructed. Until Canadian Confederation all paper was made from rags and was relatively expensive. Slates were extensively used in business and industry for calculations and, of course, in school also. One slate of the period had an oak frame and was nine inches by thirteen inches in size. School furniture usually consisted of long desks and benches extending from centre aisle to wall. Sometimes the seating was parallel to the long axis, and one row of students faced the other across a space reserved for the teacher, and the box stove. The benches and desks were of unfinished pine, made by carpenters.

In 1806 the Legislature appropriated £400 for the purchase of "a collection of instruments suitable and proper for illustrating the principles of Natural Philosophy, Geography, Astronomy and Mathematics, to be used as the Governor should direct." It is doubtful, however, if all those who could derive benefit from these instruments had an opportunity to use them. The private circulating library, founded in 1810, and the book store opened in that year are indicative of the cultural progress of Toronto since its founding.

In 1810 the settlers around Toronto were raising their children in an environment which permitted only the most rudimentary education. The schoolhouse was of logs, not larger than fifteen by twenty feet, with three windows and a door. These rural schools were often taught by men whose only qualification for their work was that they were discharged half-pay soldiers, or that they had been crippled through accidents. Sometimes a spelling-book and the Bible were the only textbooks.

CHAPTER 11

Currency

Canada in 1810 was not a united country, but merely a number of colonies. The currency in use varied with the location. In Toronto, and most of Ontario, the money was Halifax and New York currency, with the British soldiers being paid in English sterling. There was no paper money in Ontario and the coinage in circulation was that of many other countries besides that of Britain.

The industrial expansion in England was being aided by the development of private banks and there were nearly 700 of them. This private ownership led to many difficulties, but their presence inspired confidence and discouraged hoarding. Each bank issued its own paper money; indeed in rural areas, Bank of England notes were rare and sometimes looked upon with suspicion. While the financial theorists were disagreeing on policy, these banks flooded the country with paper money without proper bullion backing. England was leading the world in trade, but her money was depreciating in terms of foreign exchange. At home, however, the cheap credit which these private banks fostered enabled industry to grow and expand, and money could be borrowed at three per cent to finance manufacturing. The paper money of these banks was not used in Ontario, and English visitors were warned not to carry English paper money past Montreal.

In the United States before the Revolutionary War, the colonists used the coinage of Spain, Holland and Germany, as well as English coinage, with the Spanish dollar predominating. They also printed their own paper money for sums as low as one penny. This dollar coinage rivalled the British coinage in circulation and was much sought after. The British economic theories of the time necessitated gold in the national treasury in London, and the colonists were not supposed to trade directly with other countries. The colonists ignored this regulation and Britain, to a great extent, winked at their violations. This illegal trading brought cash into the country, and it is difficult today to thoroughly appreciate how important cash was at that period. Even with this foreign money, a large percentage of the colonists saw little cash from year to year. Tobacco, furs, and even bullets were used as a substitute. Most American colonies also issued their own paper money, which circulated at varying discount rates. But by our standards there was never enough cash to permit the average individual to make purchases of necessities without becoming involved with a storekeeper as a creditor.

The first unified American currency was the notes issued by the Continental Congress of the American Revolution. These notes soon became practically worthless, and the expression "Not worth a Continental" is still used and is a reminder of this step in the world's search for a sound medium of exchange.

In 1792, Congress passed the first Federal Coinage Act, under which gold and silver coins were minted. This coinage included eagles and half eagles ($10 and $5) which also circulated in Toronto. Much of the gold coinage was later withdrawn, for these American dollars could be exchanged in the West Indies for the heavier Spanish Dollar, which was melted down and sold at a profit to the American mint as bullion.

This new coinage and money was based upon the decimal system, inaugurated during the French Revolution, and existing money was related to it for, of course, all existing money could not be immediately withdrawn from circulation. In the State of New York, existing shillings were related to the new dollar and that dollar was related to the pound. Thus twelve pence, or twelve and one-half cents, equalled one shilling; eight shillings equalled one dollar, and two and one-half dollars equalled one pound. In Toronto, this New York state currency was called the "practical currency."

As a large percentage of the Loyalists who settled in Ontario were from New York State, and a great deal of the trading was with that state, they found it convenient to continue to use the American system. This has often confused the modern reader who does not realize it was only the American system, not the money, that was used in Ontario. In advertisements in the Toronto newspaper, and in merchants' account books we see both dollars and pounds mentioned. This had led the casual reader to suppose that the pounds were English money and the dollars were Canadian or American. In Ontario, New York currency was not represented by any banknotes, and the New York dollar and pounds existed only on paper in merchants' books. No American paper money circulated here, and when pounds are mentioned in price lists and store-keepers' books they are not English pounds. They were pounds of New York or Halifax currency. These currencies were purely money of account and all the various coins of many nations were related to them. This was quite reasonable, for the alternative would have been to give the price of every article for sale in half a dozen different coinages.

Halifax currency was also used in Toronto. This was also a money of account. It had the theoretical dollar as its basis, but there were only five shillings, instead of eight to the dollar. With this system, twenty shillings equalled a pound of four dollars. This Halifax currency was used for large accounts and for government business. It was established in 1765 and its purpose was to adopt as a money unit a shilling equal in value to an existing French coin used in Quebec. This Halifax currency was called the "legal currency."

With all the foregoing, we are impressed with the fact that all paper currency in 1810 was unstable and could not be exported – even to a colony. In all the western world there was never enough metal coinage for with few banks it was hoarded. In Canada we grasped for any metal coinage we could, and this fact makes our money system quite logical, for we had no banks. The two currencies must have entailed a great deal of book-keeping for storekeepers. In some cases they both were mentioned in the same advertisement for the same product. Here is one from the *York Gazette* in 1800:

Ashes wanted, Sevenpence Halifax currency per bushel for house ashes will be given, delivered at the Pot-ash works, opposite the

Gaol; fivepence, same currency, if taken from the houses; also eight-pence, New York currency for field ashes delivered at the works.

Generally, most transactions in Toronto in 1810 were in New York currency until about 1820 when Halifax currency became more general. In 1810, however, the official business of the government and large business transactions were always in Halifax, and British soldiers on duty in Canada were supposed to be paid in Sterling with twenty-four shillings to the pound. Sometimes the paymaster in Montreal remitted bills of exchange to Ontario on the pretext that the hard cash might be lost in transit.

As individuals bought necessities in larger quantities than today, such as snuff and liquor in kegs and pork and flour by the barrel, the plight of the storekeeper was not quite as bad as it would appear. Neither were there the thousands of articles costing a few cents that we have today. Another factor, which does not exist today, was that the customer often had something to sell as well as to buy, for stores bought fireplace ashes, furs, firewood and garden produce from their customers. These established a credit for the customer, and his next purchase was merely subtracted from it without any money changing hands.

It may be readily seen why many contemporary writers declared that the reason storekeepers failed in business was that they did not keep proper books. The system must have been a continual irritation, for the customer was forced to accept the storekeeper's price both ways, particularly when he owed him money.

An act had been passed in Ontario in 1796 making many British and foreign coins legal tender. These included the British guinea, crown, shilling and sixpence, the Portuguese moidore, the Spanish dollar and pistareen, the French crown and several other French coins, the American dollar and the New York State shilling and sixpence. There was also a variety of bronze coins. The counterfeiting or passing of counterfeit money was a felony punishable with death.

Much of this coinage was in general use in Canada until 1858, when our present Canadian coinage was introduced, and it was legal tender until 1871, when the Canadian silver coins of 50, 25, 10 and 5 cents, and the bronze cent became the coinage of Canada.

In 1810, if coins were of large enough value, they were always weighed by the storekeeper with a scale for that purpose, for before the milled edge came into use, gold coins were often cut around the circumference by unscrupulous people who stole precious metal in this manner. To make change in Toronto, coins were cut in half and in quarters with a chisel upon a stone or anvil. Since the balance of trade was against

Canada, at this time, money tended to leave the country, but this cut money stayed. It irritated the people who were forced to use it for it ruined their pockets and purses.

There was very little paper money in Canada until the issue of army bills during the War of 1812. The people of Toronto had looked with suspicion upon any American state or Federal paper money, and that of Quebec was used only locally. With these army bills, however, they regained confidence in paper and after this war demanded banking facilities, which resulted in the Bank of Montreal being granted a charter in 1822 and the Bank of Upper Canada (Ontario), in 1821. It is interesting to note that these banks did not pay interest upon deposits until 1835.

Without banks, the custom of hoarding gold and silver coins and purchasing "plate" in the form of cutlery, dishes, and silver candlesticks, was prevalent. At this time "plate" was solid silver, not plating, as most silverware is today. It was legal for silversmiths to convert silver currency into plate, since precious metal possessed the value of its actual weight. The plate upon the sideboard was a tangible evidence of wealth and solidarity. It was often given as a gift. Upon his retirement to England in 1813, because of poor health, Lieutenant-Governor Gore was voted by the Ontario Legislature the astonishing sum of £3,000 for the purchase of plate. Often the expression was a polite gesture, and the recipient simply spent the money as he pleased. In the following chapter we will see what this money of 1810 could purchase, and how much of it a man earned.

CHAPTER 12

Business and Trade

Toronto, at its inception, was commercial rather than industrial. In 1810 the town was producing proportionately no more manufactured goods than Kingston and Niagara which had a greater population, and these articles, which included barrels and kegs, wagons, sleighs and furniture, were for local use. The presence of government officials and civil servants, and the British soldiers of the Garrison stimulated business when the purchasing power of the surrounding settlers was very small. Business was also aided by the weekly market, which gave some cash to farmers to spend in town.

All of the stores were "general stores," in that they kept a variety of goods which would be sold in separate stores today. Even one of the hotels also sold general merchandise, and it was not until 1830 that a store was opened for the sale of groceries only.

The two large docks were not out of proportion to a town of such a small population, for most of the transportation of imported goods from the eastern ports and from the U.S.A. was by water. These ports were closed in winter and transportation by road with either wagons or sleighs was slow and costly. For these reasons, Toronto merchants ordered their goods well in advance, so that their supplies could be transported from Montreal or New York by water, instead of by land.

Business was competitive in 1810, the same as today, and the hazards, commensurate with the rewards, were probably greater. In that age of slow transportation and communications there was no labour-saving machinery, and no packaged foods, and the tempo of life was more leisurely, simply because these limitations forced it to be. The jolly storekeeper of past generations who had time to gossip with his customers and open the door for them is nostalgically remembered.

When a customer in 1810 bought five pounds of sugar, the storekeeper found his scoop, reached into the sugar barrel and put several pounds on the counter scale. Then he went back to the barrel with his scoop and chopped and loosened more sugar to fill it. He next weighed the sugar, taking time to adjust the weights, taking out or putting in more sugar until he had exactly five pounds. He then emptied the scale pan into the container brought by the customer, and made change from a drawer, which contained the coinage of several nations. If the customer submitted a large coin for payment, the storekeeper weighed it, or he entered the transaction in his books, figuring it out in New York currency. Sometimes he was forced to take goods in exchange for this sugar, which entailed storing it at the back of his store or in a shed on his property. As it was necessary to work up to twelve and even fourteen hours, six days a week, to make a living in this age of little machinery, he was forced to adopt a leisurely pace to ward off fatigue. During all this routine of serving, he had time to talk to the customer as he worked, and both of them welcomed this chat or exchange of gossip as a respite in their long day.

The storekeeper lived over or behind his store, which partially compensated for the long hours, if we compare his day with that of the modern man in Toronto who spends up to three hours getting to and from work. Unlike his counterpart in England, the Toronto and Canadian storekeeper was also a banker, for he often kept his customers' money in his own strongbox, although no interest was paid. Many of them made money by trading in commercial paper. Bills of exchange on London were often at a premium in New York, and they could be sold there at a profit. In contrast to shopkeepers in England, he tended to work with fewer assistants, for labour was relatively expensive.

There were two currencies used in Ontario, the legal and the practical. The practical currency, used by private business for all but large transactions, was that of New York State, in which twelve pence or twelve and one-half cents equalled one York shilling; eight shillings equalled one dollar, and twenty shillings, or two and one-half dollars, a pound. In 1810 a labourer in Toronto earned about one dollar and skilled workmen, such as a carpenter or plasterer, about two dollars a day. If we take the wage of this skilled workman and fix it at the round figure of twenty cents per hour, we have a very good idea of the cost, compared with today, of merchandise sold in Toronto stores in 1810. The following price-list of standard merchandise, in hours worked instead of in money, makes us very thankful for our modern industrial system. It explains why many people went into the woods to gather herbs for substitutes for tea and coffee, and why they did not send many letters to the old country. It also tells us why practically everyone attended auction sales to buy used furniture. They were not looking for antiques – just furniture to use. Most people made their own candles and their own ink. Some women in Toronto had looms in their homes.

Now, let's compare the cost of merchandise in 1810 with prices today. As the average man in Toronto today earns about four thousand dollars per year, this works out to about two dollars per hour. Now we are ready for the comparison. The schedule below, gives the cost of goods in 1810 in dollars and cents. For example, if an article at that time cost four shillings, New York currency, we are calling this fifty cents on our schedule as the shilling was worth twelve and one-half cents. The second column shows the number of hours at twenty cents per hour this skilled workman in 1810 had to work to purchase it. The last column lists today's prices if our average man in Toronto today had to work the same number of hours to purchase the same articles. This comparison is not sound economics, but it gives the reader a fairly accurate picture of the cost of merchandise in 1810 compared with that of today. *(See p. 142)*.

The reader might assume that, in an age of far greater class distinction than today, it is unfair to use this theoretical carpenter or plasterer as our norm. In 1810, however, North American labour was relatively well paid, for this was before the great waves of immigration

MERCHANDISE	COST IN 1810	HOURS WORKED	TODAY'S PRICE AT $2.00 PER HOUR
1 lb. tea	$1.00	5	$10.00
Bushel of potatoes	.50	2½	5.00
Gallon of vinegar	1.00	5	10.00
1 lb. tobacco	.50	2½	5.00
1 lb. snuff	1.50	7½	15.00
1 qt. port wine	.80	4	8.00
Toothbrush	.20	1	2.00
Paper of pins	.50	2½	5.00
Pair women's shoes	1.12	5½	11.00
Pair "Dog irons"	5.00	25	50.00
Woman negro slave	150.00	750	1,500.00
Boy negro slave	250.00	1,250	2,500.00
House and lot	750.00	3,750	7,500.00
Postage to England	1.00	5	10.00
Weekly newspaper per year	4.00	20	40.00

from Europe and the birth of milltowns. The reason for high wages was simply that, with the rapidly expanding economy of Canada and the U.S.A., a tradesman could more easily start in business for himself, or he could purchase land at low cost and become an independent settler. For this reason, an employer was forced to pay wages more equal to what he himself earned than in Europe.

So let's see what other people earned to buy this merchandise. A school teacher was paid only £100 Halifax currency, which would be $400. In addition, his board was supplied by the parents of his pupils. In 1800, Peter Russell, when he was the Receiver-General of the province, was paid £200 Halifax, or $800 per year. He asked for an increase to £400, but this was refused. If we figure his present salary in the same way as the merchandise, it would amount to $8,000 annually.

Office rent in 1810 appears to be very low. One office is mentioned as renting for six dollars per month, which if worked out in the same way would be the equivalent of thirty hours, or sixty dollars per month today. The area was probably 200 square feet. Office space today is rented on a basis of so much per square foot per year. This would make our 1810 office three dollars and sixty cents per square foot. Today, prestige office space above first floor rents for six dollars, with standard office space renting for from four to four-fifty per square foot. Office space in a converted warehouse, which has satisfactory lighting and heating and may be considered far superior to the office space of 1810, rents for two-fifty to three dollars a square foot.

The most astonishing example is that of the gift of "plate" to Governor Gore. This £3,000, even if in New York Currency, works out in this same way at $75,000 today. It seems incredible that such a poor province should have felt obliged to vote such a large sum to a man already in comfortable circumstances.

A feature of the times was quantity selling. This was partly due to the lack of packaged merchandise and paper bags, but it was also the consequence of the transportation of the period. The shipping container was the wooden stave keg, tightly mitred together and waterproofed, and also the barrel for such dry goods as flour and salt pork. These containers were made by coopers, and coopering was a fair-sized industry. Ocean ships did not pass Montreal, and at the docks Durham boats, bateaux and Schenectady boats were waiting to take on cargo for the long trip up the St. Lawrence to Kingston. At that town the cargo was usually placed aboard schooners, of from 15 to 87 tons, for the journey to Toronto and Niagara. The holds of these small craft and schooners were often splashed with water and had little protection from rain. Even such merchandise as snuff was shipped in kegs, and it was this container that went into the stores and was often purchased wholly by one customer. There were no wholesalers, as today, and without paper bags and cartons there was no alternative. The average house had a cellar and some had back-kitchens which contained many kegs and barrels. Canned goods and packaged food have not only changed merchandising, they have done away with the spacious kitchens and back kitchens of the past. There is no space in the modern apartment for a barrel of salt pork.

Before railroads, the transportation of freight by land was called "carrying," and this included horse- and oxen-pulled wagons and sleighs. Often a "brigade," consisting of a dozen sleighs, left Quebec or Montreal for towns as far west as Sandwich. During the war that came two years later, these brigades contained up to sixty sleighs.

Business men and storekeepers in Toronto worked under far less restriction than their counterparts in Britain, particularly in regard to taxes. There was no pauper tax, as in Britain, no tax to support the clergy, for it was intended that the church would be supported by the clergy land reserves; and no road tax, for statute labour was supposed to build roads. There was no imprisonment for debt, as in England, unless the creditor made an affidavit that the debtor intended to leave the province to avoid paying. In cases of business failure, traders were on the same footing as other debtors for there was no bankrupt law in the province. There were duties upon imported merchandise, but town taxes were very low. In fact, the total tax collected in Toronto in 1810 was only £92. The interest rate was six per cent, which was one per cent higher than the rate in New York State.

Lumber and furs head the list of Canadian exports, but these had little direct effect upon business and trade in Toronto. Quebec had been shipping yellow pine to England before 1800, and timber rafts were floating down the Ottawa River as early as 1806. On Lake Ontario, however, timber exporting was just beginning, although masts for the Royal Navy had been out for some time. When Napoleon's Continental System was in full operation in 1808, Britain turned to Canada for the timber to build her navy, as well as for industry and construction, for the war virtually halted trade in timber with the Baltic countries for about two years. Most of this timber came from the St. Lawrence and Ottawa Rivers, not from Lake Ontario. There were sawmills on the Don and Humber Rivers, but these made lumber for local use. These were waterpower mills, and used a "muley" or up-and-down saw. The circular saw was to come thirty years later. Much lumber was made at the building site with "pit sawing," with two men, one standing on a platform and another on the ground below.

Furs, the first export from Canada, had no direct effect upon the growth of Toronto, for the beaver flourished in what are still described as northern areas, where thousands of lakes and swamps provided their breeding ground. Toronto was an important shopping place on the route to the fur country and had at least one fur warehouse. The North-West Fur Company found that the route up Yonge Street was not only cheaper than the Grand River from Lake Erie, and the Ottawa River route, but it also avoided contact with the American border. The Fur Company's boats went up the Don River to York Mills, and from there via the Severn River to Georgian Bay and Lake Huron.

Some grain was exported from the settled areas near Kingston and from the Niagara Peninsula, but the greatest part was consumed in the province or sold to British army garrisons. Meat also found a market in the garrisons but none was exported to Britain.

With open fireplaces, and a few iron box stoves for heating buildings, the collection and sale of firewood was an important local industry. This firewood was usually purchased from men who bought woodland or cutting rights on the outskirts and cut and delivered cordwood to customers in town. Selling water was also a business. There were few wells or pumps, and the first public well did not come until 1823. Some townspeople had wells but most of them secured their drinking water from the Don River or the nearest creek. The majority went for it with buckets; the more prosperous had carters or water-sellers deliver it to their doors.

Wood ashes, which the settlers collected from the burning of trees to clear their land, and fireplace ashes from the houses in town were a staple product for a consumer to sell. These ashes were sold to stores or directly to the potash works. Potash was in great demand in England for the woollen industry. It was also used locally to make soft soap. The stores sold potash kettles to be placed over an open fire. They were large iron pots with handles.

Ginseng, a word unfamiliar to modern readers, is the name of a plant highly valued by the Chinese as a cure-all, although any western pharmacologist will tell us that it has little medicinal value, and that quinine is far superior. In 1714 a French priest heard about the plant from the Royal Society in London. With the increase in the Chinese population, their own ginseng could not supply the demand, and they were importing it from Korea. This priest determined to search for the plant in Canada and found it growing near Montreal. A profitable trade sprang up between Quebec and China. The search spread to Ontario, and settlers dropped their ploughs and people in Toronto went into the forests to seek it. Jacob Herchmer advertised in the *Gazette* in 1801 that he would buy any quantity, and would give two shillings New York currency per pound for well-dried ginseng, and one shilling for green. The British Government, in 1805, made an abortive attempt to have settlers grow hemp, when the supply of the Russian product was cut off. This was an important commodity when ships' anchor hawsers were often six inches in diameter. The farmers who grew it, however, found that the government had made no provision to buy and store it. Merchants refused hemp as barter and the farmers were forced to plough it back into the soil. Salt, a commodity we now take for granted, was proportionately far more important in an age of salted meat than it is today. As there were no salt mines, and Toronto was far from the sea, salt could only be obtained in a few locations where it was on the surface. In the war which came two years later, its price rose to the equivalent of 75 hours of a skilled workman's wage per hour per bushel.

Tea was the universal beverage, although cocoa was also advertised in grocery lists. Coffee was scarce and expensive, and on most lists it was not mentioned. It is probable that the demand was minimal because tea was preferred by most people. The British Government had placed a tax upon tea entering Canada which made its cost far higher than in the U.S.A. One Scotsman who travelled through the U.S.A. and Canada in 1818 reported that nearly ten thousand chests of tea were annually consumed in Canada, of which not more than two or three thousand came from Europe. The remainder were smuggled, and no doubt this condition existed in 1810 in the same proportion. This traveller declared that he knew a dealer in Newark who annually smuggled five hundred to a thousand chests of tea from the United States, and this town was probably the source of most of the tea sold in Toronto. He claimed that for every fifteen pounds of tea sold in Ontario thirteen were smuggled, and that the profit on this tea smuggling was fifty to one hundred per cent. This evasion of the tea tax was comparatively easy in a large country with a small population. The Canadian tea-dealer, after buying a few chests from Montreal with the customs mark on them, kept refilling with tea from the U.S.A. Such duplicity was hard to prove, even though the re-used chests showed signs of wear, and the ultimate consumer had little interest in preventing this smuggling for he would be the loser.

A store inventory of 1810 would list a surprising number of articles that are sold today, such as castor oil, nutmeg, lime and lemon juice, peppermint, toothbrushes, violin bows, mathematical instruments, padlocks, silk stockings and suspenders. Many of them, however, would be unfamiliar; such as bedcord, powder for dusting ink, wafers to seal letters, snuff, beaver hats, horn powder flasks, ivory combs, potash kettles, green canvas for blinds and foot-warmers. The smoker had his choice of plug, pigtail, ladies' twist, Spanish cigars, etc. Then there were other products used today whose 1810 names would confuse the modern shopper. Souchong tea was black and hyson was green tea, copperas was sulphuric acid, fustian was a kind of dark cotton cloth, muscovado was an unrefined sugar, etc.

Although advertising may appear to be a modern innovation, every issue of the *York Gazette* carried advertisements for tailors, hairdressers, barbers, tradesmen and stores. These store advertisements contained long lists of merchandise with no order or classification. Mathematical instruments were followed by knives and forks, and brass wire followed violin bows. One list ends with a span of horses. It now seems strange that in these advertisements no prices were given.

Wholesale buying and selling has always existed to some extent in the sale of commodities, for the large merchant could use his greater purchasing power and credit to buy more than he could sell in his own store, and dispose of the surplus to smaller ones at a price which enabled the small merchant to resell at a profit. At this time Quetton St. George advertised that he could supply country store-keepers "more advantageously than if they made their purchases below (Montreal)."

Shop and business signs were used extensively, and they were very necessary in an age when a percentage of the population could not read. Many of these signs were ingenious and eye-catching with anvil, sledge-hammer, horseshoe, fowling-piece, boot, tea-chest, etc., painted on them. One of the best was a double-sided watch, about two feet in diameter, which hung over the entrance to the shop of Jordon Post, the clock and watch-maker. House-numbering in Toronto did not come until 1833 and many private residences used the same device of painting some figure or emblem, as well as the name, on a board and placing it near the entrance.

Fire insurance on both residences and places of business in Toronto was not unusual, and in the *York Gazette* of March 2, 1808, the editor requests that a fund, repayable in ten years, be raised to give a loan to a merchant who was burnt out, and had no fire insurance.

In 1809, because of events in Europe, most Canadian merchants overestimated their future sales and ordered more European goods than they could sell. This commercial distress was first apparent early in 1810 and rapidly spread westward. It was at its worst in Ontario. In Toronto the pinch began to be felt in April. Prices fell rapidly and many merchants were ruined. The main reason for this temporary recession was the drop in the demand for squared timber, for which Britain was again turning to Norway and Sweden. This had little effect upon those with fixed salaries, such as government employees; it was the merchants and settlers who felt it most.

CHAPTER 13

Doctors
and Sickness

The difference between sickness in 1810 and that of today is not only in the disparity between the medical skill of that period and the present. The primeval forests of Ontario maintained a water level much higher than that of today. Great areas of swamp and moist forest land, that the sun seldom penetrated, provided a breeding ground for mosquitoes. This included the flats at the mouth of the Don River, and the rain-water barrel at the corner of every house. The people of Toronto in 1810 were victims of "Lake Fever," "Intermittent Fever," and "The Shakes," the alternating chills and fever ague of early America, now known as malaria. This disease was seldom fatal.

It was believed that malaria was inhaled from the vapour rising from swamps. People closed their windows at night, especially in August, "for the night air was dangerous." Like quite a few of the unscientific customs of our forefathers, this window closing was a successful expedient, for it kept out the mosquitoes. Malaria reached epidemic proportions along the Great Lakes in 1828, but as the land became settled, it gradually disappeared.

Pneumonia was another disease which often reached epidemic proportions and it was often fatal. It was prevalent over the whole of the United States and Canada in 1812-15. It was called by various names: typhoid, typhus pneumonia, bilious pneumonia, malignant bilious fever, etc.

We first learn of inoculation for smallpox in the issue of the *Gazette*, of January 25, 1797, at Newark, in which it is mentioned that Dr. Kerr the well-known physician would inoculate on the most reasonable terms and the poor would be treated gratis. In 1807 Elizabeth Russell casually mentions in her diary that a doctor in Toronto inoculated a patient with cow pock, so we may assume that this cure for smallpox was standard in 1810, and the disease had ceased to be a threat.

Even with their relative helplessness in epidemics, the people of Toronto were generally healthy. The poorest in Toronto had all the food they wanted, and they also had a more varied diet than the poor in England. The people rode horseback, skated and swam in the Bay, went on picnics and dug in their gardens. And what is perhaps more important, they were not health conscious. They were not continually reminded of diet or vitamins. They had no statistics upon health or the death rate, and fatalistically accepted what God had in store for them.

As the American Revolution had seldom harshly treated Loyalist members of the medical profession, only a few of them had joined the exodus to the Canadas. So there were not many practising physicians in Ontario in 1810, even in the towns. In some cases, army doctors could be secured by civilians living near their quarters. Toronto had Dr. Glenon, Dr. Baldwin, Dr. Lee, a military surgeon attached to the Indian Department, and perhaps one other. As Dr. Lee was away from Toronto most of the time, he cannot be considered a resident. It is remarkable, however, that because of the good health of the people and their ability to doctor themselves, Dr. Baldwin was forced to turn to the profession of law.

It was not unusual, at this time, for a bright boy to study with a doctor as a kind of apprentice. He lived with the doctor's family, ran his errands and groomed his horse. In return, the doctor gave him instruction and outlined a course of reading. Then the young man went to New York, or some distant place for lectures. When he returned, he went before a licensing board, and if approved by them was granted permission to practise. We say "permission" for in 1810 such a young man started his practice without any legal authority. An act to license doctors had been passed in Ontario in 1795. It had proved unworkable in curtailing the activities of quacks, and was not in force in 1810.

Bleeding appears to have been the cure-all in the medical profession. This bleeding was done with leeches which were collected or raised for that purpose. Sometimes the patient fainted with the loss of blood, and we read of fifty ounces being taken at one time. It is doubtful, however, if physicians in 1810, with their limited knowledge, succeeded much better in treating common ailments than the townspeople and settlers with their homemade remedies.

It was only in extreme emergencies that the townspeople felt the need of a doctor. There was someone in nearly every household, or a neighbour, who could be relied upon to treat common disorders. This person, usually a mother or a grandmother, was the doctor, nurse and druggist for the family. She gathered her drugs in the forest, in the form of plants, roots, berries, bark and seeds. Many of these have since been proven to have medicinal value. Others were practically worthless, except for their psychological effect. These herbs included bloodroot, catnip, cherry bark, black alder, smartwood and wormwood. They were made into remedies with the addition of lard, vinegar, resin, beeswax, etc. It was long before modern science, and such remedies were often concocted in an atmosphere of quackery and mysticism. Some people would collect these herbs in the forest only when the moon was full, or under some similar restriction.

Toronto had the beginning of a spa which, however, never materialized. In 1808, the newspaper mentioned that, "an eminent physician of York is said to have received much benefit from the use of the water." This referred to a spring in Scarborough, a few miles away. The newspaper item noted that the water from this spring resembled that in Saratoga, in New York State. Although many visitors remarked upon the damp and unhealthy situation of the town, the English settlers agreed that the province was a healthy place in which to live. They first noticed they had fewer colds than in the old land.

As elsewhere in the world, women were assisted in childbirth by midwives. These women were virtually practical nurses, whose experience in this field usually made the service of a doctor unnecessary.

Mrs. Bennet, the wife of the King's Printer, had a sign outside the door of her home, "Isabella Bennet, midwife from Glasgow." No doubt, in that age of limited vocations for women, Mrs. Bennet thoroughly enjoyed her position in society as a woman indispensable in time of need.

When we speak of dentistry, we enter a man's world, for both sexes had more confidence in a man's physical strength to pull out a tooth as quickly and painlessly as possible. No teeth were filled, for there were no dentists. Teeth were left in the mouth until agonizing pain forced their hurried removal. The instrument of extraction was the turnkey, and there was always someone from whom it could be borrowed. With men, the offending tooth was often extracted in the taproom of a hotel, so that the victim could be well fortified with liquor, and have a sympathetic audience. If a hot poultice failed to stop the pain, the turnkey was secured. The sufferer sat in a chair and grasped the rungs. The operator loosened the gum with a pocket-knife, and inserted the hook of the key. The two faced each other as the victim grimly shut his eyes and held on to the chair rungs while the operator pulled.

Contemporary letter writers and travellers, when they referred to or described friends or strangers, seldom mentioned missing front teeth. Absent front teeth, thanks to the dental profession, are so rare today we might receive a shock if we could return to the early eighteen hundreds.

Glasses, or spectacles as they were called, were expensive, and their purchase often necessitated a trip to Montreal or to the United States. They were casually loaned and passed on to others. However, as fewer people than today could read well enough to enjoy perusal of a book, they were not as necessary.

Many of the homes in Toronto had a family medical book, such as *Thompson's Family Physician, Everyman's Physician,* and *Louisa Solomon's Guide to Health.* In one merchant's advertisement in the *York Gazette,* the above books were included in the long list of drygoods, groceries and hardware. There were patent medicines, just as today, and in one newspaper advertisement in 1810 we note that "Clarendon Younger announces that he has appointed Doctor Dorland of Niagara to be his sole agent in the province for vending his Peruvian Anti-Bilious Bitters, and his truly valuable Itch Ointment."

The impression we have today of the army sick and wounded of that period being housed in tents in fields, with no medical organization, is not altogether correct. During the war that came two years later, a collection of log buildings, formerly Butler's Barracks of the War of Independence days, was used as a field hospital for the Queenston-Niagara field of operations.

We read in army despatches that convalescent soldiers were sent across Lake Ontario to the "Base Hospital" in Toronto as soon as they were well enough to be removed from the drafty barracks at Newark. We also find that the box pews in St. James' Church in Toronto were hurriedly removed to convert the building into a hospital, after the army hospital at the Garrison was full. Medical service in the army hospital was crude and inadequate, but the organization existed. When the war was over, a seventy-bed hospital was built in Toronto for disabled veterans.

CHAPTER 14

Hotels and Boarding Houses

In 1810 some residences were larger than the hotels of the town. This was typical of the period, and hotels in the settled parts of the U.S.A. were not much larger. Fewer people travelled than today in Canada, and the economic structure permitted a fair income to the owner of a hotel with only a common sleeping-room, a few bedchambers, a dining-room and a bar. To a much greater extent than today, if we exclude conventions, these hotels were used for business and some sold general merchandise and we must remember that Lloyd's Insurance Company had its origin in an inn. Auction sales were held in these Toronto hotels and they were occasionally used for church services. The Legislature even met in one of them in 1814, after the Americans had burnt the Parliament Buildings.

All had taprooms, or bars, or bars in their dining-rooms. Two of them had ballrooms where assemblies (dances) were held, and the occasional play, concert or lecture was given in these rooms. They were club buildings of sorts where men could meet their friends, listen to travellers' stories on cold winter nights around the fireplace, play whist or dominoes, smoke a clay pipe and drink ale or a whiskey punch. On occasion, these hotels were used for polling booths and even for magistrates' courts. Club activities, such as the St. John's dinner, the St. Andrew's Dinner, and the dinners following provincial elections were also held in Toronto's hotels in the period from the town's inception to 1810.

They had hanging signs over their entrances, and some regularly advertised in the *Gazette,* describing themselves as, "Beefsteak and Beer House," "House of the Entertainment," etc. All had stables, usually a wing at the rear or a separate building, but in the case of one hotel it was across the street. One of these Toronto hotels had a billiard table. Many Ontario hotels, at this time and later, had a wash-trough, which was sometimes merely a hollowed-out log, with a bucket of water located in the stableyard. Here was also located a brush and comb hanging by a string from a nail. It is probable that all Toronto hotels had shallow wells, and there were some kind of open-air washing facilities for the men in addition to the hand wash basins in the guest rooms. Guests could take a bath in a wooden stave tub or tin tub, after it had been filled with hot water brought up from the kitchen. Even a stand-up bath was a welcome luxury for a traveller. It is probable that the toilet accommodation was the same as described elsewhere for houses.

The American plan of putting the food upon a long dining-room table and permitting the guests to help themselves was prevalent in Toronto hotels for a long time after 1810. This custom of serving food without waiters was due to the shortage of servants. The guests were forced to be prompt, at the sound of the bell, to come to dinner before it was cold. This lessened the time of eating meals, which also enabled a hotel to operate with a minimum of servants. A jug of liquor stood on the table and many guests always finished a meal with a dram and a cigar. The hasty eating and lack of casual dinner conversation astonished many European travellers, who usually condemned North American hotels.

Some Toronto hotels may have followed the American custom of having a woman, preferably a young one, sit at the head of the table and act as hostess by serving food, pouring tea and creating a homelike atmosphere. Even at this date the English name of Inn had been discarded for hotel and tavern.

In 1801 it was the opinion of the Court that six persons were sufficient for "keeping tavern" in Toronto for the following year and several applications were refused. It is difficult to separate the genuine hotels from those which were merely general stores and drinking places, where the owner may also have had a room or two to rent if requested. In a few of these the drinking was probably done at the store counter, or at a few tables. These, of course, had no hotel atmosphere.

Most of these hotels in Toronto in 1810 were very small by the standards of today. Frank's Hotel near the Market, for example, was a white painted clapboarded building which could have been mistaken for a private residence. It was about thirty feet wide and eighteen feet deep, and was two storeys in height. The entrance door led to the centre hall, so that the largest room was about twelve by eighteen feet in size, or about the same area as the living-room of a moderate-sized modern residence. To the right upon entering was the room used as a barroom and dining-room and on the left the "sitting-room" or lounge and kitchen, or service room. The second floor had a common sleeping-room with a few private bed-chambers.

At the rear of Franks's was an auditorium, or "ballroom" wing, and this room was reached from the hotel stair, or from an open outside stair directly to the ballroom, for the hotel was on a corner. The auditorium appears to have been less than thirty feet wide and forty feet long. We are told that the ceiling was very low. The room had a stage and draw curtain for theatrical performances.

Hotels changed owners very rapidly at this period and many proprietors were in the business for a few years and sold out to others who changed the name. Cooper's Tavern was sold to a Mr. Gilbert of Newark in 1806, who placed the following advertisement in the *Gazette:*

> The subscriber having left the "Yellow House" at Niagara, and opened the Toronto Coffee House at York; begs leave to inform his friends and the public that he has fitted up said house in a most superior manner than heretofore; where gentlemen, travellers and others may be accommodated with genteel boarding and lodging. He is provided with the best liquors, etc., and hopes by his assiduity and attention to the commands of those gentlemen who may be pleased to favour him with their custom; to merit a share of the public confidence. Good stabling, hay and oats for horses.

Abner Miles' Inn was the first, and it was erected about 1795. The *Gazette,* however, refers to it as Miles' hotel. In 1798 the gentlemen of the town and the Garrison were requested to meet there to arrange the York Assemblies.

The most important was Jordon's York City Hotel, which was commonly called Jordon's. For many years it was the best in Ontario. This building was one and one-half storeys with dormer windows on its roof. Illustration No. 7 shows a service wing for kitchen and servants. It is probable that the six dormers on the main building represented six single rooms, although there was probably a common sleeping-room on a portion of the opposite side of the building. If we assume that the bed-chambers were eight feet six inches wide, both the "ballroom" and the lounge and dining-room which probably contained the bar, were both about twenty feet six inches by twenty-six feet in size. These two rooms probably contained two columns to support beams for the second floor joists to rest upon. Each room was heated with a large open fireplace.

Another hotel, the Half-way House, was so named because it was midway between the town and the Garrison. It was located on Front Street, between Peter and John Streets. While this hotel was larger in floor area than Frank's Hotel (excluding the ballroom), it is seldom mentioned in early writing, for it was frequented mostly by the working class and soldiers from the Garrison.

One and one-quarter miles north of the town, on the east side of Yonge Street, and just north of the present Bloor Street, was the popular farmers' hotel, the Red Lion. This building, erected 1808-10, was three floors in height and larger than Jordon's. A two-storey wing on the south side had a ballroom on the second floor twenty feet wide and forty feet long and had a wooden barrel-vaulted ceiling eighteen feet in height, but the walls were plastered. This room was lighted by three windows on Yonge Street and was heated with a fireplace at each end. It was considered a large room and was used for political meetings, banquets and assemblies. Swinging over the entrance on Yonge Street was a large sign with a fierce lion painted on it. The Red Lion was used as a hotel until 1892.

Members of the Parliament came from all of the electoral districts in Ontario to live in Toronto for the duration of the session. Many of them stayed at what was called Johnson's Boarding House, which had accommodation for twenty guests. This building, two storeys high of white painted clapboarding, was built about 1812. Mrs. Johnson was a good cook and a cheerful and hospitable woman, and many preferred her boarding house to the hotels, although the rate of three or four dollars a week was the same as Jordon's across the street.

When Ontario became a separate province, and the Loyalists came in increasing numbers, the British Government built several good hotels in Ontario. Architecturally, they were as good as the best wooden buildings in the province. Their primary purpose was to provide army storehouses and troop billets in case of war with the U.S.A. They were also used to store Indian treaty presents. A token rent of one dollar per year was paid to the Government by responsible landlords who acted as caretakers for these buildings, and operated highway hotels as private enterprises. One of these was located at Burlington, near the present city of Hamilton; another, near the mouth of the Credit River, west of Toronto.

CHAPTER 15

Newspapers

There were three newspapers in Ontario in 1810, at Kingston, Newark, and Toronto, the *Kingston Gazette* having begun publication in September of that year. As Ontario had a population of seventy-five thousand, there was one newspaper for approximately twenty-five thousand people, compared with one for fifteen thousand in New York State. This ratio gives a comparison of the development of Ontario compared with eastern United States at this time. Quebec had five newspapers, or about one to fifty thousand population.

The antecedent of Toronto's first newspaper was the *Upper Canada Gazette,* or *American Oracle,* first published at Newark, April 18, 1793. This *Gazette* was the first newspaper in Ontario. It was founded by Governor Simcoe and, although privately owned, was subsidized by the government and intended to be its mouthpiece. Its circulation was limited. In 1795 a writer and traveller stated that this paper was not subscribed to by anyone in Kingston, but that a Quebec paper was taken by two residents.

This Newark newspaper was simply one sheet folded to make four pages of printing fifteen inches by nine and one-half inches in size. It was two columns wide but by 1810 was four columns. While this appears to be small for a newspaper, the first issue of the *New York Sun,* in 1833, was only three columns in width. A modern paper is usually nine columns. This *Upper Canada Gazette* contained no illustrations, no features, no syndicated columns, no sport or financial pages, and no free discussion of public affairs. It was not sold on the street or in stores, but only to subscribers who picked up their copy at the printing office. If mailed, the subscriber paid the postage.

The quality of the paper was coarse but durable, for it was made from rags, not pulpwood. The *Gazette* was issued weekly (it was not until 1853 that the province had a daily paper), and the price was three dollars per year. The price per copy would be about sixty cents in today's money. After the subscriber had finished reading the *Gazette* he passed it along to friends and neighbours for not everyone could afford a newspaper.

European news was often five months old in the *Gazette* and most of it was simply lifted from other papers. Even news from the U.S.A. was often a month old. In 1801 one writer made the comment that the issue of November 13th contained news from Halifax, Philadelphia and Boston papers from October the 19th, New York, October 23rd and Charleston, October 1st.

There were no news stories in the modern sense of the word. A local murder could be dismissed with a paragraph. A Parliamentary speech was printed in its entirety without comment. A large portion of the paper consisted of advertisements for stores, army recruiting advertisements, help wanted notices, auction sales, lost and found notices, etc.

In 1798 the *Upper Canada Gazette* moved across the Lake from Newark to Toronto to be near the Parliament of which it was the mouthpiece. When it moved, however, the editors remained in Newark for they had grown tired of the restrictions the government had placed upon them and wished to start a newspaper of their own. They called it *The Canada Constellation,* but this new paper had a short life of about one year.

In 1801, starting from March 21st and for six issues, the *Gazette* was printed on blue paper called Government "blue stock." The stock of white paper had run out and no more could be secured until the opening of navigation. In 1807 the paper was headed *The Upper Canada Gazette,* and the words *American Oracle* were dropped. This is understandable, for there was a threat of war with the U.S.A. at this time and no doubt, the editor realized that the word American was being increasingly applied to the United States, not to the whole of North America. For over twenty years it was the official mouthpiece of the government.

Cameron and Bennett were the printers and publishers of the *Gazette* in 1810, and at this time newspapers were also job printers. The press upon which the *Gazette* was printed in 1810 was a used machine of cast iron, wood and stone. It was purchased from the *Quebec Gazette,* was reputed to have been the oldest press in Canada, and was constructed about 1780. Its capacity was sixty sheets per hour, and it was very similar in design to the one used by Benjamin Franklin when he worked as a journeyman printer in London, 1725-26. This press was in use in Toronto for job printing until 1901. In 1810 it was located in a house on King Street, near Caroline (Sherbourne) Street.

In 1813 the name was changed to the *York Gazette,* and during the occupation of the American troops the press was broken and the type scattered. Publication was suspended from 1813 to 1815, and during this period the *Kingston Gazette* was the only newspaper in Ontario.

The second Toronto newspaper was the *Observer* in 1820. Many newspapers began to appear in the province after the War of 1812, but most had a short life. There was no dearth of intelligent men with a desire to enter the field of journalism, but population was lacking to support many papers. The modern age of journalism began with the publication of George Brown's *Toronto Globe,* in May, 1844, and this newspaper was issued three times a week. It became a daily in 1853.

The third newspaper in Ontario in 1810 was the *Upper Canada Guardian, or Freeman's Journal* (1807-1812), published at Newark by Joseph Willcocks, an Irishman, who had a personal grudge against some members of the government. *The Guardian,* of course, had no government subsidy. It was four columns wide and could be described as a free newspaper, and its editor often risked a charge of treason in criticizing the government. This paper was furtively read by some in Toronto, but approvingly by many settlers. Publication ceased on June 9, 1812, when Richard Hatt, one of the founders of Dundas, bought the *Guardian* for $1,600 to silence it. In this last issue Willcocks frankly told his readers that he had sold its press and type for three times their value, and actually quoted the adage, "A fool and his money are soon parted." Scarcely two weeks later the U.S.A. declared war against Great Britain and Willcocks, who fought on the British side but turned traitor and joined the Americans, was killed in action at Fort Erie in 1813.

Before 1810 a few people in Toronto subscribed to American newspapers and these gave to an intelligent group an ever-changing picture of America's attitude toward Great Britain.

To modern readers these newspapers of 1810 are incredibly dull. Politics, a small amount of local and foreign news and advertisements were practically all they contained. They were not colourless, however, to the readers of the time for politics was news and very absorbing news when every settler's paramount interest was the improvement of his own fortune with the development of the province. The Clergy Reserves, the poor roads, the lack of schools, the bias shown in government which favoured an *elite,* were as interesting to those of that period as the financial and sport pages are to modern readers. The dullness of these early newspapers to modern readers is a tribute to the success of our democracy which we take so much for granted.

CHAPTER 16

Servants

About 13.5 per cent of the people of Toronto in 1810 were servants, including those employed by merchants, hotel owners, etc. What we would today classify as store clerks and waiters were then listed as servants on assessment rolls. The number of domestic servants might be little more than half of this percentage. One family had five persons listed as servants, but some of these were slaves. Seventy per cent of the families of Toronto had no servants.

As in the U.S.A. there was a servant problem in Toronto from the beginning which has lasted until the present, and for more than a century wealthy families made a practice of hiring newly-arrived valets and domestic servants from England for these men and women were courteous and had the proper amount of respect for their employers. They were also efficient. Some were intelligent men confined by accident of birth in the rigid class mould of the Old Land.

Those born in America, of comparable talents, were seldom valets or domestic servants for there were greater opportunities open to them in other fields. In 1810 there was much complaint about domestic servants being indolent and dirty, and not worth the cost of their keep. One man spoke of his wretch of a servant woman as being in a continual state of intoxication. In 1807 a Toronto woman, writing to her brother in New York, spoke of "the wretched state of this country as to servants." The servant problem in Ontario started with John Graves Simcoe, the first governor of the province. All of the men servants he brought with him from England left his employ as soon as they saw an opportunity to better themselves.

English visitors, upon returning to their own country, warned their friends about bringing servants to Canada. It was sure to result in the loss of the money paid for their passage. The servants remained in the new country to be hired for better wages, or found other employment in fields which had been practically closed to them in Britain. The reason, of course, was the economy of the New World which was based upon cheap land and this made men proprietors instead of servants.

One writer complained that, "The very air of Canada severs the tie of mutual obligation which bound you together." They demanded the highest wages and grumbled at doing half the work which they cheerfully performed at home. This same writer, on second thought, observed, "With all their insolent airs of independence, I must confess I prefer the Canadian to the European servant. If they turn out to be good and faithful, it springs from a real respect and affection, and you possess in your domestic a valuable assistant and friend."[10]

Simcoe had spoken with uneasiness of the election to the Legislative Assembly of men who ate at a common table with their servants (an unpardonable offence among the members of the nobility and gentry), but the relation of master to servant in Toronto, and that of settler to hired man in the clearings, in 1810, was already bringing about a subtle change which was breaking down the barriers between classes. It is probable that many of the best families were patiently waiting for the rigid society of England to be established in Toronto, and with the prosperity that came a decade or two later many servants were required for the "estate houses" which were being built. The wealthy, however, were increasingly compelled to hire servants from the recent immigrants from Britain and other countries.

CHAPTER 17

The Mail

When George Heriot became Postmaster-General of British North America in 1800 there was much room for improvement in the method of transporting and distributing mail. He could make no drastic changes, for Canada was too sparsely settled and too poor for good postal service. Even with what today appears to be an extremely high postal rate the service was indifferent, and much of the mail was carried at a financial loss to the government.

At this early date penny postage would not have solved the problem, for travelling was very slow; the winter mail was carried entirely upon men's backs, and lowering the rates and doubling or tripling the amount of mail would have merely increased the number of couriers taking the same time to cover their route. Penny postage came when railroads and steamships made conditions favourable for it.

In Ontario there was a regular mail service which had been established in 1810. Every two weeks during the winter months a courier left Montreal for Kingston and Toronto. The following year this service extended to Newark. The trip from Montreal to Toronto took sixteen to eighteen days, and the postage from Montreal to Kingston was ninepence. During the summer months the service was not as regular, for it depended upon the sailing of government-owned schooners and bateaux. By 1811 the mail went as far west as Amherstburg and Sandwich when there was enough to make a load for a carrier. By 1815-16 there was a weekly service from Montreal to Toronto and the number of post offices in the province had increased to nine.

While there were few post-offices, there were many locations along the "carrier's" route where mail was picked up or left. These locations were usually stores. It was a strict rule that letters must be ready, for the courier could not wait. They were then distributed by the storekeeper who was glad to perform this service. Sometimes the mail was taken to the nearest church and distributed after the service.

One of these carriers, Eli Corbiere, often walked from Toronto to the location of the present city of Hamilton in eight hours, and made the sixty miles from Holland Landing to Penetanguishene, on Georgian Bay, in one day. Needless to say he worked under contract, and was not an employee of the Post-office Department. It cost about a dollar to send a one-sheet letter to England, and took so long that a letter mailed from England in November did not reach Toronto until the following spring. Previous to eighteen hundred the army in Ontario had a postal service of its own for military correspondence, and two Schenectady boats carried dispatches from Kingston to the Bay of Quinte, and war vessels and military bateaux, and trusted soldiers on snowshoes, carried mail to military posts. This, of course, was for the army, and civilian mail or soldiers' letters were not carried.

The first post-office in Toronto was established in 1799. The mail was distributed first from a store but then a small log building was rented or constructed to serve as the post-office. This was probably opened only on the day the mail was received, and the remainder of the time was used as a storage depot for mail to be picked up. It is probable that mail and postal charges were accepted only on certain days. It was not until 1816 that a squared-log building, later covered with clapboarding, was built to serve as a post-office and this was located on the east side of Frederick Street, south of King Street, and the postmaster also used this building as an office for his other government duties.

The first postmaster in Toronto was William Allan. He also held offices of Inspector of Flour, Pot and Pearl Ash, and Inspector of Shop, Still and Tavern Duties. In addition, he was the Collector of Customs, and owned the Merchants Wharf, at the foot of Frederick Street. All of these duties and offices gave a living to only one man in 1810.

The inadequacy of postal service was highlighted in 1813, during the war, when British officers stationed at Stoney Creek, on Lake Ontario, presented a complaint to the Governor-General, stating that they could not write to wives and relatives in England. The Canadian postal regulations required postage to be paid from Stoney Creek to Halifax. The postage from Halifax, however, could be collected from the recipient of the letter. Their nearest post-office was in Toronto, fifty miles away, which they could not reach. They requested that a monthly bag of mail, be made up at their camp, as Wellington was doing in Portugal, and sent to England. We may imagine the restlessness of those who had left wives and sweethearts in the Old Land.

Interchange of letters with the Old Country could be speeded up by giving mail to a friend visiting New York or Boston, and having him mail the letters from those cities to England. As postage was expensive, it was common courtesy to tell friends you were about to go to England, and would personally deliver their letters, or mail them from London to parts of England you did not intend to visit. There was also an illegal way to send mail across the ocean which was cheaper and usually faster. New York and Boston ship-owners carried mail to England in defiance of the postal laws, and this method could be used by those who knew someone in those cities to forward it.

There was, of course, no postal service within Toronto. In an age before telephones many letters were written to friends in Toronto and delivered by a servant. Townspeople wrote letters to friends and relatives out of town when they found that a friend was journeying to that place. They also wrote letters to storekeepers ordering merchandise, and some-times to the newspaper. Those in love, of course, also wrote notes to each other, so there were hundreds of letters written each year in Toronto which were not sent by mail.

The father of the family might have a writing-desk, but wives and children would have their personal writing case. Writing a letter at this time involved far more than an airmail envelope, a ball-point pen and a postage stamp. The pen was a goose quill, and these were bought by the dozen or the gross. These quill pens were sharpened with a penknife. It was not until twenty-five years later that steel pen nibs came on the market, but these cost twenty-five cents when a clerk in an office earned only a few hundred dollars a year. The ink could be home-made, for one diarist mentions making a quart of ink. This may have been made from black or red ink powder advertised by the stores to be mixed with water. The ink took a long time to dry so it was sprinkled with sand-shaker, or a pinch of sand from an open dish, for blotting paper was unknown. This sand was dropped off by turning the paper upsidedown. Erasures had to be made with a sharp knife. The letter, if it was to be mailed, was usually written on one sheet of foolscap. As postage was paid by weight and one sheet was one-half ounce, everyone made an effort to write as many words as possible on one sheet of paper. One example shows forty-seven lines with thirteen words to the line – more words than a page of single-spaced typing today. Some people also wrote diagonally across the sheet over the first writing.

The paper was folded in from the sides, and then each end was folded in and lapped in the centre, and a seal was placed over this lap. The address was written upon the reverse side. Many letter writers also wrote upon all the reverse side of the paper which would be hidden from sight when the letter was folded. This seal could be a "wafer," which was a small disk of dried paste, or it could be sealing wax, a substance composed of shellac, resin, pitch and filling to which a light oil and colouring had been added. This wax was heated and applied to the lap in the paper. An invasion of privacy was thus precluded, for wax which had been melted and re-applied could be easily detected. A few letter-writers had a seal, which was pressed on the wax before it hardened. This could be the initials of the sender or simply an ornamental design.

The letter, if it was to be mailed, was taken to the post office, or to Mr. Allan, and the postage prepaid. It might then remain with Mr. Allan for a week or more until the courier passed through Toronto. The *Gazette* usually announced the time the courier was expected so that most people wrote their letters a day or two before.

CHAPTER 18

Vehicles

Except in winter, most of Ontario's freight and passenger traffic in 1810 was by water. Even in winter, sleighs carrying their loads of freight moved on the ice of rivers, or along the shore of Lake Ontario to avoid the valleys and makeshift bridges of the pioneer roads. Freight was hauled by oxen, rather than horses, and these heavy beasts were more difficult to control on steep slopes.

The first stagecoach runs between Toronto and Kingston, and Newark were not inaugurated until 1816 and 1817. Travellers used water for transport as often as possible or rode horseback over the pioneer roads. Settlers used saddle-horses also, except when they came to town on market day with their wagons drawn by horses or oxen.

The average working man did not own a horse, unless he used it to earn his living, and none possessed carriages. Men and women of the middle class might own a saddle-horse but few owned a carriage, and it is likely that there were fewer than forty carriages or "pleasure sleighs" of any kind in Toronto in 1810, most of them owned by the upper class or by prosperous merchants. In an emergency one could be borrowed, and it is probable that a few were occasionally rented to travellers at the hotels. There were no "cabs" for hire and there was no one in the business of renting carriages, or conveying people to a ball or a wedding, or to a settler's cabin on the outskirts of town.

In our age of motor cars, the term "wagons kept for pleasure," or "pleasure wagons," appears to be a contradiction of terms. We find, however, that these phrases were used on the assessment rolls up to 1834 and after. This indicated a wagon primarily for passengers, for visiting and trips to market, although freight sometimes was carried. These wagons had no springs, and were simply long wooden boxes on wheels. Passengers sat upon cross boards, or reclined upon straw on the floor. Governor Simcoe had the first carriage in Toronto, if such it could be called, for it was simply a wooden box, shaped like a boat. As there were practically no roads, and the streets were being constructed, it was principally for prestige, and he used it to visit Castle Frank on the Don River, and for state occasions. It had no top of any kind. The front wheels were smaller than those in the rear, but curiously enough, each wheel had only eight spokes. It was probably made at Newark and brought to Toronto by schooner.

Another early vehicle was the Conestoga wagon, which was brought to Ontario as early as 1799 by the immigrants from Pennsylvania. It was made by boatbuilders. The box was narrow and deep, and had the same curved lines as a boat. This wagon had a rounded canvas top, and the immigrants had a place to sleep on their long journey to Ontario. The box of the wagon was waterproof and it was so constructed that the wheels and gear could be removed and put into the wagon which was used as a boat when there were rivers to be crossed. This Conestoga wagon was the forerunner of the well-known prairie schooner of the American west. These vehicles, usually without the canvas top, were pulled into Toronto by oxen or horses on market day from the German settlements north of the town.

There were several types of carriages mentioned in the letters and diaries of the period, and these included the phaeton, the chaise and the gig. The phaeton was a light, open, four-wheeled carriage drawn by either one or two horses, with front and back seats to accommodate four people. Some had a folding canvas top. President Russell, and his half-sister Elizabeth, owned one of these carriages. The chaise was also a carriage with four wheels, very similar to the phaeton. The gig was a light two-wheeled open carriage drawn by one horse. The French-Canadian calèche, which was the first carriage in Canada, was used in the Niagara district but there are few references to its use in Toronto. It was a graceful-appearing open carriage drawn by one horse for two passengers and a driver.

For winter use there were several types of what were called "pleasure sleighs," pulled by one and sometimes two horses. These included the carriole and the curricle, which was gradually supplanted by the Ontario sleigh-cutter. These pleasure sleighs were often lined with brilliant red cloth, and had buffalo robes or bright-coloured blankets draped on the sides.

The few stagecoaches, including wheeled vehicles and sleighs were surprisingly streamlined, for some had the top curved down at the front and back. They were drawn by two pair of horses, and had leather curtains at sides and back and a large one at the rear to cover the luggage holder. Stagecoaches always carried shovels and axes to enable passengers to assist the driver in extricating the vehicle from the mud, or to remove fallen trees, on the road.

In the winter, both deep and shallow wood boxes or platforms on iron-shod sleigh runners were used with both horses and oxen to haul winter freight over the roads. Sometimes, a dozen, or more, formed a "brigade," and slowly travelled across the province and through Toronto, with their drivers wrapped in buffalo robes and their feet in straw or blankets. Two years later, when farmers' sons were enlisted to move war materials from the Atlantic, or Montreal, to distant locations in Ontario these brigades often contained as many as sixty sleighs.

We read in one source that Lieutenant-Governor, General Hunter, stepped out of a schooner at the dock and got into a waiting sedan-chair to be conveyed to the Parliament buildings, for a meeting of the Executive Council. This chair was a miniature cab for one passenger, with long poles at the sides. It was carried along the streets by two men. To the writer's knowledge, this is the only mention of a sedan-chair being used in Toronto. It is probable that Governor Hunter used it only when attending Parliament or meetings of the Council, and in his opinion it gave proper dignity to the office of Lieutenant-Governor. The conveyors were probably soldiers from the Garrison.

We may wonder why the English custom of keeping to the left side of the road was not followed in Toronto. In 1812 a statute was passed requiring vehicles to keep to the right side of the road or street: this, of course merely made legal what was being done. This year, also, a police regulation required at least two bells to be fastened to a harness. In 1817 another regulation prohibited driving or riding at an unreasonable speed, and in this same year the first parking regulation was introduced to Toronto streets. It became unlawful to leave wagons on the street for a longer period than twenty-four hours.

CHAPTER 19

The Library

Religion was the best seller in Britain and America, just as it is today. This may seem strange to modern readers who are aware that the period around 1810 was an age of callousness and selfishness, with an extraordinary amount of drinking and gambling and a lazy clergy in the established church. However, illiteracy was far higher than it is today so that books were written for a smaller proportion of the people. In the established church in England at this time religion was a mode, rather than a deep faith, so it was an interesting topic for reading and discussion.

Books of travel were a close second to religion in popularity. World trade from Britain was rapidly expanding, so thousands had a very practical reason for reading books about other countries. The subject was also an escape for millions of people trapped in the tiny world to which the prohibitive cost of travelling, even in Britain, confined them. Poetry was read by all, and some read plays, but many were proud of the fact that they had never read a novel in their lives.

There was no publishing business in Canada except newspapers, posters and documents. It was mainly the literature of the old world that was read in the new. In 1805, Quetton St. George advertised in the *Gazette* a long list, of books, recently imported. These included medical books, and *Children of the Abbey,* which was the inspiration for naming Miss Russell's house. Most of the titles, including *Devil on Sticks, Looking Glass, Dr. Witman's Egypt, Evelina,* etc. are practically unknown today, but *Tom Jones, The Vicar of Wakefield,* Stern's *Sentimental Journey,* and Smollett's works, including *Roderick Random,* are on the list. Spelling books, primers and Bibles are also mentioned. The Rev. J. Carroll, who was a boy in 1810, stated in his book, *My Boy Life,* that the entire Bible was not generally in use until after the War of 1812. Before that there had been only a large New Testament with metrical version of the Psalms, the Paraphrases, and a few hymns.[11]

It was customary in 1810 for someone, usually the father, to read newspapers, books and plays aloud to the assembled family. As newspapers were passed on to others and books were expensive and were borrowed from friends, the loaning time was cut down by such group reading.

As early as 1804, Ely Playter mentioned in his diary that it was proposed to have a library in Toronto, but this was not established until December 9, 1810. It was called a private subscription library and the books were kept in Elmsley House. The sum of £200 was subscribed toward it. When this library was less than three years old most of its books were carried off by the invading Americans, although the American admiral collected as many as he could and returned them. At this time numerous works were printed in several volumes and, of course, many of the returned books were incomplete, which helped to dampen the enthusiasm of the library board. These returned books were stored in a private house, but the library never got started again and the books were sold at auction in 1822. No list of these books has been found to this date.

As the Toronto library was established to some extent by men who had lived in Newark, it is probable that a great number of the books were identical. At any rate, a glance at the Newark list will give us an excellent idea of what was being read at this time in Toronto. Practically all of the books, including English translations of foreign writers, came from Britain, and there were only a few works by Americans. The library list includes theology, travel, history, biography, and some poetry and fiction. It extends to 1816. The first thirty volumes in the Newark list are of a religious nature, with such downright titles as *Blair's Sermons, Fordyce's Sermons to Young Women,* etc. Then we have *Cook's Voyages, Park's Travels,* and *Robertson's History of South America,* whose titles leave little to the imagination.

One book is entitled *Religious Courtship,* another, *Duty of the Female Sex.* Even a book entitled *Female Complaints* is included. Smollett's *Peregrine Pickle,* Sterne's *Sentimental Journey* and *Tristram Shandy* are on the list, but *Robinson Crusoe* (1719) is not mentioned. There are seven volumes of Shakespeare's works, and books by Milton, Pope, Goldsmith, Dryden, and Robert Burns, and Smith *(Wealth of Nations)* are included. The *Arabian Nights,* which was probably considered light reading, is listed but there are few novels. What are presumably bound annuals of monthly magazines are frequently mentioned. They included, the *Edinburgh Magazine* and the *Edinburgh Review,* the *New York Magazine,* the *European Magazine,* the *Scottish Magazine* and the *Lady's Magazine.* Most of the works of this library are obviously for the improvement of mind and morals. Nine of Walter Scott's works had been published from 1799 to 1816 but none appear to be included except *The Lady of the Lake.* One surprising item in the Newark list is *British Theatre,* 25 volumes. We may only guess at the contents, for this could be critical essays, plays, or both.

The Newark Library was founded in 1800 and it was the first in the province. If Newark's example was followed in Toronto, the library was open to subscribers who paid annual dues of six dollars. Each subscriber made his choice, "provided that nothing irreligious or immoral was contained in it." Although *The History of Tom Jones, a Foundling,* by Fielding, was for sale in Quetton St. George's store, it was not in the Newark library. One month was the borrowing limit and two books could be taken at one time. Out-of-town members were permitted to take three books for six weeks. The Newark Library contained seven hundred books in 1810, so it is probable there were at least two hundred in Toronto by the time of the American attack. At Newark, in 1810, the librarian was to be in attendance for one hour three days a week, from eleven to twelve o'clock on Tuesdays, Thursdays and Saturdays, and he received a mere token salary for his trouble. Copies of the printed catalogue were given to each member and a printed sticker was pasted in each book.

There was also a Parliamentary library, and this one was also destroyed or dispersed during the American occupation. Later, in 1816, Parliament voted the sum of £800 for the purchase of books for the Legislative Council and the House of Assembly.

In 1810, a Mr. Green Adams, an American, opened a bookstore, and a Toronto resident, J. B. Robinson, wrote to a friend, "We have quite a respectable bookstore here from the United States. Good authors but wretched editions – however, I could lay out fifty pounds very much to my satisfaction in it."[12] This bookstore was in a room in a residence.

CHAPTER 20

The Market

In 1810 the Toronto Market was simply a parcel of land south of King Street, extending from New Street (Jarvis), on the east to the present Church Street on the west, and south to Palace (Front) Street. This land had been designated a market in 1803. It comprised five and one-half acres, and a small creek ran through the centre from King to the Bay. In its westward expansion the town had jumped the area in the location of the market because of uneven ground, and maps dated as late as 1813 and 1814 show no north-south streets between Jarvis and Yonge Street. At the western limit of the market property was the jail, and on the north side of King Street, near the centre of the market property, was St. James' Church on its six-acre lot, which had been constructed in 1807.

There were probably no buildings on the market property in 1810, but a plan by George Williams, dated November, 1813, shows a building marked "schoolhouse," west of Jarvis and a few feet south of King. It may only be conjectured what school was intended and the year it was built, for the Masonic building in this location, which was used for the first common school in Toronto after the Common School Act of 1816, was not constructed until 1822. The school in the Masonic Temple occupied the first floor, and the upper floor was used by the Masons who owned the building.

In 1814 a small shelter, twenty-four by thirty-six, was erected as a market building. Toronto's first public well was dug on the property in 1823, and the market was fenced in in 1824. The recently demolished (1968) St. Lawrence Market building, erected 1904, was on the east side of the original market property. This building combined with St. Lawrence Hall, constructed in 1850 and restored in 1967, occupied only about one-third of the land area of the market in 1810.

As the market was virtually the only place for a great number of settlers to sell their produce, it was usually crowded. It was also a place for townspeople to sell their garden produce, or even a piece of furniture, and for licensed pedlars and Indians to sell their wares.

Market business was encouraged by a town bylaw which regulated market hours and ruled that no one could sell meat, poultry, butter, eggs, vegetables and fish between the hours of 6 A.M. and 4 P.M. on Saturdays except at the Market. There was a fine of fifteen shillings for storekeepers who violated this regulation.

As everywhere in the world of 1810, market day was one of excitement for young and old. It was held every Saturday, although there was probably a tacit understanding that deep snow would automatically cancel it. Some farmers were up before dawn to reach the market and others, from a longer distance had spent the night at the Red Lion Hotel, if they came from the district north of the town. With the rising sun, these settler farmers could be seen unloading their ox-carts, setting up tables on wood trestles, or arranging their produce on the ground. Pigs, cattle and fowl were confined in temporary enclosures, and oxen and horses were tethered to hitching rails or posts. Hawkers with tinware and the miscellaneous collection of small articles in daily use, and patent-medicine vendors shouted the virtues of their product. Stoical Indians displayed their game and fish, or their wild fruit, basketware and moccasins.

Auction sales and public meetings were also held at the market, including the occasional auction of a negro slave, but most auctions were held in stores or hotels. Soldiers, in their brilliant scarlet or green uniforms of British regulars, were interested spectators, even if they had little money to spend. We may presume that cash was paid for all small merchandise and garden produce, so that the prices would be lower than those of the stores.

The market was within sight and hearing of the grim stockade of the jail on its west boundary. It was in accord with the spirit of the times to set up the stocks, whipping post and pillory (the pillory remained until

1834), in the market square, so that the greatest number of persons could see the offender receiving his or her punishment. No doubt the outcries of those being whipped were also intended to have a salutary effect on those in the jail.

The market was the location for a public feast to celebrate the coronation of Queen Victoria in 1837, and a hundred-pound plum pudding, beer, military bands and fireworks illumination all contributed to make it the best market day up to that time.

CHAPTER 21

The Jail

The world of 1810 belonged to the property owners. It was the property owners who made the laws and they were not to be dispossessed. Offences against society and against individuals were not as serious as offences against property. It was a period of individualism, and the economic theories of the time condoned callousness toward one's fellow-men in business. It was inevitable that this viewpoint influenced the whole social outlook of the period, including the writing of the criminal code. Stealing, even something of little value, could be punished with death, for such theft undermined a social structure based upon privilege.

In 1810 there appears to have been very little investigation or analysis of the reasons for crime. To us today, it appears that the world of 1810 regarded crime as an evidence of man's depravity rather than, to a partial extent, at least, the inevitable outcome of unfair social conditions. We also see that because of the property and wealth bias in the making and administration of law, even respectable people often countenanced, and even engaged in, smuggling.

This attitude toward crime and prisoners was held in Canada, as well as in England, but to a less degree, for there was no wealthy class to make and enforce laws for their own benefit. Although the law and the administration of it were the same in Canada as in England, there is no doubt that both judges and juries more quickly softened the penalties. Considering the outlook of the age, the Toronto jail was typical of and certainly no worse than its counterpart in England. It was probably much better, for its limited size in a small community brought about a more personal contact between court, jail staff and prisoners. Its wood construction precluded the prison fevers mentioned by the reformer John Howard, that were inevitable in the damp masonry prisons of England.

It was typical of the age that the mentally ill in the Toronto jail were confined with those incarcerated for crimes against society, although sometimes kindhearted people took them into their homes and were paid for their keep. It was not until twenty-four years later, in 1834, that it was suggested by a grand jury that debtors be separately confined and that "lunatics" be given a property asylum.

The Toronto jail of 1810 was located on the site of the present King Edward Hotel. It was a squat, unpainted, clapboarding-over-squared-logs building, with a hip roof. It was concealed from the street by a cedar-log stockade, about sixty feet square. This stockade was about fourteen feet high and each log was sharpened with an axe at the top. The large double doors were seldom opened. A block of wood was suspended on a chain over these doors, and when it was pulled a bell rang inside.

There were no proper means of distributing heat from open fireplaces. There were no bedsteads, and the prisoners were forced to lie upon straw on the wooden floor. Although the building was only ten years old in 1810, the sheriff reported to the magistrate that the wood sills on the east side of the building were completely rotten. The illustration (No. 8) shows that the floor of this jail was only a step above grade, and it is evident that the floor joists were too close to the ground and were not ventilated.

All the prisoners got to eat was dry bread and water. Even this scanty diet was often not regularly distributed, and sometimes a famished prisoner ate three days' supply of bread in one. If the prisoner had relatives in Toronto, they were sometimes allowed to supplement this scanty diet. It was not until 1813 that makeshift straw beds, raised above the floor, were supplied to sick prisoners. There was no prison garb, and the prisoner wore the clothing he brought with him.

As the jail was located close to the market, the stocks, the whipping post, and the pillory (where the victim stood upon a platform with his arms locked between two timbers supported on a pole) were located on the market property so the prisoners could be viewed by the greatest number of people. We find that in 1804, a woman for being a nuisance was sentenced to six months imprisonment, and to stand in the pillory on two market days for two hours at a time. A man was given the same treatment for using "seditious language." "Burning in the hand," or "branding on the tongue," with a hot iron, a sentence usually carried out in the court room, had been abandoned by 1810, except for manslaughter. Some prisoners were forced to wear the ball and chain, fastened with leg irons, and this was not given up in Toronto until about 1875.

Although written records and letters are curiously reticent regarding sex it is only in police records that we learn that prostitution existed in Toronto in 1810. In one instance, three men were found guilty by the court of keeping a disorderly house, and were sentenced to be imprisoned for fourteen days.

Banishment was a sentence occasionally dealt, and it carried with it the death penalty for disobedience and return. We may presume that any prisoner so sentenced gladly went directly to the U.S.A. in the eight days he was given to leave the country.

Mud and refuse were often thrown at those in the stocks and the pillory; hundreds journeyed miles to enjoy the thrill of public whippings and public hangings; but it is no coincidence that as the common man gradually had a share in the making of the law, both he and the laws he made became less cruel. We must not blame the property owners, and the wealthy alone for the cruelties of the age, but we cannot help but conclude that the exercise of too much power by a privileged class warped their judgment in making laws, as demonstrated by the fact that stealing was a greater crime than the taking of life.

CHAPTER 22

Slavery

Many readers will be surprised to learn that there were slaves in Toronto in 1810. There were only about two dozen, however, and legislation, passed in 1793 at Newark by Governor Simcoe, was steadily decreasing their numbers.

Canada was spared the curse of slavery and time's vengeance for it because of the very practical reason that the climate was considered too cold for the coloured race, and because there was no large single-crop agriculture. Canada had slaves from the time of the first settlements.

During the French Regime they were imported from the West Indies, for the use of fur-traders and merchants. More slaves were brought in after the British conquest; and after the American War of Independence many were brought to Canada by the Loyalists, particularly to Nova Scotia. Negro slaves at any time in Canada were a tiny minority of the population.

The settlement of Ontario did not begin until anti-slavery sentiment was increasing, and many colonists from Britain brought it with them. About five thousand Loyalists came to Ontario, and thousands of American settlers soon followed. They were permitted to bring slaves into Ontario under the Imperial Act of 1790. These slaves, of course, were not citizens. Although white settlers from the U.S.A. were required to take the oath of allegiance, slaves were exempt. The act stated that slaves could be sold after one year's residence.

Many settlers from the U.S.A. were not opposed to slavery and there were no non-slave states in 1790, but being poor, few of these settlers owned any. It should be noted that the first European country to abolish slavery was Denmark, in 1792. The first state in the U.S.A. to do away with it was Massachusetts, in 1793.

The number of slaves in Ontario was so small that Governor Simcoe, who was ardently opposed to slavery, was able to introduce legislation at the second session of the Legislature at Newark, in 1793, repealing the Imperial Act of 1790. As there was some opposition, he accepted the compromise that existing slaves would remain the property of the owners until death, but that the children of the slaves born after July 9, 1793, would be set free upon attaining the age of twenty-five years (1818). It also provided that any slave who came into the province, or any slave brought into the province by his master, would automatically become free.

There were no statistics upon the number of slaves in Ontario, but in Quebec (which included Ontario) the number of slaves by the census of 1784 was three hundred and four. It is reasonable to suppose that there were fewer than one hundred in Ontario in 1793, or less than one tenth of one per cent of the population. Simcoe declared that slavery was inconsistent in a free nation, and that it should be abolished in Ontario, "so far as same may gradually be done without violating private property." The last was a concession to slave-owners who objected to the act.

Simcoe's legislation set free all children of slaves upon reaching the age of twenty-five years. Before this occurred, however, the parents were gradually being set free by their owners, and this included children. In 1803, Solicitor-General Gray, who had framed Simcoe's Act died in the sinking of the *Speedy* on Lake Ontario. His will not only gave his slaves their freedom, but also gave them legacies and land. After 1800 slave ownership ceased to be a status symbol, and was fast becoming the reverse. The bondage of one human being to another was coming into sharper focus as cruel and undesirable. Many others freed their slaves in the face of rising public opinion so that by 1834, the year slavery was abolished in all British possessions, there were no slaves in Toronto or Canada to free. It is not known when the last slave in Toronto was freed, but it was probably before 1820.

The slaves in Toronto were household servants and handymen. It is very evident that they received better treatment than the field slaves of southern United States plantations, under the whips of white overseers. They were generally faithful and goodnatured, but advertisements in the *Gazette* reveal that it was not unusual for them to run away. A minor tragedy of slavery is revealed in a letter written in Ontario in 1793. The writer asks his friend in another town to be on the lookout for his boy slave. He had sent his son and two Indians in pursuit. He states, "As the boy's mother lives in your town, he may call to see her." From time to time slaves were jailed for stealing their master's property and they sometimes drank too freely, but did not commit proportionately more vicious crimes than white men.

Most negroes had Christian names, only, such as Peggy, Dorinda, Black Sal, Pompadour, Coachly, Simon, Jupiter, etc., to mention some in Toronto. Pompadour's daughter, was known as Amy Pompadour, so that in time they assumed the double names of whites. An exception to the custom of having single names was Robert Franklin, a free negro in the employ of Peter Russell, who came to Toronto with him as a senior servant. Most of the free negroes were employed by storekeepers, tradesmen, and hotel owners, and the slaves worked in private homes, although there were sometimes free negroes and slaves in the same household. Obviously, as soon as some negroes were free and others slaves in the same household, emancipation was not far away. Although negroes have traditionally been considered to lack initiative, there was some co-operation and enterprise among them in Toronto, for as early as 1799 they jointly assumed a road contract. After 1810, Toronto's first ice company consisted of a lone negro who cut ice from a mill pond north of Bloor Streeet and delivered it to customers in town.

The judicial view in 1810 was that slavery was inconsistent with the laws of Canada, but there were also other reasons which militated against slavery. The first was that except for use as household servants, slavery was economically unsound in Ontario. There was no intensive cultivation of one crop or plantations of thousands of acres in extent, as in the South. In 1810, one-third of the population of South Carolina, for example, were slaves. In such an older locality, plantations could be financed on borrowed money to provide the land, the buildings and the slaves, for it was close to transportation by ship to England for an ever-increasing market for cotton. The second reason was that the cost of a slave was too high for the primitive economy of the country, for there were no banks in Ontario and most of the population saw little cash from year to year. One newspaper advertisement asked one hundred and fifty dollars for a woman and two hundred and fifty for her son. A skilled workman in Toronto earned about twelve dollars per week. A slave would cost him forty per cent of his yearly salary. The settlers earned far less and had little cash. Most of the slaves in Toronto were owned by high-ranking civil servants. Expressed in terms of the money of today the boy slave would cost $2,500.

When American soldiers returned from campaigns in Canada during the War of 1812 to their homes in the South, the news quickly spread that no slaves could be imported into Ontario, and that any slave who reached Canada would be free. Negroes soon began to appear in Ontario around Niagara Falls and the Detroit River. Fugitive slave entrance into Canada reached its greatest volume in the 1840s. After the passing of the Fugitive Slave Act, by the American Government, it became unlawful for the northern states to harbour escaping slaves. Thus was born the "Underground Railroad," operated by Quakers and others to assist southern negro slaves to escape to Canada. It is believed that as many as five thousand crossed the international border in the years 1850-51.

The reader has heard of the indented servants of the thirteen American colonies, whose service was purchased for a term of years for the passage money across the Atlantic. This custom became so prevalent that the colonists could literally buy them from sea captains. In 1700 there were more white indented servants in Virginia than black slaves. Indenture for the Atlantic passage began to decline after this date, however, for a slave gave a greater return upon the money invested. A vestige of indenture still remained in Toronto in 1801, for we find a business man writing to his brother in Scotland to be on the lookout for a lad of about fifteen years of age who would be willing to come to Canada as an indentured servant. In this case the boy was to be paid a small salary as well as his passage money and his board, but he would be under contract and could not leave his employer to better himself. No doubt, the higher cost of living in Toronto was not mentioned to the boy when the salary was quoted.

It was not unusual in Ontario for a settler with a large family to sign an indenture with another to place his boy with him for a period of ten years. The boy was treated as one of the family, and sometimes the reason for the exchange was not financial but to ensure a disciplined son through the experience of living with others.

CHAPTER 23

Duelling

The first duel in Toronto was in January, 1800, when Mr. Small met Attorney-General John White. Mr. Small's wife and a Mrs. Elmsley disapproved of Mrs. White for some reason. They saw fit to snub her at a public gathering. This act aroused the ire of Mrs. White's husband who made some uncomplimentary remarks about Mrs. Small to his friend Mr. Smith. In the heat of his anger, the Attorney-General also told his friend Smith that he could repeat the remarks, if he wished, to Mrs. Elmsley. Such pique, jealousy and unkind remarks are, of course, just as common today. Mr. Smith held his tongue for six months, but then repeated the Attorney-General's remarks to several people in Toronto. One of them told Mr. Small, who called upon Attorney-General White and demanded satisfaction. The two men, with their seconds, met the next morning. Both fired their pistols at the same instant. It was Attorney-General White who died in agony several hours later. As usual in such cases, Small was tried for murder but acquitted.

There were also two duels which did not end fatally. In July, 1801, Joseph Wilcocks, of Toronto, was challenged to a duel by a Mr. Weeks. It seems that Weeks had accused Wilcocks of being an informer. Wilcocks called Weeks a liar and Weeks challenged him. That night Wilcocks slept with his second to be ready at the place appointed at 5 A.M. On the way to the duelling rendezvous he was placed under arrest and was then forced by the court to give security to keep the peace for six months. The "informer" accusation was probably correct for Wilcocks was emotionally unstable. Thirteen years later he was killed at Fort Erie fighting on the American side – a traitor to his country.

In April, 1812, Colonel MacDonell who died with General Brock ascending Queenston Heights, had a quarrel with Dr. Warren Baldwin and the two men crossed the Bay to Gibraltar Point to fight a duel. When the time came MacDonell refused to fire at his old friend and Baldwin discharged his duelling pistol in the air. After this sobering experience they shook hands cordially and returned to town the best of friends.

In 1806 a fatal duel between two Canadians took place on the American side of the Niagara River, across from Newark. This was between William Dickson of that town and William Weeks of Toronto. Weeks was a lawyer and a member of the House of Assembly when he was killed. He had resided in Toronto since 1798.

In 1813 a duel took place between two regular army men stationed at Fort George at Newark. This was between Dr. Shumate and Lieutenant Smith of the 16th Regiment. They settled their difference near the lighthouse, and it was the challenger, Dr. Shumate, who was fatally shot.

The second and last duel in Toronto took place in 1817 and it was a showery dawn in July as two young men and their seconds waited in a barn for the rising sun to give a better light. The younger, John Ridout, son of a prominent family, was a student in his brother's law office. At fourteen years of age he had served as a midshipman in the lake navy during the War of 1812. He was tall and well built for his eighteen years. His second, James Small, was also in his teens.

The other duellist, Samuel Jarvis, seven years older than his opponent, was also from one of the "families," and the parents of both of the young men were friends. Duelling, of course, was against the law and Ridout's second, James Small, was a lawyer who had taken the oath to uphold it. Ironically, he was the son of a man who had killed his opponent in a duel in 1800.

The shower stopped. The four men emerged from the barn, and the duellists took positions eight yards apart, and listened to the formal instruction which the duelling code demanded. As they grimly faced one another both men remembered in vivid detail the quarrel that had brought them to the spot.

John Ridout, on behalf of his brother, had been conducting a civil suit against Samuel Jarvis' father, and he had attempted to make a settlement with Samuel out of court. A quarrel arose, and Samuel had ordered the younger man out of his office. Hot-tempered young Ridout waited in the street until Jarvis came out and then struck him with a cane, breaking the bone of his right hand. The injured Jarvis then knocked young John Ridout down. A few days later, Ridout had his second call upon Jarvis and challenged him.

Jarvis' second tensely explained to both that he would count "one, two, three, fire," and reminded them they were not to shoot until they heard the word "fire!"

Both men sighted their pistols and waited for the count. On the count of two, the young and excitable Ridout fired and missed. He asked for another pistol, but this was not permitted by the duelling code. Jarvis now had his opponent completely at his mercy. He took deliberate aim and fired. Ridout fell to the ground mortally wounded.

Jarvis was tried for murder and acquitted. But the death of Ridout was to haunt him all of his life. If both had fired at the proper time, the duel might even have brought him some respect, for it was the other man who had challenged. But to kill young Ridout while he had him at his mercy shocked the people of Toronto. Years later, Jarvis felt it necessary to distribute pamphlets, giving his version of the duel to vindicate himself, and his second was belatedly tried as an accessory to murder in 1828. This scandal had such an effect that the Jarvis-Ridout duel was the last in Toronto.

The circumstances of this duel made it the last, but there were also forces at work which were bringing an end to duelling in all civilized countries. A new class was emerging to take over the leadership of society and that was the business men who had more important things to think of than the "honour" of gentlemen which had dominated previous centuries. The rise of the middle class also created a mass mind more rational than in the past, and the taking of life to prove something or other came to appear ridiculous as well as cruel and stupid.

CHAPTER 24

The Fire
Department

In an age of wooden buildings heated with open fireplaces, fire was always a hazard. In addition to fires started by carelessness or overheated fireplaces or the few stoves, there was the danger of forest fire spreading to the town. Some of these forest fires were, of course, started by lightning, so that this source could not be controlled. Fire often started from brick chimneys above open-fireplaces, for often the mortar pulverized with the extreme heat and permitted the escape of flames to roof construction, or attics.

Every settlement in America had its fires at this period, and in the year 1805 the town of Detroit was almost totally destroyed by fire. In May, 1806, a forest fire to the northwest of Toronto came dangerously close and burnt 250 panels of split rail fence as well as grass and stacked hay on a farm between the present Queen Street and Bloor Street, west of Bay Street. As usual, in such cases, the army came to the aid of the townspeople until the danger was passed.

It did not take long for fire regulations and fines for non-compliance to be brought into effect. In the year 1802, eight years after the first frame house was constructed in Toronto, a police regulation directed every house to have two fire buckets of wood, leather or canvas (the canvas was to be painted on the outside and covered with pitch on the inside), holding at least two gallons of water, hanging in a conspicuous place, and available if the occupants were not in. These "fire buckets" were to have the owner's name marked on them, and were not to be used for any other purpose. The leather buckets were the most popular. These were not as unsophisticated as the material might suggest, for they had leather-covered wooden hoops at the rim and leather-covered rope handles. Theye were lighter than wood and more durable than canvas.

Ladders to reach roofs and chimneys were also required. Each house was to have at least two. One was to reach the eave, and could be left hanging in a conspicuous place; the other was to be permanently fastened on the roof slope, below the chimney, with "hooks or bolts." The fine for non-compliance with this act was forty shillings, which, if in New York currency, would compare with $50 today.

After the disastrous fire in Detroit, the premium of Toronto fire insurance was raised. One letter writer, in complaining about this increased premium to a business associate, stated that all Toronto buildings were isolated, and stood upon a lot that was usually at least an acre in extent; and that all buildings had fire buckets and ladders, and were a short distance from the Bay or a creek or well. The board fences between the buildings, he explained, could be removed in less than five minutes. In his opinion, Toronto was far less subject to a destructive fire than Detroit.

The first organized effort to put out fires was the bucket brigade. It was self-preservation as well as neighbourliness that brought all men and boys into the streets with their buckets at the first sign of a fire. A double line of men formed from the fire to the nearest creek or well, or the bay. Filled buckets were passed along one line and empty ones passed back on the other. Venturesome men and youths carried these filled buckets up the ladders, on the outside of the building, and handed them to others near the chimney to be emptied into the flames. If the fire had a good start, however, such well-meant efforts were of no avail, and the firemen spent their time dousing outbuildings, and sometimes tore down fences to keep the fire from spreading. Buildings in Toronto were not contiguous, and the fire usually consumed one building only.

In 1802 this bucket brigade was superseded by a fire engine, although there were still instances of minor brigades putting out fires before its arrival upon the secene. This hand-operated engine was a vertical pump on wheels. It was worked by two crews of volunteers who stood on each side and raised and lowered long horizontal spars. The water came from barrels on wagons, whose drivers had hastily secured it from the bay or the nearest creek. Most of these drivers were professional carters. Upon the ringing of the alarm bell, which was the bell of St. James' Church, or the first sign of smoke, they raced to the nearest water to fill their barrels, for a reward was given to the first cart to arrive at the fire engine. In their eagerness to win the award, the first wagon often reached the fire engine with half the water slopped out of the barrels.

This fire engine was a gift to the town from Lieutenant-Governor Peter Hunter. It was carried off by the Americans during the attack upon Toronto in 1813, and is now in a Washington Museum. To show their appreciation of the generous bequest a subscription was immediately put forward to raise money for a building to house the fire engine, and a shed was constructed.

In 1826 the first volunteer fire company was formed, and its members were merchants and tradesmen who dropped their work to attend to their fire duties. The taxpayers provided an engine house. This building became a kind of club for these volunteers spent much time in it, playing cards, etc. Gradually a nominal sum per month was paid to these men for their part time volunteer services, but it was not until 1875 that a permanent professional fire brigade was organized, and this full-time brigade employed fifty officers and men.

The first fire of any account in Toronto was the burning of the Parliament Buildings, by the Americans, in 1813. The greatest fire to the present day was a two-day fire in the downtown manufacturing district, in 1904, which brought additional firemen from as far away as London and Niagara Falls. Eighty-six warehouses, covering an area of fourteen acres, were destroyed.

CHAPTER 25

Indians

Unlike Quebec and the eastern United States, Ontario never passed through a frontier period with settlers ploughing their fields within reach of a musket. The forts in Ontario in 1810 were for defence against white Americans – not for Indian attack.

A large proportion of the Indians of Ontario were Loyalists, for along with white men they had been driven from the U.S.A. for being loyal to Britain during the War of Independence. As with white Loyalists, the British Government supplied them with food and utensils and presented them with hunting grounds purchased from the Mississaugas. Land for white settlement was purchased, not wrested by force, from the original and the Loyalist redmen, and there were no Indian uprisings in Ontario with the coming of white settlers.

By 1790 the Mississaugas were the principal neighbours of the whites in Toronto for a radius of one hundred and fifty miles. The first purchase of land in Ontario was from the Chippewa tribe in 1781. The second, the Toronto Purchase, was from the Mississaugas in 1787. Robert Gourlay, an English writer of the period, estimated there were little more than three thousand Indians in southern Ontario in 1817, so that in 1810 the Indians comprised less than four per cent of the total population.

The Indians of America had been in the stone age before the coming of the white men. They were eager for his firearms and his tools of copper and iron, and it was not the white man's fault they had no immunity to his diseases. The cheating in trade and the debauching with liquor in the early settlement of both the U.S.A. and Canada is not a pleasant phase in North American history. But we must remember that the more the Indian was in contact with whites the less he engaged in the senseless wars of extermination with other tribes. It was a rough age prior to the nineteenth century. The plight of the victimized Indian was more picturesque, but perhaps no greater than that of the new exploited factory class in England.

The cunning of the Indians, which has been their most characteristic trait in fiction, sprang from a law of necessity due to their savage life. Their sense of hearing was remarkably acute. They had rich musical voices and spoke low and quietly, seldom speaking to strangers and only in moderation to whites. One observer tells of an Indian at a council meeting making a speech that lasted five hours. He said that the Indian's delivery was similar to that of a Roman orator.

Ontario was covered with Indian "trails" or paths worn on the ground from centuries of use. They walked in single file, and on new trails all but the leader had a path to follow. This habit persisted when they walked the streets of Toronto. One contemporary writer said they were truthful and never forgot a kindness. There were no words of blasphemy in their language. They had a great affection for their children and respect for the aged. Indians seldom quarrelled with whites unless insulted by them but were very quarrelsome among themselves. One woman writer, who knew them as neighbours, was astonished at their innate politeness. Although they used their fingers when eating with their own people, she noted that when they dined at her farmhouse they waited to see how she used her knife and fork and gravely imitated her. They did not help themselves but waited to be served.

When drunk they still showed savage traits. They had no tradition of drinking and the white man's liquor brought out the worst in them. In 1810, trouble with Indians was usually brought about when they entered settler's cabins when the men were away, and attempted to obtain liquor by force. Their squaws took the precaution of securing their hunting-knives when they drank. They were not thieves, however, and when they camped upon a settler's clearing they did not steal. They closed gates and left everything as they had found it.

The Mississaugas were coming under the influence of the Christian faith in 1810, and there were many Christians among the Mohawks who had come as Loyalists to Ontario. By 1825 drunken brawls and shiftlessness had been succeeded by tilled fields, and log houses and barns instead of teepees. It is interesting to note that in 1810 a great number of these Christianized Indians did not use intoxicants at all whereas practically all whites drank to some extent. Except when Christianized, however, their morals had declined from contact with white men. One contemporary writer spoke of the "deplorable want of chastity in their women."

Mrs. Simcoe was impressed with the tall muscular men of the Mohawk tribe. She relates in her diary, "Jacob, the Mohawk, was there. He danced Scottish Reels with more ease and grace than any person I ever saw, and had the air of a prince . . . I never saw so handsome a figure."[13] The Mississaugas, however, were perhaps the least impressive of all Indians at this time, and were only of average height. She describes them as an "unwarlike, idle, drunken, dirty tribe." These Mississaugas were the Indians most often seen by the people of Toronto in 1810.

They had low receding foreheads, large ears, sharp eyes wide apart, prominent cheek bones and long flat noses. Their mouths expressed ferocity and sullen determination. Their teeth were dazzling white. A traveller of the period relates that from their habit of greasing their bodies to ward off mosquitoes, they were "exceedingly malodorous." The women carried their babies loosely strapped to their backs on a "papoose board," which could be set down and leaned against a tree.

Although savages, the Indians had always been eager for the benefits of white civilization. As early as 1793, Augustus Jones employed Indians on his surveying parties. In 1810 they were fitting into the economy as trappers and fish-catchers to sell to white men, bateaux men, making canoes for sale, and occasionally working as mail-carriers. They even worked for wages to assist whites in building log cabins. Sometimes they earned money at harvest time, but were restive when attempting to do a full day's continuous hard labour for others.

No Indians in 1810 wore the entire ensemble of white men's dress. Even Joseph Brant, the highest chief of the Iroquois nation, who had visited England and was the guest of the best society, could be recognized by his selection of clothing.

As partly civilized savages they, no doubt, felt uncomfortable with their bodies tightly covered. The complete dress of the whites, including top boots, pantaloons, vest, ruffled shirt and waistcoat, was not acceptable to them. When dressed for market in cool weather, they could wear the boots of the settler, and his deerskin or linen or flannel pants. But the gaudy trade goods calico shirt was covered with a blanket instead of a coat. They still painted their bodies for ceremonial dances, and were often seen on the streets with paint or soot upon their faces, a custom which might have a pagan or a tribal significance.

No Indians actually lived in Toronto, and none worked as servants for white masters. They were often seen on the streets, however, or at the market on Saturdays, selling their wild fruit, fish, basketware and moccasins, which whites used as house slippers. They came from the reserve of about two hundred Indians west of the town, which extended from the Humber to the Etobicoke River, and they came from their farms on the Kingston Road. They could also be seen at the "island" for the fresh lake breezes were supposed to have curative powers.

CONCLUSION

In the preceding pages we have continually called attention to the early colonial status of Ontario, and the effect which it had upon the people of Toronto. We may now contemplate the effect of Toronto's history upon the city of 1970. To do this we will review the slow emancipation from colonialism.

The War of Indepedence in the American Colonies was the first setback to democracy in Britain and Canada. The French Revolution gave it another. Those in Britain who made the decisions, and those in Canada who were selected to govern Canadian provinces, were invariably men who considered Canada to be a colony, and their interpretation of the duties of their office was to make this country, as far as possible, a transcript of Britain, and to protect it from the detested democratic ideas which had brought about the French and Ameircan revolutions.

Those who came from the American colonies as Loyalists, and those who came later as American immigrants, brought with them a spirit of progress which had been nurtured in the thirteen colonies. With two modern world revolutions fresh in the minds of the British statesmen, they decided that too much freedom was dangerous, and that safeguards were necessary to prevent a repetition in Canada. Most of the political power in Ontario was in the hands of the British officials or colonists from Britain – not Loyalists or American immigrants. This power did not come from the Canadian people, but from the Colonial Office in Downing Street.

Two years after 1810, Canada was engaged in a war with the U.S.A. This war was quickly forgotten as a humiliating experience by the Americans, whose armies were driven from Canada. It was also unknown to the hundreds of thousands of European immigrants to the United States.

In Canada, with however one-tenth of the population of that country, this War of 1812 had the effect of inciting fear of another attack, for it was the second attack upon this country. This anxiety, which lasted for half a century, together with our colonial status was not the best stimulus to progress. It is clear today with the perspective of one hundred and fifty years that free land, available to all, and self-government was making the U.S.A. prosperous and progressive; that free land in Canada precluded a social system identical to that of Britain; that on the spot actual representative government was required to solve problems intrinsic to the country.

Colonial rule may raise an uncivilized or a backward country to a high level of comfort and industry. In practice it assumes that the colonizers are more intelligent than the colonists. Those who came to Canada, however, were already civilized and progressive. British rule in Canada had the effect of semi-stagnation compared with that of the United States, for after losing her most valuable colonies she took precautions to prevent its occurring again. Even the best colonial rule of a civilized people precludes the chaotic upheaval, the adjustment to new values and a new economy, and the settling-down process, all of which occur with the birth of a nation.

In Toronto, particularly, the class with wealth and position attempted to be as British as possible, for the magic of royalty was represented by a Britisher from Britain. Repudiation of this British pattern and example would have brought social ostracism. This class, by their example, retarded the development of a truly Canadian identity, and this colonial dependence precluded the spiritual revolution which would have come if Canada had become independent. We early formed the habit of looking to Britain, as children look to their parents, for example and guidance. After the Rebellion of 1837 the advance toward a more progressive type of Canadian was accelerated, but it was then too late to offset the initial advantage of the U.S.A. in the competition for settlers.

During the last century most of our leading scholars and educators came from Britain. Choir leaders, organists and musicians of all kinds came from that country to find ready employment here, for the standards were that of Britain. Leading men in Canadian branches of British merchantile houses were generally British, and these men often antagonized their staff by clinging to the protocol of British business offices. Ambitious Canadian employees of many business firms found they could not compete with recent British immigrants for senior positions, and left for the United States where merit was accepted without prejudice.

During this nineteenth century, those in Toronto heard many reports of life in the U.S.A. which did not meet with their approval. Bank failures, political graft and corruption, disrespect for law, and ill-treatment of factory workers were noted in screaming headlines in most American newspapers. The conditions recorded by their press were never much worse than reported, for the structure of American life based upon the Declaration of Independence was such that no faction was strong enough to censor it. Meyers *History of the Great American Fortunes,*[14] written in our century, has verified these ugly facets of American life from colonial times. The period of yellow journalism in that country, however, had the saving grace of revealing the facts so that the evils of American life were known and could be combatted.

It is no wonder that during the past century this revelation of American life engendered a complacency in Torontonians, whose social system was more like that of Britain than the U.S.A. We envied their success, but we told ourselves we did not wish to be like them. We often repeated the explanation that our population was small because of our lack of arable land. Any Canadian school child could glibly explain that during the ice age most of our fertile soil had been pushed across the international boundary. Many who were not satisfied with the relative inertia and the protocol of Canadian life went to the U.S.A. to better themselves. Professional men, such as doctors, architects and engineers, usually found an easy success in that country and they were welcomed. Writers and artists found success there, also, while they had received little or no recognition in Toronto. Most of those from Canada became American citizens and remained in that country. Approximately 3.3 million Canadians have imigrated to the U.S.A. since Confederation, and 60-70 per cent of these were Canadian-born.

Up until World War Two, visitors to the United States from Toronto found their visit a stimulating experience which made them take a second look at their own city. Although all aspects of American life did not meet with their approval, they wondered why we could not retain the solid virtues we considered we possessed, and also have the prosperity of that country.

Then, after World War Two, something happened which the business forecasters had not predicted. Many Canadian manufacturers had expanded their plants to fill war contracts. They had expected to be forced to lease this additional floor space to others when the war ended. Instead, they started construction upon additional floor space, and began to look around the city for locations for still larger factories. A building boom, which began with the war has, with few setbacks, continued ever since. Population flowed into Toronto, and with our generous immigration laws, Toronto has become the city of opportunity for hundreds of thousands from Europe. Multiple-storey office buildings and apartment buildings are rising everywhere on the Toronto skyline. One of the tallest buildings in the world has been completed, and still taller buildings have been designed for construction at an early date.

The reader may wonder if the expansion of our business and our population since World War Two is a passing phase. Will it stop precipitously – or merely slow down? Are we about to have a decade of recession? Will the one hundred and fifty years of slow growth, compared with the rapid growth of the United States, continue?

In the past we have looked for our answer in the pages of business surveys, financial reports, and the statements of economists and others whom we have looked to for guidance. Most of their short-time forecasts were correct. They were based upon the immediate past. They now, however, appear to be overlooking subtle and indiscernible forces which are working to accelerate the growth of Canada and greatly increase our population. This stimulus is not shown on financial reports, for it is spiritual, rather than temporal, psychological rather than economic. The source of this new force may be revealed only by reviewing the gradual winning of freedom, from the perspective of 1970. Because of our colonial status, Canada has taken one hundred and seventy-five years to win the nationhood that the United States achieved in one war. We believe that the population of Canada and Toronto will be much larger in the future, and it will be a greatly accelerated increase caused by forces already at work.

Canada is now a self-governing nation – not a colony. It was not until World War Two, however, that the spiritual transition from colony to nation was finally completed. The climax of this transition was inevitable, and would have come later, if not during this war, for the British from the end of the nineteenth century were pursuing contradictory ideals – the ideal of Empire and the ideal of self-government, which connotes the dissolution of Empire. An attempt to pinpoint the climax of our spiritual dependence upon Britain could place it on the day when Winston Churchill made his famous "Blood, toil, tears and sweat" speech in 1940.

Although our colonial and semi-colonial status during the nineteenth century and after produced a less aggressive type, and a lower standard of living than that in the U.S.A. during that long period, our slow growth to maturity has actually benefited those living in Toronto today. Our modest economy never created the sprawling and ugly industrial complex which may still be seen in large American cities. Our conservatism and caution did not permit us to use frame construction for residences and commercial buildings; we have escaped the large blighted areas of unpainted and decaying buildings found in many American cities.

With our rapid expansion occurring during this present period of clean power, as represented by electricity instead of coal, and industry upon our streets instead of railroad sidings, we have escaped another blight. Our industrial growth has consisted of clean areas, with industrial buildings behind restriction lines, with landscaping between building and street. The relatively small "downtown" area which represents the original city, is now being transformed with multitudes of tall shafts of new buildings in open areas. Our slow growth has also given Toronto a tidiness which has not been lost in our rapid expansion. The English love of gardens has placed more flower beds around our public buildings and residences than in most American cities.

We have seen the affluent society of the United States living midst rivers and lakes of decay and filth, so our late start in population expansion has enabled us to learn the salutary lesson of water contamination and we have been warned of air pollution, before it is too late.

The proportion of negroes to whites in Canada, at present, is about one in six hundred; in the U.S.A. it is about one to nine and a half. The white inhabitants of Toronto, who comprise close to one hundred per cent of the population, do not have to be wooed away from a deep-seated belief that a great mass of their fellow men are second class citizens. No imprint of hundreds of years of legal and social discrimination has left its spiritual mark upon our citizens; no black ghetto deforms this city and no black race riots have ever occurred. For this we claim no commendation; but if Toronto had been founded earlier, and if we had been a self-governing nation before the last century, there is no doubt we would have had a larger percentage of negroes, and could be reaping time's vengeance as in the United States. History is on the side of the Toronto of today.

It is hoped that the Toronto of 1810 presented in this book has enabled the reader to better understand and appraise the city of 1970, and be proud to be a Canadian citizen following Centennial Year, a century after the birth of Canada and one hundred and sixty years after 1810.

[1]*Richardson's War of 1812,* edited by Alexander Clark Casselman. Toronto: Historical Publishing, 1902. P. 293.

[2]*Lake Ontario,* by Arthur Pound. The American Lakes Series. Indianapolis: Bobbs-Merrill, 1945. P. 201.

[3]*Ten Years of Upper Canada in Peace and War, 1805-1815,* being the Ridout Letters, with Annotations by Matilda Edgar. Toronto: William Briggs, 1890. Page 41.

[4]*Travels in Canada and the United States in 1816 and 1817,* by Lieut. Francis Hall. London: Longman, Hurst, Rees, Orme & Brown, 1818. P. 200.

[5]*Religion in the Development of American Culture, 1765-1840,* by W. W. Street. New York: Scribners, 1952. P. 94.

[6]*The Diary of Mrs. John Graves Simcoe,* edited by John Ross Robertson. (Toronto: William Briggs, 1911). Toronto: Ontario Publishing, 1934. P. 41.

[7]*Statistical Sketches of Upper Canada for the Use of Emigrants,* by William Dunlop. London: Murray, 1832. P. 48.

[8]*A Year's Residence in America,* by William Cobbett. London: Chapman and Dodd, n.d. P. 230.

[9]*Jesse Ketchum and His Times,* by E. J. Hathaway. Toronto: McClelland & Stewart, 1929. P. 100.

[10]*Roughing It in the Bush,* by Susanna Moodie. Toronto: Hunter Rose, 1871. Pp. 241-43.

[11]*My Boy Life,* by Rev. John Carroll. Toronto: William Briggs, 1882. P. 99.

[12]J. B. Robinson to John Macauley, *Macauley Papers.* Quoted in *The Town of York,* by Edith Firth. Toronto: University of Toronto Press, 1962. P. 210.

[13]*The Diary of Mrs. John Graves Simcoe,* edited by John Ross Robertson. (Toronto: William Briggs, 1911). Toronto: Ontario Publishing, 1934. P. 307.

[14]*History of the Great American Fortunes,* by Gustavus Myers. New York: Random House, 1907-1937.

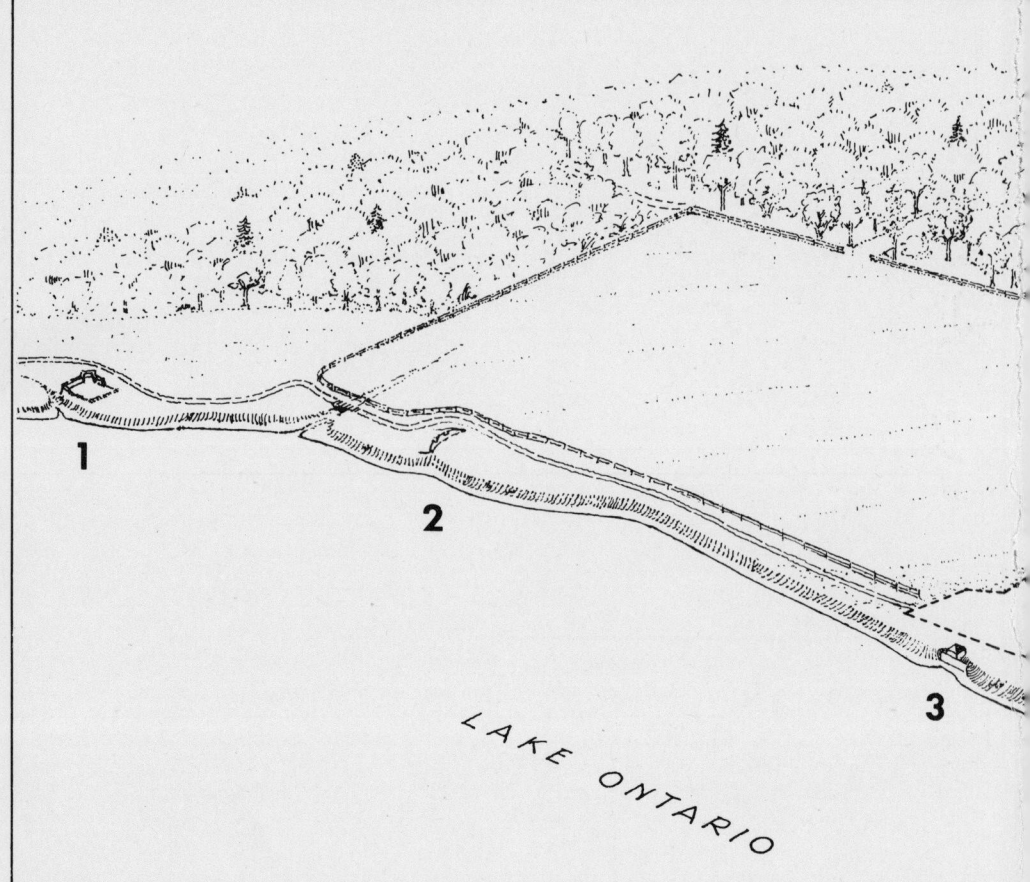

Aerial perspective of the garrison in 1810,
with broken line indicating fort constructed late in 1813.
Numbers indicate gun batteries, etc., as follows:

1. *Western Battery*
2. *Half Moon Battery*
3. *Magazine blown up April 27, 1813*
4. *Lieutenant-Governor's residence*
5. *Government House Battery*
6. *Ravine Battery*
7. *Blockhouse*
The large cleared area to the left
was called the Garrison Reserve.